Clause Structure

Clause Structure is the most widely studied phenomenon within syntactic theory, because it refers to how words and phrases are embedded within a sentence, their relationships to each other within a sentence, and, ultimately, how sentences are layered and represented in the human brain. This volume presents a clear and up-to-date overview of the Minimalist Program, synthesizes the most important research findings, and explores the major shifts in generative syntax. As an accessible topic book, it includes chapters on framework, the clause in general, and the semantic, grammatical, and pragmatic layers. Designed for graduate students and researchers interested in syntactic theory, this book includes a range of examples taken from acquisition, typology, and language change, alongside discussion questions, helpful suggestions for further reading, and a useful glossary.

Elly van Gelderen is Regents' Professor of English in the Department of English at Arizona State University.

KEY TOPICS IN SYNTAX

"Key Topics in Syntax" focuses on the main topics of study in syntax today. It consists of accessible yet challenging accounts of the most important issues, concepts, and phenomena to consider when examining the syntactic structure of language. Some topics have been the subject of syntactic study for many years, and are re-examined in this series in light of new developments in the field; others are issues of growing importance that have not so far been given a sustained treatment. Written by leading experts and designed to bridge the gap between textbooks and primary literature, the books in this series can either be used on courses and seminars or as one-stop, succinct guides to a particular topic for individual students and researchers. Each book includes useful suggestions for further reading, discussion questions, and a helpful glossary.

Already published in the series:

Syntactic Islands Cedric Boeckx

Clause Structure by Elly van Gelderen

Forthcoming titles:

Argument Structure by Alexander Williams

The Clitic by Francisco Ordóñez

Ellipsis by Kyle Johnson

Syntactic Agreement by Roberta D'Allesandro

The Evolution of Syntax by Brady Clark

Studying Syntactic Change by Thomas McFadden

Clause Structure

ELLY VAN GELDEREN

CAMBRIDGE
UNIVERSITY PRESS

University Printing House, Cambridge CB2 8BS, United Kingdom

Published in the United States of America by Cambridge University Press, New York

Cambridge University Press is part of the University of Cambridge.

It furthers the University's mission by disseminating knowledge in the pursuit of education, learning and research at the highest international levels of excellence.

www.cambridge.org
Information on this title: www.cambridge.org/9781107659810

First published 2013

Printed in the United Kingdom by Clays, St Ives plc

A catalog record for this publication is available from the British Library

Library of Congress Cataloging in Publication Data
Gelderen, Elly van.
Clause structure / Elly van Gelderen.
pages cm
Includes bibliographical references and index.
ISBN 978-1-107-01774-0
1. Grammar, Comparative and general – Clauses. 2. Grammar, Comparative and general – Syntax. 3. Principles and parameters (Linguistics) I. Title.
P297.G44 2013
415–dc23 2013013922

ISBN 978-1-107-01774-0 Hardback
ISBN 978-1-107-65981-0 Paperback

Additional resources for this publication at www.cambridge.org/9781107017740

Contents

Figures

Tables

Preface

This book has as its basis the question of how a syntactic derivation is built: top-to-bottom, i.e. representational, or bottom-to-top, i.e. projectionist. Representative sides of this debate are the Cartographic approach, as in Cinque (1999), and the bare phrase structure approach, as in Chomsky (1995). In much literature, these two approaches are assumed to be compatible, but this compatibility is not spelled out. The book is organized Cartographically, i.e. the three layers are examined in great detail, but the underlying message is general cognitive factors should be responsible for the ordering of the phrases in the layers.

Another issue that has caused a lot of debate is whether the argument structure is projected from the verb and then mapped to the syntax, as in e.g. Reinhart (2002), or imposed by the environment of a vP-shell, as in e.g. Borer (2005a, b). In either approach, the issue of how to order the arguments is again crucial: the Thematic Hierarchy and the Uniformity of Theta Assignment Hypothesis (UTAH) take care of this in the projectionist approach; the ordering is Cartographic in the constructionist approach.

Features are central in the Minimalist Program. How are they acquired, are they bundled, and do they project? I discuss various aspects of features and hope that I contribute to a clearer analysis of the TMA features connected with affix-hop. I argue that, unlike in the case of phi-features in English, tense, mood, and aspect features are interpretable on the verb once verb is joined with a certain suffix. It is thus the *-ing* that has interpretable aspect, the infinitive that has irrealis, and the *-ed* that has anterior or passive meaning. This provides a more consistent picture of how interpretable and uninterpretable features are used in connection with C, T, ASP, and M.

I have added facts from the history of generative linguistics in many of my discussions. I think it is important to see that some problems remain problems, e.g. the ditransitive construction, affix-hop, and the representation of the imperative, and also to be able to read older work. Chapter 1 discusses a lot of this history. It explains the underlying philosophy of Generative Grammar, namely to not only be descriptively adequate but to be explanatorily adequate. In recent years, the emphasis has shifted to asking the "why" question, i.e. beyond explanatory adequacy or why the rules are the way they are.

From teaching "baby" syntax, I know that sometimes basic terms such as complement, adverbial, and modifier are not always concrete for students. They have heard the terms but don't know how to use them. The distinction between function in the sentence and name of the phrase is also something that needs consolidating. That's why I have added Chapter 2 as a review of more traditional terminology and how concepts from traditional grammar are relevant to Generative Grammar. I have also added an analysis of relative clauses since it enables me to touch on a number of issues, such as islands and the Linear Correspondence Axiom (LCA). Sometimes, I discuss the same topic in two separate chapters but from a slightly different perspective. The grammatical subject is such a topic. It is relevant to defining the clause (Chapter 2), the semantic roles (Chapter 3), and case and agreement (Chapter 4). This leads to some repetition but also to consolidation (I hope).

For practical reasons, the book will focus on the clause in the English language. Where relevant (e.g. to explain AGRs and AGRo and the various topic positions), I add data from other languages, but this cannot be comprehensive. Chapters 2 to 6 have short sections that discuss a few areas where languages vary. Each chapter is also followed by a set of keywords, discussion points, and suggestions for further reading. Please note that important topics new to the discussion of a chapter are in **bold** type. Since this is more of a textbook than a monograph, I use the pronoun "we" to include the reader in the activities and sometimes "I" when it is more something I personally suggest. I have tried to indicate the major innovators, e.g. the various scholars that came up with the split VP, TP, and CP, but there is so much common knowledge that it is often hard to track the first person to argue a particular point or term. My main contribution is to focus on the various layers and, within the three main layers, to focus on the features and their acquisition, and on asking how we get the ordering that we do.

I occasionally make use of authentic corpus examples for a variety of reasons: (a) It makes the examples more interesting for the reader, and, (b), where variation among native speakers occurs, it provides evidence that at least some speakers use the construction. The main corpora used are Mark Davies' *Corpus of Contemporary American English* (COCA) and the *British National Corpus* (BNC). I also use the *World Atlas of Linguistic Structure* (WALS) database, mainly to provide cross-linguistic comparisons. The corpora and WALS are easy to use in case students want to check a construction, so I need not provide a guide to them.

The audiences for this book that I have in mind are advanced students (taking a second or third generative syntax class) and colleagues. I have tried to make the issues accessible for anyone with a basic knowledge of generative/Minimalist syntax. I therefore assume a familiarity with generative syntax and Minimalism which Radford (2009), Carnie (2007), Adger (2007), or other syntax textbooks supply. I also assume basic linguistic concepts and will consider as grammatical prescriptively incorrect English, e.g. split infinitives, stranded prepositions, and object *who*, without further comment.

Thanks very much to Werner Abraham, for emphasizing the syntactic importance of information structure so many years ago, to Terje Lohndal for many suggestions, references, and for using several chapters in a seminar, to Hui-Ling Yang and Mohammed Al-Rashed for numerous references and data, to the ASU Syntax Reading group for suggestions and support for a number of years, namely Mohammed Al-Rashed, Mariana Bahtchevanova, James Berry, Carrie Gillon, Daniela Kostadinovska, William Kruger, Robert LaBarge, Claire Renaud, Uthairat Rogers, Olena Tsurska, Anne Walton-Ramírez, Jing Xia, Hui-Ling Yang, and Yidan Xu. I tried out this book in an advanced syntax class (with Naomi, Anne, Daniela, Lin, Qin, Sadique, Robert, Eleonore, Dawn, Carolyn, Tatiana, Amanda, Annette, Youmie, and Bethany) and am grateful to the students in that class. Thanks also to two anonymous referees, Johanna Wood, Marijana Marelj, Jay Myers, David Medeiros, Christina Sarigiannidou, Chris Jackson, Gnanadevi Rajasundaram, and Helen Barton, whose visit in 2009 prompted this book. Jan Koster was the first (as far as I know) to point out clearly that there is a real mismatch between Cartography on the one hand and Merge-only Minimalism on the other, so many thanks to Jan.

Abbreviations

A	Agent; also used to abbreviate "Answer"
ABS	Absolutive
ACC	Accusative
Adv	Adverb or adverbial, depending on the name or the function
AGR	Agreement
AGRo	Agreement with the object
AGRoP	Agreement with the object Phrase
AGRs	Agreement with the subject
AGRsP	Agreement with the subject Phrase
ASP	Aspect Phrase
AUX	Auxiliary
BNC	*British National Corpus*, with references cited using the BNC codes
BP	before present
c	Causer, used for theta-role features
C	Complementizer
C-I	Conceptual-Intentional
CL	Classifier in gloss
COCA	*Corpus of Contemporary American English* (http://corpus2.byu.edu/coca)
CP	Complementizer Phrase
CSE	*Corpus of Spoken, Professional American-English* (www.athel.com/cspatg.html)
D	Determiner
DEF	Definite
DP	Determiner Phrase
dur	durative features
EA	External Argument
ECM	Exceptional Case Marking
EPP	Extended Projection Principle
ERG	Ergative
Exp	Expletive

F	Generic Functional Category; future in gloss; feminine in gloss, e.g. FP feminine plural
Fin	Fin(ite) Phrase
FOC	Focus
fut	interpretable future features
FUT	future in gloss
G	Goal (theta-role)
GEN	Genitive
H	Head
HT	Hanging Topic
I	Inflection
i-	interpretable feature, e.g. [i-fut] is interpretable future, [i-past] is interpretable past, and [i-pres] is interpretable present
IMPF	Imperfective in gloss
ind	indicative
INFL	Inflection
Int	Interrogative
IP	Inflection Phrase
irr	irrealis
LCA	Linear Correspondence Axiom
LDT	Left Dislocated Topic
LF	Logical Form
m	mental, used for theta-role features
M	Mood
MP	Mood Phrase
Neg	Negation
NMZ	Nominalizer in gloss
NOM	Nominative
NPI	Negative Polarity Item
Num	Used as a functional category for Number
obj	an uninterpretable feature, indicating the case relationship between a transitive verb and its object
OBL	Oblique
OCC	Occurrence, alternative term for EPP
OED	Oxford English Dictionary
P	Preposition; plural in gloss
PART	Particle
pf	perfective
PF	Phonetic Form

PHON	Interface from the Narrow Syntax to the Sensorimotor system
PRO	empty subject argument of a non-finite verb
pro	empty subject argument of a finite verb
Ps	Used as a functional category for Person and as a feature
PST	Past in gloss
Q	Question particle in the gloss; and used to abbreviate "Question"
RelT	Relative tense; used for the perfect in English
S	Sentence (now TP); singular in gloss
SEM	interface from the Narrow Syntax to the Conceptual-Intentional system
S-M	Sensorimotor
Spec	Specifier
STAT	Stative
SUBJ	subjunctive
SV	Subject Verb order
SVO	Subject Verb Object
T	Tense
Th	Theme
TMA	Tense, Mood, Aspect Marking in the clause
Top	Topic
TP	Tense Phrase
u-	uninterpretable features, e.g. [u-T] is uninterpretable tense in T; also used on nouns for case checking
UTAH	Uniformity of Theta Assignment Hypothesis
v	light verb
V2	Verb-second
VP	Verb Phrase
vP	small VP
VPISH	VP Internal Subject Hypothesis
VS	Verb Subject order
WALS	*World Atlas of Language Structures* (wals.info)
*	ungrammatical, or repeatable more than once
#	pragmatically ill-formed when in front of a sentence; also the number feature
1	first person
2	second person
3	third person

1 Introduction

Much has been written on what constitutes a clause cross-linguistically. In English, main clauses minimally contain a finite verb and a subject, whereas subordinate clauses may lack an independent subject or a finite verb. Before discussing the descriptive characteristics of the clause in Chapter 2, I first present a brief overview of Generative Grammar and some of the main issues of the moment: Universal Grammar, Principles and Parameters, and the status of phrase structure rules.

Chomsky (1965 and later) emphasizes descriptive and explanatory adequacy. By that, he means that our models need to describe what the grammar of a language is and how children learn it. In recent years, he has emphasized a third question, namely why the grammar is the way it is. This question is also known as going "beyond explanatory adequacy" (Chomsky 2004), and I will discuss it in Section 1.1 of this chapter, though it is not the focus of this book.

The chapter is organized as follows. In Section 1.1, the focus is on Universal Grammar, the early instantiations of phrase structure rules, and the Principles and Parameters approach that is still the basis for Minimalism. In Section 1.2, I sketch the changes from phrase structure rules through X-bar theory to bare phrase structure and to the current problematization of projection. I also outline the changes from transformations to Move-alpha to Agree and features. In Section 1.3, I introduce Cartography and, in Section 1.4, we look at word order issues. In Section 1.5, we return to what might be feature parameters of the clause.

1.1 GENERATIVE GRAMMAR AND UNIVERSAL GRAMMAR

In this section, we first examine Universal Grammar and how Universal Grammar interacts with Phrase Structure Rules, then the Principles and Parameters approach, and finally some recent issues.

1.1.1 Universal grammar

The first half of the twentieth century is, among other things, known for its precise descriptions of languages. Leonard Bloomfield and Zellig Harris are among the most influential linguists using a descriptive, structuralist approach. Psychology and learning theory are at that time dominated by behaviorism. Noam Chomsky and the generative model he develops offer an alternative, starting in the late 1950s, to descriptive linguistics and behaviorism and bring about a revolution in the fields of linguistics, psychology, and cognitive science. Chomsky continues to stress descriptive adequacy but adds explanatory adequacy to emphasize the interest in how the language faculty is represented in humans.

In the new model, the focus is on the mind of the language learner/user (the **competence**) and ceases to be on the structures present in the language produced (the **performance**). The input to language learning is seen as poor, a phenomenon known as the "poverty of the stimulus". The basis for this phenomenon is that speakers know so much more than what they have evidence for from the input. For instance, speakers of English have never been taught that sentences of the type in (1a) are grammatical but those in (1b) are not. Yet, they can judge this difference in grammaticality.

(1) a. Who did I hear **that** John met?
    b. *Who did I hear **when** John met?

In (1a), *who* originates as the object of the verb *met* and is fronted to form the *wh*-question; in (1b), the same is true, but somehow changing *that* to *when* makes the sentence ungrammatical. We'll talk about *wh*-movement more in Chapter 2, where relative clauses are concerned, and more generally in Chapter 5.

How is acquisition of, for instance, (1) possible? We may never have heard (1a) and still know that it is grammatical, and we certainly haven't been taught that (1b) is ungrammatical. The answer to this problem of impoverished input, **Plato's problem** in Chomsky (1986a), is Universal Grammar, the initial state of the language faculty. This biologically innate organ helps the learner make sense of linguistic data and build an internal grammar (I-language), which then produces the sentences a speaker utters (E-language). See Figure 1.1.

The innate language faculty, when "stimulated by appropriate and continuing experience ... creates a grammar that creates sentences with formal and semantic properties," according to Chomsky (1975: 36). Thus, our innate language faculty (or Universal Grammar) enables

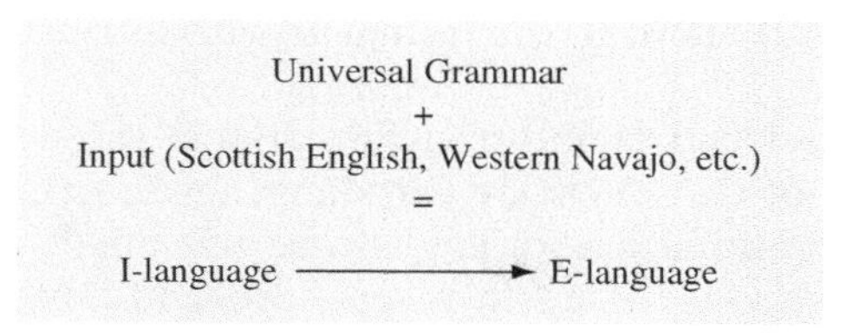

Figure 1.1 Model of language acquisition

us to create a set of rules, or grammar, by being exposed to (rather chaotic) language around us. The set of rules that we acquire enables us to produce sentences that we have never heard before. These sentences can also be infinitely long (if we have the time and energy).

Language acquisition, in this framework, is not imitation but an interaction between Universal Grammar and exposure to a particular language. "Learning is primarily a matter of filling in detail within a structure that is innate" (Chomsky 1975: 39). "A physical organ, say the heart, may vary from one person to the next in size or strength, but its basic structure and its function within human physiology are common to the species. Analogously, two individuals in the same speech community may acquire grammars that differ somewhat in scale and subtlety ... These variations in structure are limited." (1975: 38).

As I mentioned, Chomsky, in various publications, has talked about descriptive and explanatory adequacy. With the first, he means that we have to be able to **describe** the grammar of a particular language; with the second, he means that we have to be able to **explain** how the child acquires its language. In the last decade, he has added that we have to look at why language is the way it is. This is also known as "Beyond Explanatory Adequacy," see e.g. Chomsky (2004). In the remainder of the book, I will not focus on the "why" question, but I will return to it in Chapter 7.

Having briefly introduced Universal grammar, I'll provide a brief overview of how Universal Grammar deals with clause structure.

1.1.2 Phrase Structure and transformations

The implementation of the model in Figure 1.1 has seen a number of major changes. Between the 1950s and 1970s, a generative transformational model was developed that uses recursive phrase structure rules (to derive the deep-structure) and transformations (to derive the surface structure). These rules use substantive and formal universals. The substantive universals concern universal categories (V, N, etc.)

and phonological features; the formal universals relate to the nature of rules.

Both phrase structure and transformational rules of the internalized grammar of the 1960s are very language-specific. For instance, two Phrase Structure rules for English are given in (2) and for Persian in (3). The Verb and NP are in reverse order in (2b) and (3b), since objects follow verbs in English but precede them in Persian.

Phrase structure rules:

(2) a. Sentence → NP + VP
    b. VP → Verb + NP (Chomsky 1957: 27)

(3) a. Sentence → NP + VP
    b. VP → NP + Verb

An example of a transformation is given in (4). This rule derives an English passive from an active sentence. It is again very language-specific.

Transformational rules:

(4) If S1 is a grammatical sentence of the form
    NP1 - Aux - V - NP2,
    then the corresponding string of the form
    NP2 - Aux + be + en - V - by + NP1
    is also a grammatical sentence. (Chomsky 1957: 43)

Universals in this system of deriving the clause structure are the categories used in the phrase structure rules and the way the rules are written. (Categories are currently no longer part of Universal Grammar, and the term "universal" is no longer used in this framework except in the phrase "Universal Grammar".)

The input and output of the Phrase Structure Rules are not constrained, and one could have a rule like that in (5), for instance. Such lack of restrictions is not desirable.

(5) VP → S PP N V PP

Therefore, to remedy this lack of constraints, the system in (2) to (4) becomes increasingly generalized and abstract, starting in the 1970s. Insights into phrase structure from Chomsky (1970) and Jackendoff (1977) replace such rules as (2) and (3) with X'-theory, again applicable cross-linguistically. We'll see more on X-bar in the next section. And after Ross' (1967) work discovers **islands**, domains from which movement cannot take place, such rules as (4) are replaced by "move alpha" (= move anything anywhere). Such rules are applicable in any language. The consequence of all this is a system that invites cross-linguistic comparison, and, as a result, Universal Grammar comes to be seen in the late 1970s and early 1980s as consisting of Principles (true in all languages) and Parameters (choices to be made depending on the language).

1.1.3 Principles and Parameters

Principles can be pretty model-specific. I will list a few without elaborating on them further. They include the Subjacency Principle (Chomsky 1973), the Structure Preserving Hypothesis (Emonds 1976), the Head Movement Constraint (Travis 1984), Relativized Minimality (Rizzi 1990), the Phase Impenetrability Condition (Chomsky 2001), the Inclusiveness Condition (Chomsky 1995: 225–228), the Extension Condition (Chomsky 1995), No Tampering (Chomsky 2004: 117; 2008b: 138), the Head Preference Principle (van Gelderen 2004), and many others.

Many of the principles restrict how movement is constrained. For instance, Subjacency limits movement to crossing no more than two phrases of a particular kind; the Structure Preserving Hypothesis states that transformations, i.e. movement, can only move elements to positions that could be generated by means of phrase structure rules; the Head Movement Constraint says that heads only move to head positions; Relativized Minimality claims that heads are related to other local heads and phrases to other similar local phrases; and the Extension Condition requires that syntactic operations extend the tree at the root.

Some of these principles have been abandoned, e.g. Subjacency and Structure Preservation, although you will still see references to them in the literature. You will also see mention of some of the others in this book, e.g. head movement and Relativized Minimality, but not all will play a role. Principles continue to be valid to the present, although their location and level of specificity are debated. At the moment, the emphasis is on principles not specific to the language faculty (Universal Grammar), but to "general properties of organic systems" (Chomsky 2004: 105), "third factor principles" in Chomsky (2005; 2007). Thus, Chomsky identifies three factors crucial in the development of language.

Three factors

> (1) [G]enetic endowment, which sets limits on the attainable languages, thereby making language acquisition possible; (2) external data,

> converted to the experience that selects one or another language within a narrow range; (3) principles not specific to FL [the Faculty of Language]. Some of the third factor principles have the flavor of the constraints that enter into all facets of growth and evolution . . . Among these are principles of efficient computation (Chomsky 2007: 3)

The first factor is the traditional Universal Grammar with Principles and Parameters, and the second factor is the experience that we saw in Figure 1.1. The third factor marks a new emphasis but is somewhat related to the first factor. The third factor is favored above the language-specific first one (for reasons of simplicity) and can be divided into several types, including principles of efficient computation, which are "of particular significance in determining the nature of attainable languages" (Chomsky 2005: 6). Economy Principles are probably also part of more general cognitive principles, thus reducing the role of Universal Grammar even more.

Early examples of **parameters**, determined by the first factor, are pro-drop (Rizzi 1982), headedness (Stowell 1981), and movement of *wh*-elements (Huang 1982). **Pro-drop** is the cover term for a set of related phenomena, and there are many ways to account for having empty subjects. Not many linguists, however, believe that the phenomenon involves a +/– setting of an actual parameter called 'pro-drop'. Pro-drop is a collection of related phenomena: the absence of the subject of a finite verb, as in (6), subject-inversion, long *wh*-movement of the subject, etc. (see Chomsky 1981: 240).

(6) *tiene* *un* *bolígrafo* =pro-drop Spanish
have.3S a pen
'S/he has a pen.'

Headedness is a way to characterize a language, with Arabic and Irish being head-initial, and Japanese and Korean head-final. Following work by Kayne (1994), however, headedness has been abandoned as a formal parameter. In this framework, the basic word order is SVO, and other word orders come about through movement. I come back to issues of basic word order in Section 1.4. Likewise, the ***wh*-movement parameter** is now often seen as dependent on the character of the C or on an Extended Projection Principle (EPP) feature.[1]

[1] Setting the Binding Domain (Chomsky 1981: 225, fn 35) and finding the relevant barriers for Subjacency (Chomsky 1973) are two other early parameters. They are now part of a theory of phases or of an Economy Locality Principle.

Though most introductory generative syntax books continue to cite this set of three parameters, pro-drop/null subject, headedness, and *wh*-movement, these are often used in very descriptive ways to describe the typological characteristics of a language, not to explain what goes on in language acquisition. Since Chomsky (1995), a major question is how these parameters would have arisen in the brain. If the shift in humans from no language to language was immediate, it makes sense that there is one crucial change in the way the brain functions, and that change could have been the introduction of Merge. Complex parameters of the pro-drop variety don't fit in this non-gradual picture of evolution.

In addition, especially since Borer (1984), parameters consist of choices of feature specifications as the child acquires a lexicon (Chomsky 2004; 2007). The computational system of every language is seen as the same. Thus, all parameters are lexical, and they account for the variety of languages. If the child has evidence for gender in the language it hears, gender will be included; if not, it won't be. Baker, while disagreeing with this view of parameters, calls it the Borer-Chomsky-Conjecture.

(7) Borer-Chomsky-Conjecture

> All parameters of variation are attributable to differences in the features of particular items (e.g., the functional heads) in the lexicon (Baker 2008a: 156; 2008b: 3).

There have to of course be restrictions as to how much freedom the child has in selecting or ignoring the features and on how to bundle them. I will come back to this in Section 1.5.

The next section will examine changes in Generative Grammar in more detail and show how the move to (7) is possible.

1.2 FROM PHRASE STRUCTURE TO MINIMALIST FEATURES

In this section, I outline the system of the early 1980s (the Government and Binding framework, so called after the title of Chomsky's 1981 book) and subsequent changes up to and including Chomsky's Minimalist Program. In Section 1.2.1, I emphasize the changes in phrase structure rules, because this is crucial to the current Minimalist Program. In Section 1.2.2, we look at transformations and how their character changes due to features. Section 1.2.3 finishes with a typical Minimalist derivation.

1.2.1 Phrase Structure and X-bar

The phrase structure rules of Chomsky (1981) do not differ crucially in form from those of Chomsky (1957). Thus, (2) above and (8) are quite similar.

(8) a. VP → V NP
b. S → NP INFL VP (Chomsky 1981: 25)

A tree using (8) would look as in (9).

(9) 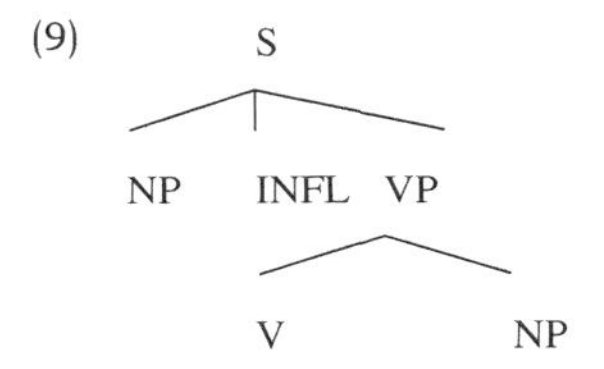

Though the actual Phrase Structure Rules aren't very different, the rationale behind (8) had become more principled, more universally applicable. With Chomsky's (1970) paper "Remarks on Nominalization", X-bar theory had been introduced, which, at least for the lexical categories, did wonders to make the system less language-specific. Jackendoff (1977) refines this system even more. Crucial to X-bar theory is that all phrases look alike, with a head, a complement, a specifier, and possibly an adjunct. Rather than having separate rules for NP, VP, PP, etc., (10) generates rules for any lexical category.

(10) a. XP → YP X' (YP = Specifier)
b. X' → X ZP (ZP = Complement)
c. XP → WP XP (WP = Adjunct)
(where X, W, Y, and Z stand for N, V, A, and P)

Chomsky had also worried about the redundancy between the lexicon and very specific phrase structure rules, such as (11), to accommodate such verbs as *give*. If *give* is in the lexicon with three arguments, that and such rules as (10) should be enough to project any space needed. The redundancy is then eliminated.

(11) VP → V NP (NP) (PP)

In tree form, (10) looks like (12a), where the X projects up and is the only head category. In (12b), an actual VP (X=V) is provided, although the subject doesn't appear as the specifier of the VP until the mid 1980s.

(12)
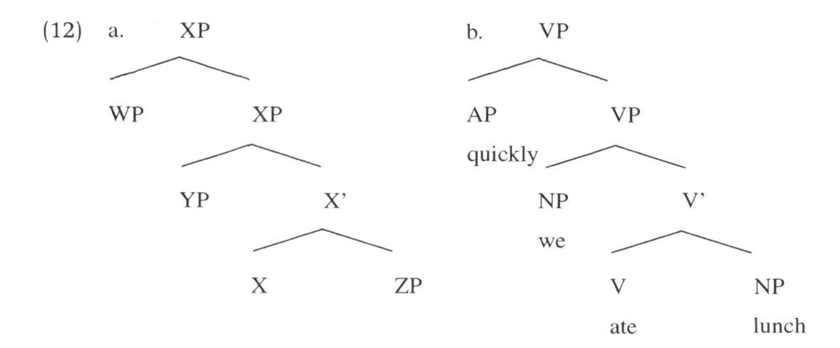

In the mid 1980s, work by den Besten (1983), Fukui and Speas (1986), Abney (1987), and others leads to a change where functional categories, C, INFL, and D are considered on a par with lexical categories and head their own projections. Taking the X-bar structure of functional categories into account as well, (8) is reformulated as (13), with INFL changed into I(nflection) and later into T(ense), and the NP argument always as part of a DP with a D head.

(13)
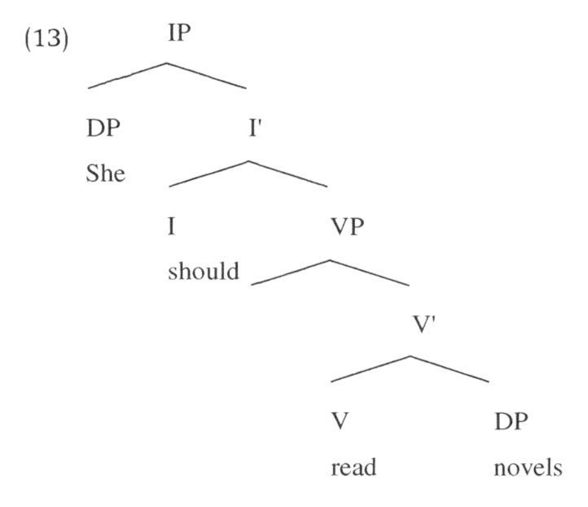

This structure has been the basic (non-expanded) structure of the clause since 1986, although most syntacticians assume a CP above the IP, as in (14), even if the clause does not include a *wh*-pronoun (typically in the Specifier of CP) or a complementizer (in the head of the CP).

(14)

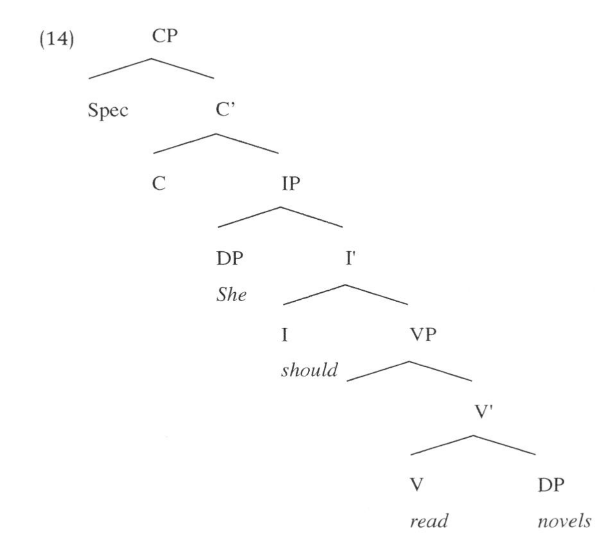

Pollock (1989) suggests splitting up I into T and AGR(reement), known as the "Split Infl Hypothesis," and Chomsky (1989) ends up with an AGRs and an AGRo. English doesn't show much agreement, so we'll use Spanish to exemplify these two categories. AGRs is used for agreement with the subject, *-án* in (15), T for the future *-r*, and AGRo for the feminine plural *-das* on the V. (I have placed the passive auxiliary in T, but that has moved from a lower position.) The tree structure of (15) is given in (16).

(15)	*Las casas*	*se-r-**án***	*vendi-**das***	*(el mes próximo)*	Spanish
	the houses(F)	be-FUT-3P	sold-FP	the month next	
	'The houses will be sold (next month).'				

(16)

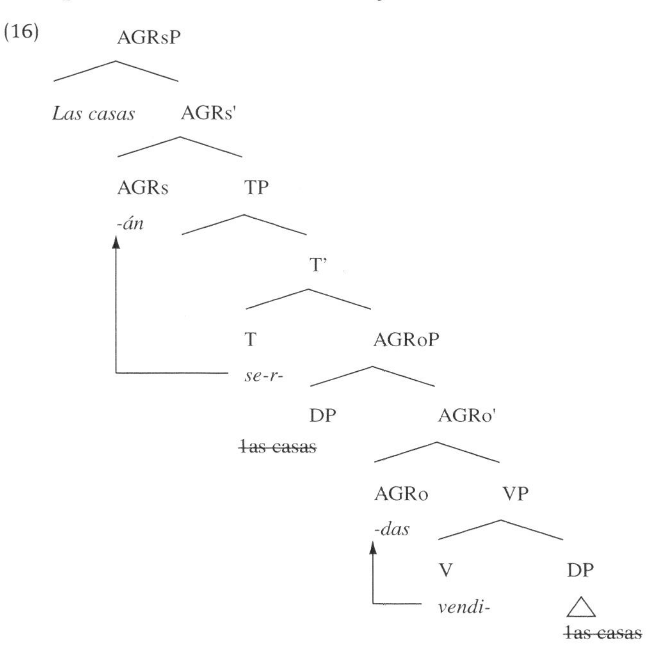

The DP *las casas* is indicated as having moved from a low position (where it receives a theta-role) to higher positions. Just like the V and the T, the reason behind the movement of the DP is to check certain features, mainly case. When did this checking first appear in syntactic thinking?

In a famous letter from 1977 (published as Vergnaud 2008), Vergnaud noted that NPs - now these would be DPs - occur in positions of case assignment, e.g. as subject of a finite verb. This became known as the Case Filter, as in (17), and gave NPs a reason to move, a "last resort".

(17) **Case Filter** (in the PF)
*NP if NP has phonetic content and has no case (Chomsky 1981: 49)

Since the early 1980s, case and agreement have become very important. In a tree such as (8) above, a c-command/sister relationship takes care of both case and agreement (although in e.g. Chomsky 1981 a slightly more complex system was employed). However, once we have a structure as in (13), (14), and (16), using c-command between two sisters is no longer possible to bring about case assignment, since the subject is no longer a sister to I, or T. It is therefore argued in the late 1980s that case is checked in a Spec-Head relationship of the kind in

(16). Chomsky (1986b: 24) assumes that Spec-Head agreement "is a form of 'feature sharing' ... sharing of the features person, number, gender, Case, etc." This sharing is exemplified for AGRs in (18) where the DP shares the verb's case and the verb the DP's agreement features.

(18)
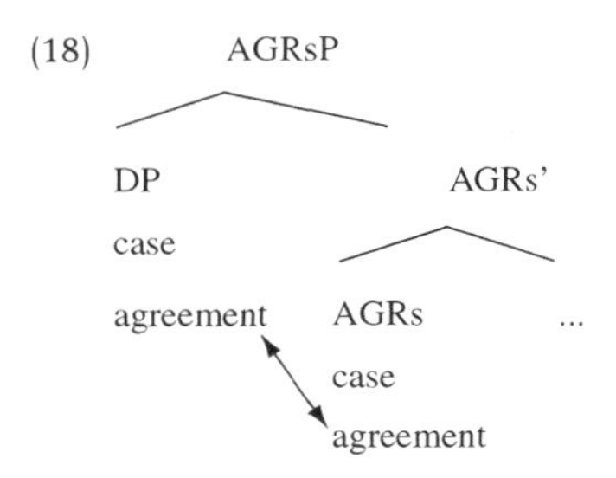

This gives movement an entirely new purpose: as last resort for an NP (now DP) to receive case. In early generative work, transformations are used for changes between the deep- and surface-structures, e.g. for passive, *wh*-movement, and existential constructions. As we saw, transformations are generalized as Move alpha ("move anything anywhere"). This movement rule achieves much more cross-linguistic insight. With the extension of X-bar theory to functional categories, there are suddenly lots of specifier positions for DPs to move to, and now there is a reason: checking of case and agreement.

Much empirical evidence for AGR is not discussed by, for instance, Chomsky (1989). One of the advantages of postulating AGRs (and AGRo) is theory-internal: It is now possible to say "that structural Case generally is correlated with agreement and reflects a government relation between the NP and the appropriate AGR element" (Chomsky 1989: 149). "We now regard both agreement and structural Case as manifestations of the SPEC-head relation (NP, AGR)" (Chomsky 1992: 10). Kayne (1989: 97), talking about AGRo, notices the same relationship between the specifier position and case/agreement: "when there is agreement, that agreement is due to the NP having moved to (or through) a position governed by an abstract element AGR generated as sister to the VP headed by the participle." This correlation had been noted by Greenberg to occur cross-linguistically for SV as opposed to VS orders. It is exemplified with an example from Arabic, where the subject in a VS structure (19) does not agree in number, though it does in an SV structure (20). I have marked the nominative and accusative, but they are not important here, so you can ignore that.

(19)	a.	*akal-at*	*l-banaat-u*	*al-taʕm-a*	Arabic
		eat-3FS	the girls-NOM	the-food-ACC	
	b.	**akal-na*	*l-banaat-u*	*al-taʕam-a*	
		eat-3FP	the girls-NOM	the-food-ACC	

(20)	a.	*al-banaat-u*	*akal-na*	*al-taʕam-a*	Arabic
		the girls-NOM	eat-3FP	the-food-ACC	
	b.	**al-banaat-u*	*akal-a t*	*al-taʕam-a*	
		the girls-NOM	eat-3FS	the-food-ACC	
		'The girls ate the food.'			(Mohammed Al-Rashed p.c.)

Chomsky (1995) abandons the AGR position because it makes no semantic contribution and, rather than using IP, starts using TP. This then also leads to a system of probing by a c-commanding head for a Goal rather than of Spec-Head agreement, as we'll see in Section 1.2.2.

A last detail to add on clausal phrase structure is the **VP-shell**. Larson (1988), Sportiche (1988), and Koopman and Sportiche (1991) contribute in very different ways to this. Larson, in examining the double object alternation in English, accommodates both (21a) and (21b) with a doubled VP.

(21) a. She gave him a book.
b. She gave a book to him.

Larson's tree (1988: 384) opens up the way for all arguments in a three-place predicate to be accommodated in an expanded VP. I will modify the expanded VP for (21) using a vP-shell as in (22).

(22)

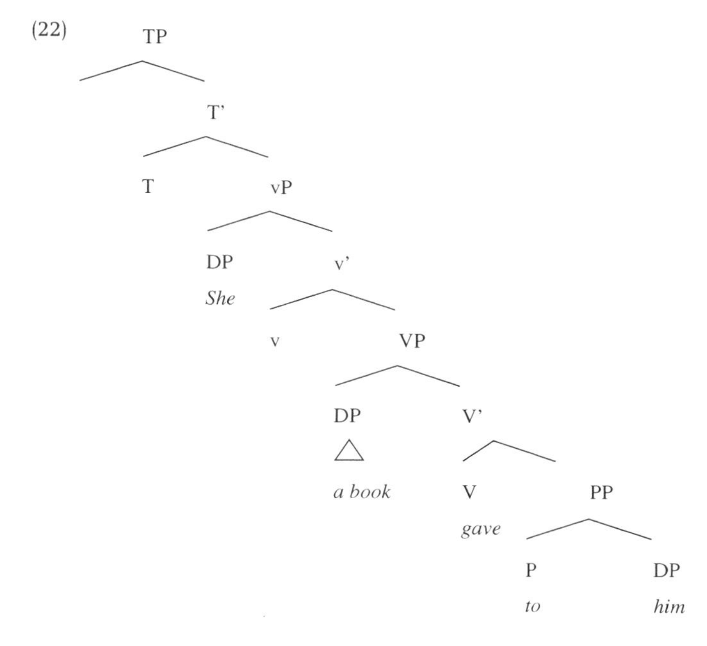

In (22), the V moves to v as well, and this gives (21b); the derivation of (21a) will be discussed in Chapter 3.

Sportiche (1988), in his work on quantifier float, and Koopman and Sportiche (1991), in their work on the position of subjects, show that all arguments originate in the VP. This is the so-called **VP-Internal Subject Hypothesis**, or VPISH. They argue (not using vP yet) that the subject originates in the specifier of the VP and moves to the specifier of IP (not TP then yet). I have indicated this position of the (subject) Agent in the shell in (22) and also updated the IP as TP.

Empirical evidence for the VPISH is provided by quantifier float. In quantifier float, it was assumed that the quantifier *all* in (23) and (24) "floated" to the right, away from the DP *the children*.

(23) The children may **all** have painted a picture.

(24) The children may have **all** painted a picture.

Quantifier float is now seen as a process whereby the DP leaves the quantifier behind as the DP moves from inside the VP to the left. If the quantifier *all* starts out together with the DP *the children*, (23) and (24) show where the DP *the children* has in fact moved from a lower specifier position to a higher one. Positions where *the children* were not base generated cannot have *all*, e.g. (25).

(25) a. *The children may have painted a picture **all**.
b. *The children may have painted **all** a picture.

Thus, the extension of X-bar rules to functional categories leads to an increase in the use of functional categories and into how we view case and agreement. This use of functional categories for case and agreement leads to seeing the role of movement as changed: Movement exists to check case in a Spec-Head relationship. Economy Principles are formulated that reflect this view, for instance, "Last Resort" and "Greed." By the late 1990s, this approach is abandoned in favor of the operation AGREE, where a head looks for matching features in its c-command domain. We'll see this in the next two sections.

1.2.2 Features and AGREE

Structures such as (16) assume that all functional categories have a one-to-one relation between a morphological feature and a functional category, although we could split up the agreement features into gender, person, and number. However, as mentioned, Chomsky (1995: 349ff.) argues, in opposition to earlier work, that there is no direct evidence for AGRs and AGRo in English and that they are not semantically relevant. Agreement expresses a relationship instead. The only clausal functional categories that Chomsky currently uses in the clause are C, T, and v (and presumably NEG and ASP etc. when needed). We'll talk about the issue of the number of functional categories in relation to Cartographic models in Section 1.3. I'll now show how abandoning the various functional categories also leads to another view of checking, namely through AGREE.

First, I'll add a little more on **features** and the role of morphology. There are many types of feature: semantic (e.g. abstract object), phonological (e.g. the sounds), and formal (Chomsky 1995: 230ff., 236, 277ff.). The formal ones are relevant to syntax and are divided into intrinsic or optional. The intrinsic ones are "listed explicitly in the lexical entry or strictly determined by properties so listed" (Chomsky 1995: 231) and include categorial features, the case-assigning features of the verb, and the person and gender features of the noun. The person, number, and gender features are usually referred to as **phi-features**.

Optional features are added arbitrarily and are predictable from linguistic Principles (e.g. nouns need case or some kind of licensing). They include the tense and agreement features of verbs and the number and case features of nouns. An example of a noun with its features is provided in Figure 1.2. Typically, the intrinsic ones are valued and the optional ones get a value assigned to them by checking/matching.

The "much more important distinction" (Chomsky 1995: 277) is that between **interpretable** and **uninterpretable features**. The interpretable ones are relevant for interpretation at Logical Form (LF), and

	airplane		*build*	
semantic:	e.g. [artifact]		e.g. [action]	
phonological:	e.g. [begins with a vowel; two syllables]		e.g. [one syllable]	
formal:				
intrinsic		optional	intrinsic	optional
[nominal]		[number]	[verbal]	[phi]
[3 person]		[case]	[assign accusative]	[tense]
[non-human]				

Figure 1.2 Features of *airplane* and *build* (adapted from Chomsky 1995: 231)

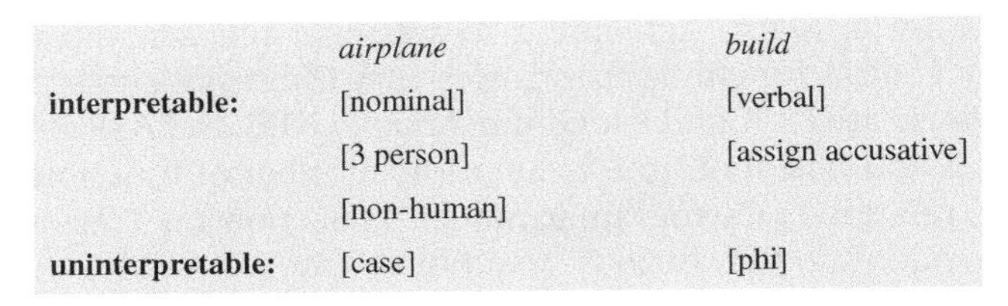

	airplane	*build*
interpretable:	[nominal]	[verbal]
	[3 person]	[assign accusative]
	[non-human]	
uninterpretable:	[case]	[phi]

Figure 1.3 Interpretable and uninterpretable features of *airplane* and *build* (adapted from Chomsky 1995: 278)

include categorial and nominal phi-features. They are not deleted or erased after they are checked because they are relevant to the interpretative component. In fact, semantic and formal features "intersect" (Chomsky 2001: 10). Uninterpretable features receive a value when they search and find an interpretable feature. These valued features are not interpreted at LF; they just go to the PF and, in English, involve the case features of NPs and verbs and the phi-features of verbs.

There are a number of reasons behind the distinction between interpretable and uninterpretable features. Some features (e.g. phi-features of nouns) remain visible after checking and hence cannot be deleted. This is the reason nouns (and of course the phrases they head) can move cyclically and provide the phi-features along the way (Chomsky 1995: 282). This is not true of the uninterpretable case feature. Once case has been checked by a DP, that DP cannot move to check case elsewhere. Figure 1.3 provides the interpretable and uninterpretable features of the noun *airplane* and the verb *build*.

Note that many intrinsic features are interpretable, but that connection isn't absolute. Note also that uninterpretable features cannot be on their own in a sentence. There has to be something valuing them.

There are different views on the role of morphological marking on nouns and verbs. Chomsky often assumes a lexicalist approach, where words are taken out of the lexicon fully inflected and then checked. This is very possible in English, since it is a morphologically impoverished language with no overt case on nouns and very little agreement on verbs. In languages with a lot of morphology, e.g. Turkish or Navajo, the morphemes may occupy independent positions in functional heads. In these languages it is not clear that we need both uninterpretable and interpretable features; just the latter may do.

Now let's return to the actual checking. In connection to features and movement, there is a major change after 1995 (Chomsky 2000, but originally proposed in 1998), namely checking through Spec-Head agreement is replaced by a **probe-goal checking** system based on the c-command relationship. Functional categories in need of feature checking search down the tree for a Goal DP that will value their features. An advantage of this shift is a simplification of the existential construction in English (and other languages that have this). The pre-2000 derivation of (26) involved invisible Raising of the postverbal DP *many buffaloes* to the specifier of TP for agreement with the verb in T. The invisibility was achieved by means of LF-Raising of the DP or movement of the features of the DP, both very ad-hoc procedures.

(26) a. There were **many buffaloes** in the room.
b. There was **a buffalo** in the room.

The AGREE-version of (26a) is given in (27). The uninterpretable agreement features in T find the DP in the specifier of VP (i.e. vP), and the interpretable features of the DP value the phi-features of T, plural in the case of *many buffaloes*, of T. (The T also has tense features, but I leave those out for now.)

(27)

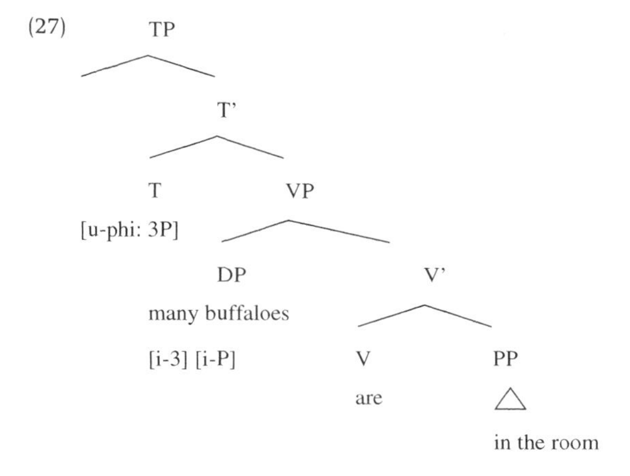

AGREE is done by an uninterpretable feature, a probe, searching in its c-command domain (i.e. down the tree) for a Goal with appropriate interpretable features. This means there is no movement to the specifier position for reasons of case and agreement. The subject moves to the specifier of the TP in English, but this is now because of the EPP, a relatively stipulative condition that we also come back to in Chapter 4.

1.2.3 Derivations through Merge

Apart from an emphasis on features and AGREE, another major change in Minimalism is that explicit phrase structures, such as the structure in (14) that descends from CP to TP to VP, are abandoned in favor of a general rule **Merge** with bare phrase structure. I assume **bare phrase structure** in this book, but often draw Cartographic trees because they are more specific. In this section, I give a derivation that is more or less the current version of a Minimalist derivation, using pure Merge but still labeling the nodes.

In a Minimalist approach, a Modern English derivation proceeds in four steps. First, items are selected from the lexicon. Chomsky (2007: 6) suggests the lexicon has "atomic elements, lexical items LI, each a structured array of properties." Abstracting away from features, a lexical array could be {saw, it, T, Martians}. Second, the elements are merged, e.g. *saw* and *it* in (28), and one of the heads (in this case V) projects to a higher VP.

(28)

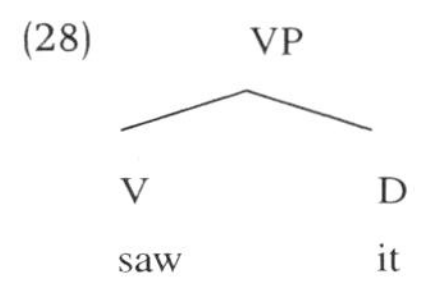

The Merge in (28) is external Merge because the lexical items are taken from the lexical array. If elements are moved, they are said to be internally merged or remerged.

Already in Chomsky (1995), there is some debate as to whether there is an additional labeling operation and which elements are selected for Merge. Labels, such as VP or V', introduce new elements into the derivation and are therefore not allowed by the Inclusiveness Condition. The **Inclusiveness Condition** bars material that wasn't initially selected from the lexicon from being introduced. Instead of labels, the actual lexical item should be projected, as in (29), a really bare structure.

(29)

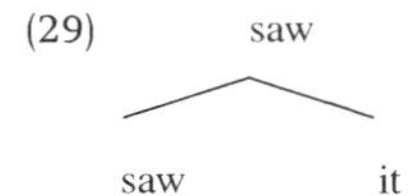

There is also some discussion as to whether it always has to be the head that projects (e.g. Chomsky 2005: 14), and this becomes a focus of attention in Chomsky (2011). I will continue to use labels as in (28) and elsewhere for convenience only (cf. Chomsky 1995: 244; 2004).

Third, after adding a (small) v and subject *Martians* to (28), as in (30), the functional categories T and C are merged to vP. AGREE ensures that the uninterpretable features on v and T find a noun with matching (active) features to check agreement. When agreement is checked, so is what is often referred to as case (at least in many Indo-European languages, but see Baker 2009 and Section 1.5 below for languages without this connection). Following Pesetsky and Torrego (2001),[2] I will refer to this case as [u-T] rather than nominative and as [u-obj] rather than accusative. More on this in Chapter 4.

So, v and T probe (search) for a nominal that they c-command to agree with. The v finds this nominal in *it*, and T finds this nominal in *Martians*, and each element values its uninterpretable features, which then delete. As T and v value their phi-features, the [u-T] and [u-obj] on the nominals is also valued. The valuation of the phi-features on v is not visible in English, but we assume it, based on other languages where participles agree in number and gender, as we've seen in Spanish (15) above.

The final structure looks like (30), where the features that are not marked by "strike through" are interpretable and not subject to elimination from the interpretable component, i.e. they are relevant at the semantic interface. The features that are struck through have been valued (also shown here) and go to the phonological interface. The subject moves to Spec TP: it is merged from an internal position, through Internal Merge, for language-specific reasons (EPP or OCC, to be explored in Chapter 4).

(30)

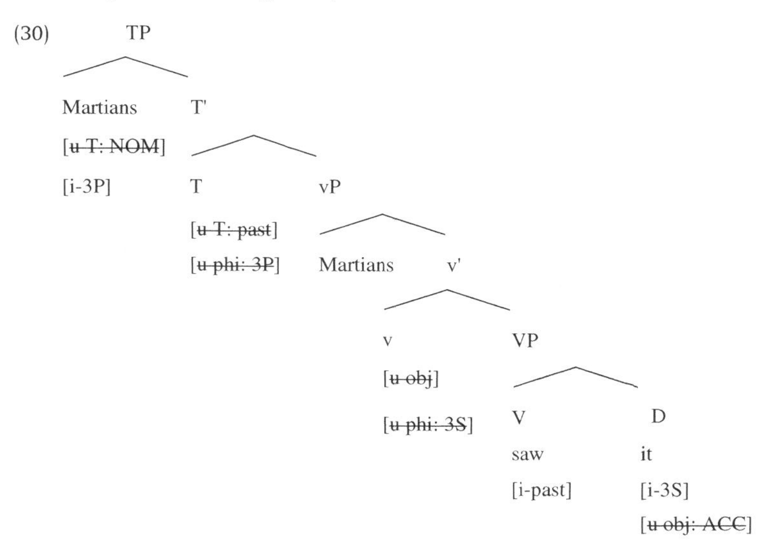

[2] Williams (1994: 11–12) is perhaps the first to argue that an NP has tense: "Nominative NPs are simply tensed NPs."

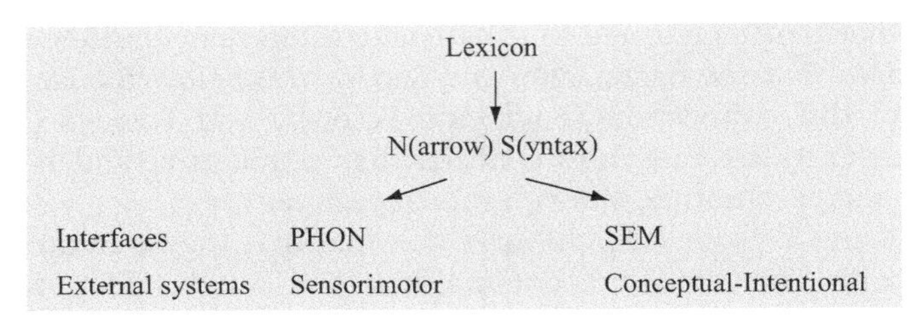

Figure 1.4 Interfaces

According to Chomsky (1995: 277–278), the case features on T and v are uninterpretable, as are the case features on the DPs. Case in English carries no meaning whatsoever. The derivation in (30) uses early lexical insertion, as in Chomsky (1995; 2004), but nothing hinges on this. The CP-Layer is not indicated in (30), although C is crucial in "giving" tense to T, as we'll see in Chapter 4.

At some point, the derivation has to be handed over to the **Sensorimotor** (S-M) and **Conceptual-Intentional** (C-I) systems external to the syntax. This is done through the interfaces PHON and SEM, corresponding to PF and LF in older frameworks. Figure 1.4 shows these interfaces.

The transfer to the interface levels proceeds step-wise as the derivation proceeds (see phases in Section 1.4). What is actually pronounced is "externalized," and there are ways to decide which copy of e.g. *Martians* in (30) to pronounce (again see Section 1.4 for further details).

This emphasis on language-external systems is formulated as the Strong Minimalist Thesis.

(31) **Strong Minimalist Thesis**

Language is a perfect solution to interface conditions (Chomsky 2007: 3)

Thus, the syntax has to satisfy the requirements of the external systems, which is achieved via the interfaces PHON and SEM. The former is responsible for linearization and externalization, e.g. what is spelled out or pronounced (see Nunes 2004 for an account on how to decide which copies to spell out).

For the C-I system, two aspects are very relevant: the theta-structure and the status of the information provided. The theta-structure must be mapped to the syntactic structure (more in

Chapter 3). In English, the highest theta-role inside the vP/VP will end up as the grammatical subject, so the theta-roles can be read off in terms of their hierarchy. In other languages, special morphological cases may indicate the theta-roles. Information structure refers to topic and focus, sometimes seen as old and new information, and can be determined through definiteness markers (typical for topics) or through position. In Chinese, there are no definite and indefinite articles. Indefinite objects and indefinite subjects appear towards the end of the sentence, as (32a) and (33a) show; definite subjects and objects appear pre-verbally, as in (32b) and (33b). So, although there are no definite and indefinite articles, whether the information is new or old is encoded through word order.

(32) a.

chi	*le*	***fan***	Chinese
eat	PF	rice	

'I ate some rice.'

b.

fan	*chi*	*le*
rice	eat	PF

'I ate the rice.'

(33) a.

Lai	*le*	***yi***	***ge***	***ren***	Chinese
come	PF	one	CL	man	

'A man came.'

b.

Ren	*lai*	*le*
person	come	PF

'The person has come.' (Li and Thompson 1981: 20)

As Chomsky (2002: 113; 2008a) points out, the semantic component expresses thematic as well as discourse information:

> In "what John is eating what," the phrase "what" appears in two positions, and in fact those two positions are required for semantic interpretation: the original position provides the information that "what" is understood to be the direct object of "eat," and the new position, at the edge, is interpreted as a quantifier ranging over a variable, so that the expression means something like "for which thing x, John is eating the thing x" (Chomsky 2008a: 8)

What is actually spelled out, i.e. pronounced, linearly differs quite a bit in specific languages because it depends on whether or not the features trigger movement. These are the (infamous) so-called **EPP** features (or OCC). I agree with Butler (2004), Reinhart (2006), and Stroik (2009: 7) that these features are relevant semantically. This would make them interpretable; it is not clear how they trigger

XP-movement, however. Chomsky (2011) pursues an approach that has to do with projection requirements, to which we return in Chapter 4, when we look at the EPP in more detail.

This section has provided a sketch of a current Minimalist derivation: starting a derivation at the bottom of a tree and going up, emphasizing features, and being pretty bare in structure. I will now contrast this with a different approach.

1.3 MERGE AND CARTOGRAPHY: FEATURES AND CATEGORIES

Within Minimalism, it is common to recognize three layers; see e.g. Chomsky (2000: 102). The idea for the three layers is an old one and is known from the Germanic literature on *Vorfeld*, *Mittelfeld*, and *Nachfeld* (see e.g. Drach 1937; Bech 1955). Since the mid 1990s, there is, however, a lot of work that splits up each layer, and, in this section, I will argue that this **representational** approach does not seem compatible with the approach sketched so far, namely the **derivational** bottom-up approach.

The work that splits up each layer more uses functional hierarchies such as (34ab) and (35b). I have added (35a) to account for the auxiliaries, for instance, in English, where the features will become more precise later on.

(34) CP-Layer

a.	...	Force ...	Topic ...	Focus ...	Fin	TP
		[ind]	(DP)	(*who*)	[tense]	

b.	Mood $_{\text{speech act}}$	Mood $_{\text{evaluative}}$	Mood $_{\text{evidential}}$	Mod $_{\text{epistemic}}$
	frankly	*fortunately*	*allegedly*	*probably*

((a) is from Rizzi 1997: 288 and (b) from Cinque 1999: 107)

(35) TP-Layer

a.	T	M	ASP
	[T]	[M]	[ASP]
	did	may	have

b.	T_{past}	T_{fut}	$Mood_{ir}$	Mod_{nec}	Mod_{pos}	ASP_{hab}	ASP_{rep}	ASP_{freq}
	once	*then*	*perhaps*	*necessarily*	*possibly*	*usually*	*again*	*often*

((b) is from Cinque 1999: 107)

This approach of assigning each category a precise position is known as **Cartography**, and a typical (partial) tree is provided in (36).

(36)

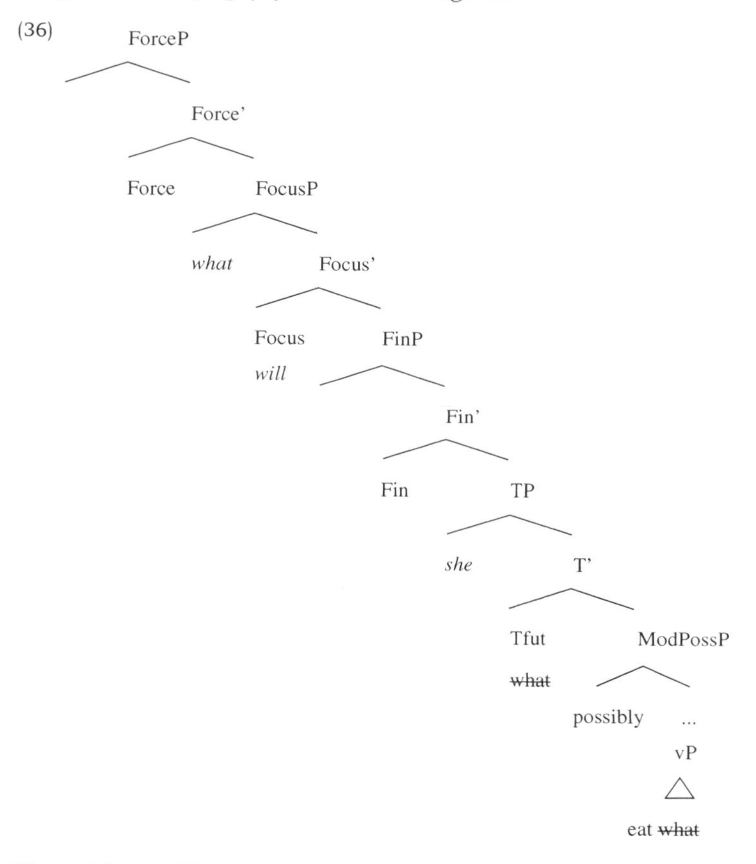

These hierarchies are representations of the functional structure of the clause that are cross-linguistically valid. However, in e.g. Cinque (1999), there is no mention of how a structure is arrived at, and, with such a wealth of functional categories, a purely derivational approach is hard to imagine. A projection from bottom to top would have to encode through the scope of features which functional category is merged first and which later.

In current Generative Grammar, Cartography is used side-by-side with the derivational, bare phrase structure approach. These two approaches, simple Merge and Cartography, towards clausal architecture are in principle incompatible. Minimalism using Merge comes up with as little structure and labeling as possible; the Cartographic approaches use "hundreds" of categories, as we'll see. Bare phrase structure abandons the distinction between specifiers and heads of

X-bar theory, whereas the Cartographic (36) relies on such projections. Adriana Belletti and Luigi Rizzi in a 2002 interview ask Chomsky how the Cartographic endeavor can "relate ... to the topics and goals pursued by the minimalist program?" Chomsky replies by dodging this question (to my mind) and says that the Cartographic approach has "led to fascinating results." He lists a few empirical facts about the layers in the clause and suggests that:

> [t]his kind of work leads us to inquire more closely into the nature of interface relations ... And beyond that it leads us to investigate the "external" systems themselves, and the conditions they impose on a well-designed language faculty. (Chomsky 2002: 123)

Mostly, Chomsky ignores the layers:

> Ignored as well are the "peripheral" systems outside TP; I will use C and T as surrogates for richer systems. On these matters see Rizzi 1997, Cinque 1999, and many other studies on the CFC [Core Functional Categories] systems and others. (Chomsky 2000: 143, fn 31)

As Shonksky (2010: 426) puts it, "[t]he tension between Minimalism's impoverished structures and the richness of Cartographic representations is a real one." Cinque and Rizzi themselves agree there is a tension, but they suggest that the tension indicates a difference in focus. In their own words:

> There is, at first sight, an inherent tension between the complexity of the Cartographic representations and the simplicity of the generative devices that minimalist syntax assumes, somehow reflected in the structural poverty of the representations typically found in the minimalist literature. We believe that there is no contradiction between these two directions of research, and the tension, where real, is the sign of a fruitful division of labor. Minimalism focuses on the elementary mechanisms which are involved in syntactic computations, and claims that they can be reduced to extremely simple combinatorial operations, ultimately external and internal Merge, completed by some kind of search operation (Chomsky's Agree) to identify the candidates of Merge. An impoverished computational mechanism does not imply the generation of an impoverished structure: a very simple recursive operation can give rise to a very rich and complex structure, as a function of the inventory of elements it operates on, and, first and foremost, of its very recursive nature. The very simplified structural representations often assumed in the minimalist literature, expressed by the C-T-v-V system, are sometimes taken literally, as substantive hypotheses on the nature of clausal configurations, but the structure of the arguments rarely implies a literal interpretation, and often is

Table 1.1 *Possible features and functional categories, based on Heine and Kuteva (2002: 317)*

permissive, possibility, agent, comparative, material, partitive, past/near, A-possessive, since (temporal), superlative, complementizer, dative, infinitive, Patient, purpose, temporal, until (temporal), only, NP-and, subordinator

> compatible with an interpretation of C-T-v-V as a shorthand for more complex Cartographic structures (a fact explicitly acknowledged, e.g., in Chomsky 2001, fn. 8), with C, T, and v taken as "abbreviations" standing for complex zones of the functional structure. (Cinque and Rizzi 2008: 49)

Cinque and Rizzi also discuss the question of the number of functional categories. There are thirty-two in Cinque (1999: 130) and around forty in Kayne (2005). Cinque and Rizzi, using Heine and Kuteva's 2002 work on grammaticalization, come up with 400 features that are targets in Heine and Kuteva. Cinque and Rizzi don't list these targets, the first twenty of which are provided in Table 1.1.

Benincà and Munaro (2010: 6–7) note in this connection that syntax has reached the detail of phonological features. These formal and semantic features would have to be innate. If we delegate language variation to the lexicon, the child needs help in acquiring this lexicon. Chomsky (1965: 142) already writes that "semantic features ... are presumably drawn from a universal 'alphabet' but little is known about this today and nothing has been said about it here." Later on, he says that vocabulary acquisition shows poverty of the stimulus (Chomsky 1993: 24), i.e. it is impossible to acquire the rich vocabulary without some help from Universal Grammar. I'll come back to this in Section 1.5.

So, Minimalism focuses on the derivation and Cartography on the overall structure of this derivation. This debate between derivation and representation is of course not new. For instance, Koster (1978; 1986; 2007) advocates a representational model without movement operations, but one where dependencies are indicated. The crucial argument for movement being superfluous, i.e. in favor of the representational approach, has been that constraints on movement operations (e.g. locality) are very similar to what we need, for instance, for reflexive binding (Koster 1986: 4). In Koster's model, the most important "notion of the theory of grammar is the dependency relation" (1986: 8), where two elements share a property. These relations are then subject to locality constraints. The relationship between a DP and its trace (or copy) can be one of these dependency relations, as is binding theory.

Key to much of Koster's thinking has been the Structure Preserving Hypothesis, which "entails that for each output of movement rules, the same output is available on the basis of phrase structure rules only; hence the complete redundancy of movement rules" (Koster 2007: 5). Chomsky (2011), without referring to Koster, handles this problem by getting rid of the last vestiges of X-bar theory, namely the labeling mechanism.

Having sketched two major approaches to a derivation in current generative syntax, I now turn to a few more issues that provide some background for the remainder of this book, namely word order and phases.

1.4 THE LINEAR CORRESPONDENCE AXIOM AND PHASES

In this section, I discuss two further refinements of the Minimalist Program, namely the issue of linear as opposed to hierarchical order, important since about 1994, and the question of phases, in the picture since 2001. Note that we'll talk about SVO but, for convenience, use S(ubject) as thematic/semantic as well as grammatical role, and the same with O(bject).

1.4.1 Linear or hierarchical order

As mentioned, X-bar theory makes it possible to see that the position of the X head is variable cross-linguistically. If an XP is headed (by a head), it makes sense that some heads are initial and others final in that phrase. If syntax is a system that relates sound and meaning, it is only the externalized part of language (the sounds) that puts words in a particular order. The semantic side of a derivation may not care about linear order at all; it is the hierarchical structure that counts (see especially Chomsky 2011). Kayne's Linear Correspondence Axiom makes a mapping from hierarchical to linear order possible.

With regard to parameters and Universal Grammar in general, Chomsky (2004; 2007) tries to limit their role and to ascribe as much as possible to the non-linguistic principles. This skepticism as to parameters holds for the headedness parameter as well. Chomsky (2008: 7) says, "I think that there is by now substantial evidence that ordering is restricted to externalization of internal computation to the sensorimotor system, and plays no role in core syntax and semantics."

Kayne (1994) argues that linear order is read off the hierarchical structure. If an element *a* c-commands *b* but not vice versa, this is an asymmetric c-command relation, and *a* has to precede *b* at spell-out, as (37) shows.

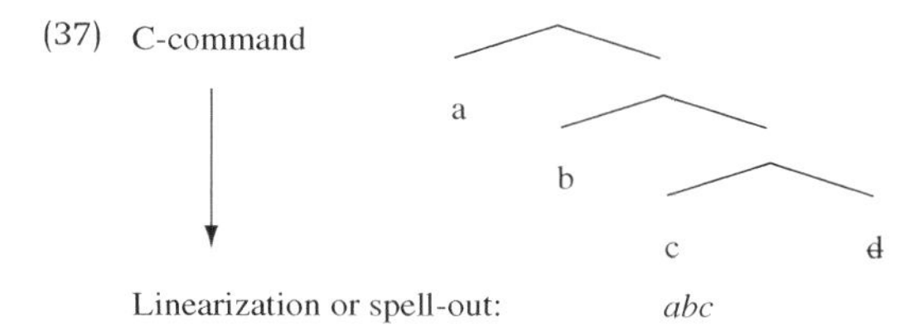

Note that, in a bare phrase structure model, one of the lower elements must be moved, since *cd* in (37) cannot be linearized when they c-command each other. I have indicated that as a crossed-out *d*, but haven't shown where *d* moves to. (Other solutions involve self-merge[3] of *d*, which creates more structure above *d* so that *c* c-commands *d* but not the other way around.)

The structure in (37) works well with heads. What if *a* contains a phrase, as in (38), where I have equated *b* with T and a phrase appears in the Spec TP? The elements *k* and *l* are asymmetrically c-commanded by *b*, so a subject DP could never be spelled out before a T, and this is not empirically correct, at least in English!

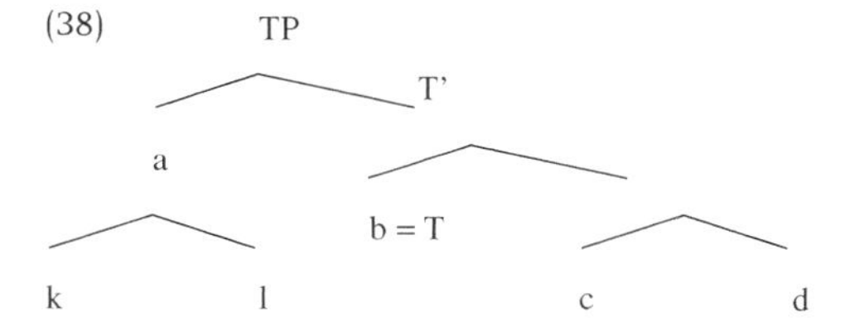

Based on May (1985), Kayne (1994: 15–16) therefore develops the notion of a segment and argues that T' is a segment that cannot enter into a c-command relationship. Once that is assumed, the problem of T having to precede *k* and *l* disappears. The model does lose its elegance, and the problem of the specifier hasn't been adequately resolved up to now (see Uriagereka 2011 for an alternative).

The linearization principle in (37) is known as the Linear Correspondence Axiom (LCA), or Universal Base Hypothesis, and has

[3] For more on self-Merge, see Guimarães (2000).

been used in a number of ways. The way this is usually understood is that word order is just relevant to the spell-out (at the S-M interface), but that c-command is the basic notion (at the C-I interface).

As to word order, the LCA predicts that languages branch either to the right or to the left, as in (39a–b). That way the c-command relations can be translated directly into linear order. For instance, in (39a), *a* asymmetrically commands *b* and therefore linearizes as *ab*, and *b* asymmetrically commands *c* and therefore linearizes as *bc*; in (39b), *d* asymmetrically commands *c* and therefore linearizes as *dc*, and *c* asymmetrically commands *b* and therefore linearizes as *cb*.

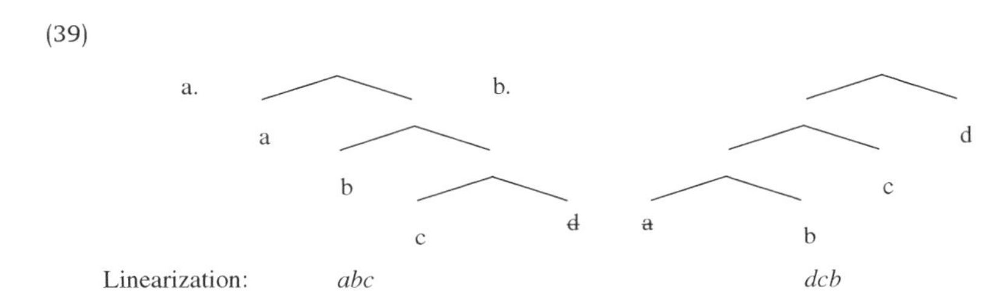

Because subjects are more frequent in initial position, Kayne (1994) chooses (39a). Kayne (2010) gives more empirical evidence for (39a). He also raises the question as to why it would be that way and finds the reason in the directionality of the probe-goal relationship.

Let's assume Merge ends up with a basic order of SVO in the VP, as in (40a), and that certain features (EPP) are responsible for the differences in word order that we encounter in (40b–f).

(40) a. SVO: basic (but probably XP movement of S)
  b. S[O]V: XP movement of O
  c. [V]SO: head movement of V
  d. [VO]S: XP movement of the VP
  e. [O]SV: XP movement of O
  f. [O][V~~O~~]S: XP movement of VP followed by XP movement of O

How do we get all the different word orders? I assume there is both head movement of V to v and further up, as well as phrase (or XP) movement to XP positions[4]. Thus, SOV in (40b) and OSV in (40e) derive

[4] It has been claimed, e.g. in Chomsky (1995), that head movement does not occur in the Narrow Syntax and is only relevant at the level of spell-out. See Roberts (2010) for arguments that head movement has semantic consequences and therefore takes place in the Narrow Syntax. We will discuss reasons for head movement in Chapter 4.

through movement of the object to a position more to the left; VS in (40c) through movement of V; and VOS in (40d) through movement of the entire VP to a position before S.

I'll give the full derivation of the more complex OVS (40f) in (41), although I leave out the Topic head for simplicity. First, V and the Object (i.e. Theme) are merged, after which a little v and the Subject (i.e. Agent) Merge. The VP is then (internally) merged to the vP, or possibly the TP, after which the object is fronted, resulting in OVS.

(41)

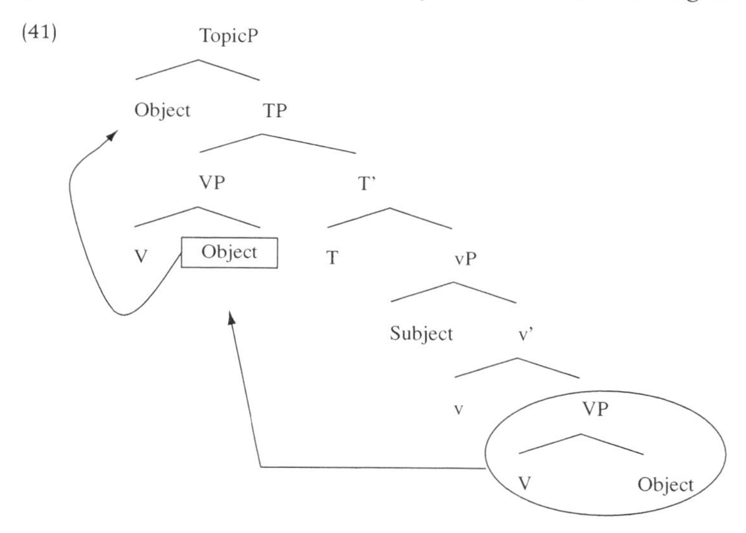

Note that many other possibilities exist; some people avoid head movement in favor of phrasal movement, as in (41). See Chomsky (1995: 367) for the claim that verb movement occurs at PF, and that is certainly a possibility. If only XPs are internally merged, the VS in (40c) could be derived first through object movement out of VP and then movement of the rather empty VP. The latter movement is called **remnant movement**.

1.4.2 Phases

The notion of **phase**, having been introduced in 1998 (but published as Chomsky 2000), becomes prominent in Chomsky (2001). It is a way to reduce the computational burden. Once Select takes lexical items (feature bundles) out of the lexicon, Merge chooses two and puts these together. Phases are a way to make complex derivations manageable. There are two phases in a clause: the CP and the vP. The TP is not a phase and inherits its tense features from the C. Once a vP is finished, it will no longer stay active in the computation and be handed over, or transferred, to the interface systems.

Apart from determining when a string will be handed over to SEM or PHON, phases are important for Internal Merge and Agree. Internal Merge of the phase head (C and v) and its specifier with a higher position is possible, but material inside the VP or TP is not accessible to the probes outside the relevant vP and CP respectively. In (42), it is not possible for the *wh*-element to move to the specifier of the CP in one move; it will have to adjoin to vP first. The reason is that C cannot probe directly into VP. (I ignore the split CP and features here.)

(42)

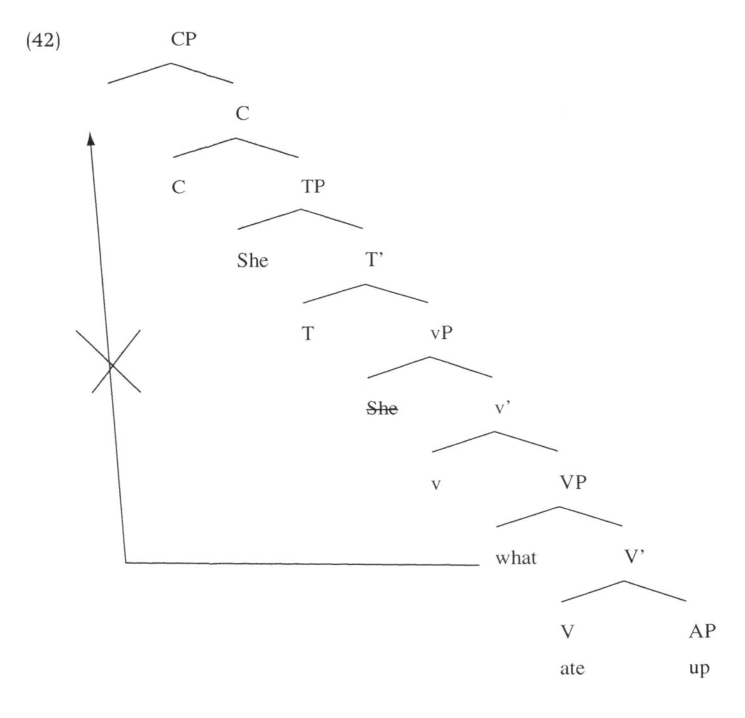

This restriction is known as the Phase Impenetrability Condition, and its effects are very similar to cycles in earlier work and of course to Principles such as Subjacency, which restricts movement across more than one CP or TP.

(43) **Phase Impenetrability Condition**

The domain of H is not accessible to operations outside HP; only H and its *edge* are accessible to such operations. (Chomsky 2001: 13)

Phases (CP and vP) constitute two of the three clausal layers, and the third layer (TP) is recognized as a weak phase. I will not emphasize phases in this book because the main emphasis is on the structure, and not so much on the exact movement restrictions. I will be dividing the clause into three layers: the highest/outer CP-Layer, where pragmatic information is provided; the middle TP-Layer, where grammatical agreement is marked; and the inner vP/VP-Layer that provides mainly lexical and thematic information. The outer layer is responsible for encoding discourse information and linking one clause to another; the inner layer is involved in the marking of tense and agreement through morphology or auxiliaries; and the lowest layer determines the thematic roles. Each layer can be expanded: when the sentence is negative, a Neg(ative)P is added. This division into three layers is descriptive but also necessary in approaches that use phases as well as Cartographies.

1.5 FEATURE PARAMETERS

In this section, we return to the parameters. We discuss the problem how, if parameters are only relevant for the lexicon and are feature-based, language learners can acquire these features. Because the term **universal** is imprecise, I will only use it when talking about work in typology that uses it or, as mentioned, as the adjective in Universal Grammar.

In Minimalism, cross-linguistic variation in the clause only arises from the lexicon: the feature inventory, so to speak, differs from language to language. Chomsky does not hazard a guess as to the number of features. We have seen that Kayne (2005) suggests about 40, and Cinque and Rizzi (2008), taking the Cartographic approach not to differ in this respect from Minimalism, suggest 400. If these features are universally present, not all languages would be using 400 features, so there is room for parameters in that way. How would we make this a little more structured so that the child would have some guidance as to which features to pick? An even more important question is how the child has access to the inventory of features. These features would have to be based in cognition and presumably antedate the appearance of language in humans. I'll first introduce the idea of a macroparameter, then adapt this to features, and then return to the acquisition of features.

Let's return therefore to the features we used in Section 1.3 and see how these would fare in a cross-linguistic picture. What we see is that

Table 1.2 *Languages with and without case and agreement*

	Agreement	No agreement
case	Yaqui, Amis, Urdu, Basque	Japanese, Korean, Khoekhoe
no case	Navajo, Zulu, Lakhota, Ainu	Sango, Haida, (French), Thai, Haitian Creole

case and agreement are not necessarily connected. Baker (2008a) argues this, and Table 1.2 shows the facts for different languages.

Agreement is the more basic phenomenon in language, more widespread than case and quite different. Thus, Siewierska (2008) estimates that 70 percent of languages have (subject) agreement, whereas Siewierska and Bakker (2009: 299) say that "case marking of arguments is overall considerably less common cross-linguistically than agreement marking." In this context, it may help to introduce the distinction between head and dependent marking languages. Head marking languages indicate the relationship between elements on the head of a phrase (e.g. on the verb), whereas dependent marking languages do so on the dependent (e.g. the DP). It is possible to formulate a macroparametric hierarchy in terms of head marking and dependent marking and see some differences between languages as different feature choices. We call these macroparameters, following Baker (2001), who in turn follows Edward Sapir in arguing a language has a basic character. If a language is polysynthetic, this will determine many other characteristics. An attempt is made in Figure 1.5.

This means that languages could be head-marking, dependent-marking, both, or neither, and that is what we find in Table 1.2. The model in Figure 1.5 goes against the current thinking that both phi- and case features are relevant for all languages. Other attempts to parametrize features are found in Biberauer and Richards (2006), Richards (2008), and Roberts and Holmberg (2010).

I'll now come back to the acquisition of semantic and grammatical features. With phonetic features, we know that children babble sounds they haven't heard but that are somehow dictated by internal mechanisms. This may be the case for features and functional categories as well, though "Syntactic Feature Babble" has never been observed. A child needs to have lexical input for grammatical categories to appear but also needs some sense as to what to look for. Chomsky (1995: 230, 381) suggests that "formal features have semantic correlates and reflect semantic properties (accusative Case and

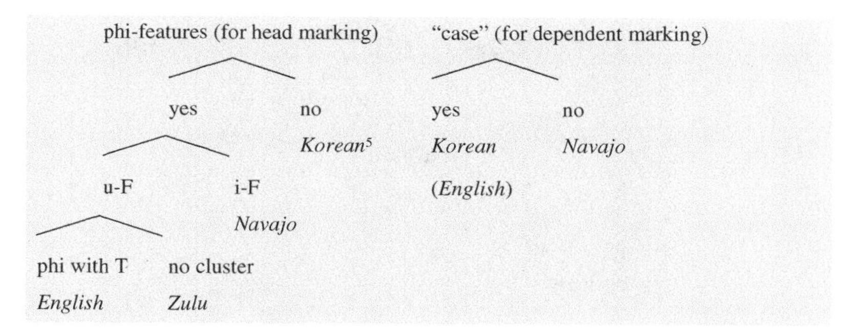

Figure 1.5 Feature macroparameters[6]

transitivity, for example)." I interpret this to mean that, if a language has nouns with semantic phi-features, the learner will be able to hypothesize uninterpretable features on another F (and will be able to bundle them there). Initially, a child would use lexical categories (as well as demonstrative pronouns) with interpretable features (see Radford 2000) which then would be experimented with as uninterpretable features. A third factor principle, such as (44), seems to be at work, with (44b) adapted from Muysken (2008: 46).

(44) Feature economy
 (a) Utilize semantic features: use them as for functional categories, i.e. as formal features.
 (b) If a specific feature appears more than once, one of these is interpretable and the others are uninterpretable.

If a child uses semantic features such as [animate], [future], [abstract] to learn words and concepts - and this acquisition is very fast - the (ancient) question arises where our knowledge of these features comes from. I am assuming with Chomsky (1965: 142) that "semantic features ... are presumably drawn from a universal 'alphabet'" (although, as mentioned above, Chomsky continues that "little is known about this today and nothing has been said about it here"). Thus, innate concepts such as time, cause, agent, etc., together with the data available to the child (modality or past tense), trigger the

[5] Baker (2008a: 39, 153) argues that T is not a probe in, for instance, Japanese, which is similar to not having probing phi-features. In these languages, I assume that independent subjects may be absent too, with radical pro-drop as the result.

[6] What isn't captured in Figure 1.6 is that [i-F] is often linked to [no-Case].

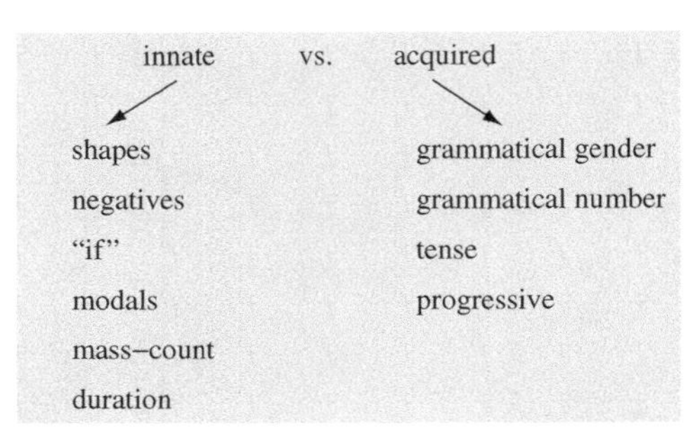

Figure 1.6 Innate vs. acquired features

grammaticalization of the semantic features into interpretable and uninterpretable ones.

In Chomsky (1993: 24), there is the very cryptic statement that vocabulary acquisition shows poverty of the stimulus. That means Universal Grammar has to give some concepts and structure. When a child looks at the world, it knows how to categorize things; it is not just abstracting from its environment. This is clear with logical concepts, as the philosopher Geach (1957: 22–23) writes: "[a]bstractionists rarely attempt an abstractionist account of logical concepts, like those of *some*, *or*, and *not*" ... "In the sensible world you will find no specimens of alternativeness and negativeness from which you could form by abstraction the concept of *or* or of *not*." In a figure, learned and innate categories can be represented as in Figure 1.6.

The ability to categorize is not unique to humans. Certain animals are excellent at categorization, e.g. prairie dogs have sounds for specific colors, shapes, and sizes (Slobodchikoff 2010). Jackendoff (2002: 238–240), based on Bickerton (1990), suggests that pre-linguistic primate conceptual structure may already use symbols for basic semantic relations. This may include spatial and causal concepts: "Agent First, Focus Last ... are 'fossil principles' from protolanguage." Homo erectus (1 million BP) may have had protolanguage. Even though the question of the acquisition of semantic features, words, and concepts is fascinating, I will now look at the acquisition of functional categories a little more.

In approaches such as those represented in Figure 1.5, the choices are not as deep and are feature-based. This means that the child may get hints to pay attention to certain features. For instance, if modals are in the input, a child might postulate an MP and will then need to decide on the types of features connected to it, e.g. deontic or epistemic, and interpretable or not. The parametric differences expressed in Figure 1.5 are also in accordance with the view that parameters are only relevant to lexical and grammatical items, the approach used in this book. We'll look at some data from acquisition.

I will argue below that there exists a mechanism for the acquisition of formal/syntactic features where the child abstracts away from the semantic features, as suggested by the Feature Economy Principle in (44). An instance of this is given using data from the CHILDES-Kuczaj corpus (Kuczaj 1976) of a child by the name of Abe, who abstracts away from a preposition to a complementizer. Abe initially uses *like* as a lexical category only, as in (45) to (47), which he uttered when he was 3 years and 7 months (and 5 days) old.

(45) **like** a cookie (Abe, 3.7.5)

(46) no the monster crashed the planes down **like** this **like** that (Abe, 3.7.5)

(47) I wan(t) (t)a show you something # I mean **like** this thin ? (Abe, 3.7.5)

He starts to use *like* as a complementizer, as in (48a–b), when he is a year older. The earlier (49) is in between the preposition and complementizer because having a pet is a nominalization.

(48) a. watch it walks **like** a person walks. (Abe, 4.9.19)
b. Daddy # do you teach **like** you do [//] **like** how they do in your school? (Abe, 4.10.1)

(49) I feel **like** having a pet do you? (Abe, 4.8.20)

The use of *like* in (48a–b) is all the more interesting in that the caregivers in the transcript only use *like* as a C after *sound* or *look*, as in (50). Although the child may have heard the use of *like* as a C in another context, it is more likely to be a spontaneous invention by the child guided by principle (44).

(50) Abe's father: it looks **like** some birds have eaten some of the bread. (Kuczaj file 206)

The situation with *for* is similar to that of *like*, although *for* is used by the caregivers both as complementizer and preposition. Initially, the preposition is used by Abe to express benefactor semantic role, as in (51) and (52). Later, this meaning is extended to time, as in (53), and more abstract use in (54) and (55).

(51) Mom # this white one **for** me? (Abe 2.7.18)

(52) this picture is mine **for** myself (Abe 2.7.18)

(53) how long you grow up **for** a minute (Abe 2.9.27)

(54) Mom # I'm glad you are making a rug **for** out in the hall. (Abe 2.8.14)

(55) this uh be a cave **for [/] for** # what you say? a Thanksgiving one this uh be a cave. (Abe 2.11.6)

The first target-like C is in (56). Another month and a half later, Abe produces his second one (at least on the transcripts we have), namely (57), and three months later the third one (58). The first two can be seen as "waiting for," i.e. a prepositional use, but the third one has to be a complementizer.

(56) yeah and I said I was waiting and waiting **for** you to come and I [/] (Abe, 3.2.1)

(57) this crocodile was standing around waiting **for** someone to drop around and what did he see when he saw it? (Abe, 3.3.18)

(58) yeah maybe it's time **for** it to rain we'll have a storm. (Abe, 3.6.26)

All languages make use of person and number features of some kind, so phi-features would be universally present, extracted from the semantic features of lexical items. Case marking is more varied across languages. Whether these features are interpretable or not is a parametric setting that a child has to decide upon.

1.6 CONCLUSION

In this chapter, an introduction has been given to generative syntax. It provides a short history of shifts in what is included in Universal Grammar, what principles and parameters look like, and how phrase structure and movement rules are regarded and formulated, and the tension between Minimalism and Cartography. It introduces the three layers and discusses the status of features.

Keywords

Universal Grammar, Principles and Parameters, descriptive and explanatory adequacy, macroparameter, Minimalist Program, Cartography, phrase structure rules, bare phrase structure, transformations, semantic features, interpretable and uninterpretable features, AGREE, (internal/external) Merge, S-M-C-I, linearization, phase

DISCUSSION POINTS

1. a. Discuss the difference between first and third factor that we have seen in Section 1.3. Is Merge a Universal Grammar Principle or a third factor principle?
   b. Chomsky (2011: 7–8) rearranges the three factors. Do you see a shift, or is he saying the same as was quoted in Section 1.3 above?

   > We can distinguish three factors in this process: (I) external data; (II) genetic endowment, which determines the general character of growth and development, and in the cognitive domains converts external data to experience; (III) organism-independent factors, including principles of natural law, which play a crucial role in development as in evolution: e.g., the laws of physics that determine that cells divide into spheres rather than cubes, and for computational systems like language, principles of computational efficiency that may well be reducible to laws of nature. For language, we can distinguish three components of the second factor: (a) language-specific endowment, Universal Grammar; (b) other cognitive processes; (c) conditions imposed on language by the structure of the brain, though too little is known to draw far-reaching conclusions, despite interesting recent progress in neurolinguistics.

2. If you remember traces from earlier frameworks, explain how e.g. the tree in (30) for *Martians saw it* would look with traces. The reason traces were abandoned was the Inclusiveness Condition: Once you select material from the lexicon and start a derivation, new material cannot be added.
3. Draw a tree for (1) using interpretable and uninterpretable features and bare phrase structure.
   (1) Unicorns eat peanuts.
4. Think about the role of interpretable features and explain why in English (2) might still be understandable.
   (2) Me sees she.
5. How would you draw the trees for the VS in (40c) above? Use either the head movement or the remnant movement derivation.
6. The *World Atlas of Linguistic Structures* (http://wals.info/feature/81A) has the following data on the relative frequency of the six word

Table 1.3 *Frequency of word orders (Dryer 1992)*

SOV	(565 languages)	SVO (488 languages)
VSO	(95 languages)	VOS (25 languages)
OVS	(11 languages)	OSV (4 languages)
No dominant order	(189 languages)	Total: 1,377

orders we have seen in (40). Does this distribution surprise you, considering our discussion of the derivation of various word orders?

7. We will use two kinds of glosses for other languages: a morpheme-by-morpheme gloss, using abbreviated symbols, and a freer translation, enclosed in single quotation marks. Both are not always provided if the meaning is clear. The glosses list morphological features such as accusative (ACC) in cases where relevant for our discussion. Hyphens are used when we can clearly see the morphemes; periods if they are fused. Explain in words what the glosses in (2) mean.

(2)	***mẽ***	*kahaanii*	*likh-tii*	*hũ*	Urdu/Hindi
	1S.NOM(F)	story.F	write-PR.1SF	be.PR.1S	

'I am writing a story.'

(Much stricter glosses are suggested at www.eva.mpg.de/lingua/resources/glossing-rules.php)

SUGGESTIONS FOR FURTHER READING

For more on Universal Grammar and parameters, read Chomsky (1965 chapter 1) and Newmeyer (2005). Boeckx (2008) provides a great introduction on bare phrase structure.

If you are interested in interfaces, Reinhart (2008) examines several areas of the interface, e.g. quantifier scope and focus. She wonders what makes the computational system legible to the other systems at the interface.

Muysken (2008: 6) finds "the generative literature on functional categories rather vague," and provides additional information on functional categories and features.

Markman (1994) argues that constraints on word learning are not specific to language, and B. Landau (1994) shows that children have a shape bias that helps them acquire words.

For an alternative on feature checking, see Stroik (2009 chapter 1), and see Fong (2005) on Minimalist parsing.

2 The clause: a description

In this chapter, we'll discuss the clause in a broad sense. Main clauses can function independently, and we'll examine what makes them independent. In many languages, this independence is the result of an independent tense. Other factors include a specially marked subject, an overt indication of the mood of the clause, and a complete expression of all the arguments of the verb.

The outline is as follows. In Section 2.1, we examine the basic, minimal components of the simple clause, focusing on English. In Section 2.2, we review semantic, grammatical, and pragmatic functions and roles. Grammatical roles are important for deciding if a clause is embedded or not. In Section 2.3, we explore some of the variety found in English clauses that have more than one lexical verb, i.e. where one is embedded in the other. In Section 2.4, we look at the three layers of the clause and, in Section 2.5, a brief overview of clauses in other languages is provided. Section 2.6 is a conclusion.

2.1 THE MAIN CLAUSE

In this section, some characteristics of main clauses are discussed. Main clauses in English have a certain mood, and they need to contain a tensed verb and a subject that agrees with the verb. This set of characteristics anchors an event in place and time and to a speech event, and is known as **finiteness**. We'll also put this together in a tree using the familiar CP and TP.

2.1.1 Mood

Mood signals the speaker's "take" on the content expressed in the sentence. It shows if the speaker is sure or unsure of what s/he is saying and how the speaker obtained the information. Bybee

(1985: 170) defines mood as having force or as indicating a commitment to the truth, as (1) shows. She follows a traditional distinction where the unmarked mood is the indicative and is hence not listed.

(1) Mood
Illocutionary force: imperative, optative, admonitive (warning), prohibitive, interrogative
Commitment to truth of assertion: subjunctive, dubitative, probable, potential, conditional

Main clauses across the languages of the world indicate **indicative**, **interrogative**, and **imperative** moods. These moods represent different pragmatic functions: statements, questions, and commands respectively. Examples of some moods in English are given in (2) to (4).

(2) I saw her in the garden. indicative mood

(3) Where did I see her? interrogative mood

(4) Meet her in the garden! imperative mood

Many moods have a special syntax that goes with that particular mood: In (2), there is the unmarked Subject Verb word order; in (3), a *wh*-word is fronted and an auxiliary is moved; and, in (4), the subject is left out.

Other moods are possible, e.g. exclamative, indicating surprise, as in (5ab), and optative/subjunctive, indicating a wish, as in (6).

(5) a. How interesting those buildings look! exclamative mood
b. What a nice book this is!

(6) May she live long! optative/subjunctive mood

Syntactically, these are marked by the fronting of *how* and the adjective in (5a), of *what* and the DP in (5b), and by an initial modal in (6).

2.1.2 Finiteness: tense, agreement, and case

In English, a simple main clause contains at least one lexical, finite verb and a grammatical subject, e.g. *went* and *she* respectively in (7a). Auxiliary verbs, *has* and *been* in (7b), can be added.

(7) a. She went.
b. She **has been** gone (a long time).

In a main clause, as in (7a–b), there is one finite verb (*went* and *has*) and one lexical verb (*went* and *gone*).

Sentence (8) shows an unfinished "fragment," with a non-finite verb and no subject. This fragment can be used as part of another sentence, or as an answer to a question, but not on its own.

(8) To go there.

Finite verbs in (standard) English agree with the subject of the clause, which happens to be visible only in the third person singular present tense on most verbs. The verb *to be* is an exception, of course. Finite verbs are also marked for present or past. Their subjects have nominative case, which can only be seen in Modern English when the subject is a pronoun, i.e. the subject pronoun of finite verbs must be nominative *I*, *you*, *he*, *she*, *it*, *we* and *they*, not accusative *me*, *him*, *her*, *us*, or *them* (*you* and *it* are both nominative and accusative), as in the ungrammatical (9).

(9) *Me have been going there frequently.

Note that, in some varieties of English, sentences without a nominative subject, such as (10), and without an agreeing verb, as in (11), are grammatical.

(10) **Me** gotta go. (Jamaican English)

(11) He **like** it, **do** he? (East Anglian English, Trudgill 1974)

In these varieties, case and agreement have been lost completely, something that the English language has been doing over the last 1,000 years.

Two more points about English: Modal auxiliaries, as in (12), count as finite even though they show no agreement or tense, and imperative clauses, as in (13), count as having a hidden (nominative) subject and are therefore finite as well.

(12) She **may** have gone.

(13) (**You**) Go there!

Finiteness is scalar, according to Givón's scale reproduced as Figure 2.1, and some clause types show more finite characteristics, e.g. the indicatives in (2) and (7), and some fewer, e.g. the subjunctive in (6) and the modal in (12). Indicatives are therefore more often independent clauses; subjunctives may be; but participials, infinitives, and nominalizations are never independent.

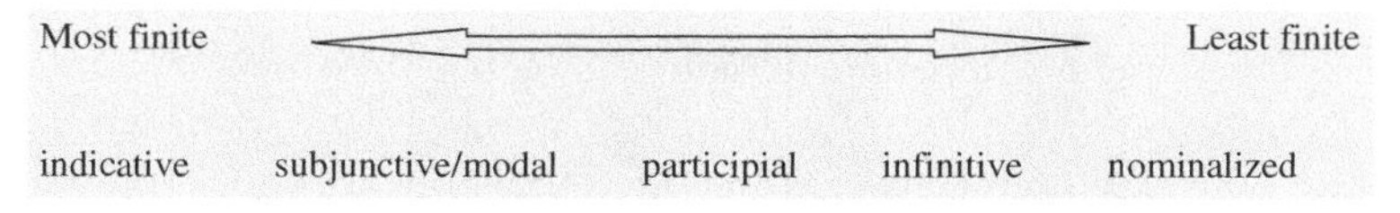

Figure 2.1 Degrees of finiteness (from Givón 1990: 854)

English uses all of these possibilities in its independent and dependent clauses, but some languages like to nominalize a subordinate clause, e.g. Russian and Navajo. Let's see where we mark finiteness and mood in the tree.

2.1.3 CPs and TPs

In this section, we add basic mood and tense features to the tree that we've seen in Chapter 1. Chapters 4 and 5 will go into much more depth.

The CP, as in (14), is the bearer of the mood of the sentence (indicative, imperative, interrogative, subjunctive, or exclamative). We can indicate mood by means of interpretable indicative features, which also means that the clause is finite. I have marked this by [i-ind] and [u-T] on C. The latter means we need a T with valued tense features, i.e. one that can check with an element that is [i-past] or [i-pres], or, in the case of modals, [i-fut]. Having an indicative C thus ensures a finite TP with agreement and tense on the verb and nominative to the subject. The T position acquires the valued tense position by probing down the tree. I will add agreement and case in later trees, and a full set of auxiliaries in Chapter 4. For simplicity, I leave that out here.

(14)

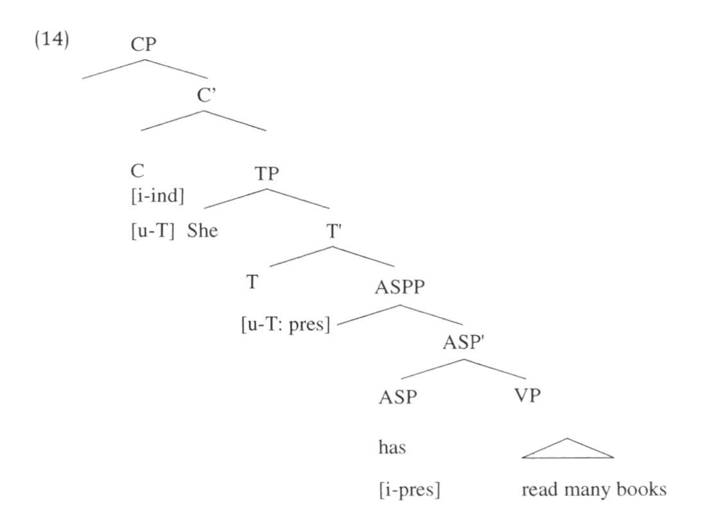

In the case of a main clause, as in (14), [i-ind] appears on C, but, when the clause is embedded, C has [u-mood], as we'll see.

Because main clauses indicate mood, assumed to be in CP, every main clause includes a CP, even in English, where there isn't that much evidence for it. In languages with second-position effects (e.g. the Germanic languages other than English), there is more evidence.

Having defined an English independent clause as finite and as having mood, we'll turn next to grammatical functions and semantic roles of elements in the clause. Having a particular grammatical function in another clause is what distinguishes the embedded, i.e. dependent, clause from the main clause.

2.2 FUNCTIONS AND ROLES

Phrases (DPs, PPs, etc.) play a grammatical **function** in a clause and bear a semantic **role**. They may also play a pragmatic role, such as topic or focus, to be ignored in this section. Each of the roles/functions is indicated in a different layer and in fact provides some rationale for the three layers. Keeping the semantic and grammatical roles separate is tricky but essential, and we discuss ways to do that here.

Semantic roles include Agent, Instrument, Theme, and Goal. In Chapter 3, we come back to semantic roles in great detail. Grammatical functions include: subject; direct, indirect or phrasal object; subject or object predicate; adverbials; and modifiers. In this section, I mainly focus on grammatical functions, to help you see the structure of the clause. Some functions are obligatorily expressed, and others are optional. The word order of certain functions in English is also much stricter than that of other languages.

2.2.1 Roles and functions

One frequent answer to the question "What is the subject in a sentence?" is that it is the actor or doer of the action. This is correct in some sentences, but not in all, as the variety of semantic roles that can function as subjects in (15) shows.

(15) a. **They** ate waffles.
Subject = Agent
b. **The book** sells well.
Subject = Theme
c. **Many books on this subject** have been written.
Subject = Theme (passivized)
d. **It** rained.
Subject has no semantic role; *it* is an expletive

Table 2.1 *Some grammatical functions in traditional grammar*

Functions in addition to subject	Example verb	Example sentence	Verb name
-	swim, arrive	She arrived (early).	intransitive
Direct object	see, eat, read, love	She saw me.	(mono) transitive
Direct and indirect object	give, tell	I gave him flowers.	ditransitive
Subject predicate	be, become	She is nice.	copula
Direct object and object predicate	consider, know	I consider her nice.	complex transitive
Prepositional object	refer, glance	He glanced at the book.	prepositional
Direct object/-	switch on/ give in	She turned off the light. He gave in.	phrasal
Prepositional object	get down to	He got down to business.	phrasal prepositional

Verbs seem to determine the semantic roles the noun phrases play (again more in Chapter 3), but morphology and position in the sentence determine the grammatical function. Thus, a verb like *eat* has an entity that eats (the Agent) and something that is eaten (the Theme or Patient). In an indicative, finite sentence, all the roles that a verb has are expressed and play grammatical functions such as subject and object.

English **subjects** agree with the finite verb and have a nominative case, and usually precede the verb; **objects** follow the lexical verb and can be passivized. In Table 2.1, some examples of functions other than subjects are provided. This is the list of the (traditional) obligatory functions, also known as **arguments**; **adverbials** are optional and are not added in this table.

As mentioned, two major differences distinguish arguments (subjects, objects, object predicates, and so on) from adverbials, namely their obligatoriness and stricter word order. Let's take a simple clause, as in (16), and determine the grammatical functions of its parts.

(16) They fed the elephants with great enthusiasm for the entire evening.

In (16), there are two obligatory nominals, the subject *they* and the object *the elephants*. Leaving them out results in (17), which is at best a fragment. Leaving the adverbials out, as in (18), leads to a less informative but complete sentence.

(17) Fed with great enthusiasm for the entire evening.

(18) They fed the elephants.

As for the stricter word order of arguments, subjects typically precede the verb and can only be separated from their finite verbs by certain adverbials, as in (19), but not by all adverbials, as (20) shows. Nominal objects are difficult to separate from the verb by any adverbial, as (21) shows.

(19) They **often** fed the elephants with great enthusiasm for the entire evening.

(20) *They **in the evening** fed the elephants with great enthusiasm.

(21) *They fed **often/in the evening** the elephants.

The position of adverbials is freer, although, as we'll see, they too have a preferred order. A note on terminology is in order. I will use "adverbial" when emphasizing the function of the PP but "adverb" when I mean the category of words like *often*, *soon*, *now*, etc.

A third difference between objects and adverbials is that adverbials can appear after *do so*, as in (22), but objects cannot, as in (23).

(22) We read books in the garden and she **did so** in the attic.

(23) *We read books in the garden and she did so journals in the attic.

An account for the latter two characteristics (the word order and *do so*-replacement) is easy in a pre-bare phrase structure system. There one can argue that the order is strict because the object has to be the sister of the V, that the subject must be in the Spec of the TP, as in (24), and that *do so* replaces the V' but not the V. Adverbials are adjoined as sisters to V's and are therefore freer.

(24)

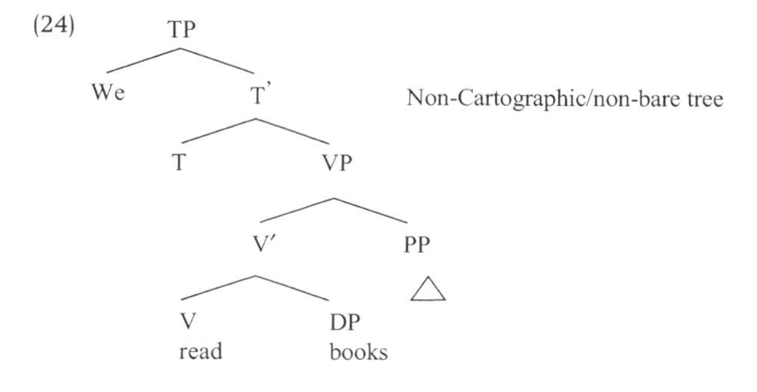

Currently, the distinction in grammatical function is harder to make in a tree because V, V', and VP are no longer distinguished in bare phrase structure. The distinction between objects from adverbials underlies a lot of syntactic thinking. In Chapter 3, we'll see that the former have semantic roles connected to them and are recognized at the C-I interface as different from adverbials.

2.2.2 Subordinate and coordinate clause functions

Complex clauses include more than one lexical verb. Sentences that are part of another sentence, i.e. that have a function in that sentence, are often referred to as dependent or embedded clauses, where the embedded clause is seen as **subordinate** to the other. There are also **coordinated** clauses which involve at least two clauses (and two lexical verbs) that are joined by *and* (or another coordinator), and both coordinated clauses are of (almost) equal importance. Frequently, one of the coordinate clauses is dependent on the other clause, however, as we'll see.

Examples of clausal functions are given in (25) to (30). In (25), the embedded clause functions as direct **object**; in (26), it is a **subject**; in (27), a subject predicate; and in (28), a phrasal object. An adverbial and a relative clause modifying a noun are given in (29) and (30).

(25) I noticed [that some recipes call for prahoc]. (embedded object)

(26) [That we saw a Kline] was nice. (embedded subject)

(27) The problem is [that too many homes were built]. (embedded subject predicate)

(28) I figured out [that it didn't work]. (embedded phrasal object)

(29) He read books [because it was required]. (embedded adverbial)

(30) The books [that she reads] are forgotten books. (relative clause)

Other terms that you'll see are **complements** and **modifiers** for object and relative clauses respectively. Clauses do not function as indirect objects, or as objects of prepositional objects, or as object predicates.

The main defining characteristic of coordinated clauses is that they have no function in another clause. They are on an equal footing, most argue, with each other. This is clearly true in (31), but less so in (32).

(31) [The ocean is green] and [the moon is red].

(32) [The food arrived] and [they ate].

In (31), the two clauses are totally independent of each other, although they have a coordinator *and*. Hearing this sentence, one wonders what kind of connection the speaker wants to make, or if it is uttered as a joke. In (32), the clauses are more closely connected, and the *and* here really means "and then," which renders the second clause almost subordinate to the first. The two clauses also have the same subjects and the same tense. However, if we consider [they ate] as a subordinate clause, that clause would have to function as adverbial, and that is not correct either.

Another indication of a difference between (31) and (32) is that, if we reverse the order of the clauses, as in (33) and (34), we notice that (33) is still strange, but not because of the reversal of the order. Sentence (34), however, has a different meaning, since we assume that now they ate before the food arrived.

(33) [The moon is red] and [the ocean is green].

(34) [They ate] and [the food arrived].

Coordinate clauses can be made into two independent clauses, as in (35), and although that sounds very "choppy," it is better than doing the same with an embedded clause, as in (36).

(35) The food arrived. They ate.

(36) They noticed. He left.

Coordinated structures, especially the ones with a closer connection between the clauses, often leave out the second subject if it is identical to the first, as in (37). This is analyzed as ellipsis, i.e. deletion, of the second subject. It is possible to repeat the subject, as in (38), but this is done only if you want to emphasize the subject.

(37) [Dinosaurs arrived] and [ate arctic anchovies].

(38) [Dinosaurs arrived] and [dinosaurs ate arctic anchovies].

In (37), we can see that one clause is dependent on the other, since it has lost its own subject. As an alternative to analyzing (37) as a case of ellipsis of the subject, we could argue that it involves the coordination of two VPs.

The different types of coordination in English are not so complex; they are listed in Figure 2.2. According to this, sentences such as (33) are the most independent of each other and sentences such as (37) the least.

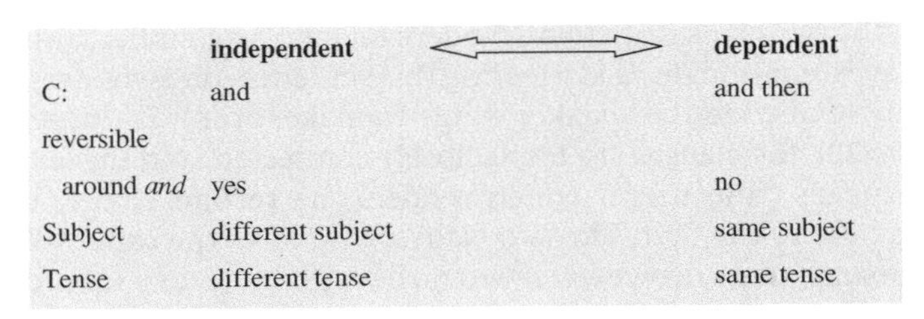

	independent	dependent
C:	and	and then
reversible around *and*	yes	no
Subject	different subject	same subject
Tense	different tense	same tense

Figure 2.2 The relative (in)dependence of coordinated clauses

In conclusion, grammatical functions such as subject and object are different from semantic roles such as Themes and Agents. Grammatical functions are relevant to defining finite clauses since subjects are obligatory in English finite clauses. Grammatical function is also relevant to distinguish subordinate from coordinate clauses: Only subordinate clauses have a function inside another clause. In the next section, we turn to those.

2.3 THE TYPES OF SUBORDINATE CLAUSE

If there are two **lexical verbs**, there are two clauses, one dependent on the other and functioning as subject or object or adverbial in the other sentence. Since a subordinate clause is dependent on another clause, it can be less complex than an independent clause. Verbs determine the mood and finiteness of their complements through marking the C or T of these complements. We will therefore pay special attention to these functional categories and show how the clausal complements differ in complexity. Adverbial clauses are much freer, but the C is crucial for them as well. Finally, we look at clauses that modify and complement nouns.

2.3.1 C(omplementizers)

Complementizers join two clauses where one clause is subordinate to the other. Examples of complementizers are *that*, *since*, *whether*, *if*, and *because*, as in (39).

(39) Kristen and Jan left [**because** Anna was about to arrive].

Many complementizers have one specific task. For instance, *because* in (39) can only introduce an adverbial clause of reason, and *after* and *before* only temporal adverbial clauses. This is thanks to their very

Table 2.2 *A few English complementizers*

after, (al)though, as, because, before, for, how, if, in case (that), in order that, in that, lest, like, now that, once, provided (that), so (that), (rather) than, that, till, unless, until, when, whenever, where(as/ever), whether, while, why, yet

specific semantic features. The complementizer *that* is more general and is connected to finiteness in (40) and *for* to future and irrealis, as in (41).

(40) **That** they laugh a lot shows **that** they are happy.

(41) I expected **for** them to do that.

Like prepositions, complementizers are invariable in English (i.e. never have an ending), but complementizers introduce a new clause, whereas prepositions are connected to a noun. Some examples of complementizers are provided in Table 2.2. Chapter 5 will come back to the features of some of these.

When prepositions, such as *before* or *after* in (42), introduce a clause, they are then complementizers rather than prepositions.

(42) He left [**after** she arrived].

In the case of complementizers such as *when*, *where*, *why*, and *how*, we could argue they are adverbials moving to the specifier of the CP, so technically not Cs. Some of these are in the process of being reanalyzed as Cs, as in (43), where *how* is an embedded C.

(43) Dwyer told the players **how** he wanted to win.
'D. told the players that he wanted to win.'
(from the BNC as given by Willis 2007: 434)

In short, complementizers help decide the function of the clause and, in the case of *for*, *if*, and *that*, are selected by the higher verb. *That* is the most frequent and typical for introducing objects, as we'll see next.

2.3.2 The object clause

Sentences (25) to (30) show that clauses can function in many ways. The most frequent of these are the object, as in (44), and adverbial, as in (42).

(44) [I should have noticed [**that** Zelda doesn't like Zoltan]].

Auxiliaries, such as *should*, *have*, and *does* in (44) are not relevant for determining the number of clauses or sentences; only lexical verbs are. The verb *notice* has a full CP complement with the complementizer *that* in C. Typically, however, embedded sentences are less complex than main clauses and may depend on the latter for their mood and tense. Examples (45a) to (45c) contain complements to the verb *want*: a non-finite CP in (45a) and reduced CPs (possibly TPs) in (45b) and (45c). Note that the subject of the embedded clause cannot be passivized, as shown in (45d).

(45) a. I wanted very much [for him to leave].
  b. I wanted [him to leave].
  c. I wanted [to leave].
  d. *He was wanted [to leave].

Want is a deontic verb that selects an irrealis CP complement and cannot have an indicative or subjunctive clause as its complement, as the ungrammaticality of (46) shows. This wasn't always the case, as Old English (47) shows with *willan*, the predecessor of *want*, which has a subjunctive present verb.

(46) *I want that they (should) do that.

(47) *Ic wille . . . þæt þu forgyt-e þæt ic þe nu secge*
  I want that you forget-SUBJ that I you now say
  'I want you to forget what I am telling you now.'
  (*Byrhtferth's Manual* 154.14, Visser 1963–73: vol. II, 841).

Sentences that consist of two or more clauses differ tremendously in the possibilities they have to link these clauses to each other. The verb *try* differs from *want* in that it cannot have a subject expressed in its complement clause, as (48a) to (48c) show, and cannot therefore passivize this subject, as (48d) shows.

(48) a. *I tried [for him to leave].
  b. *I tried [him to leave].
  c. I tried [to leave].
  d. *He was tried [to leave].

The usual explanation for the difference is that both have a CP complement but that *want* allows an overt or covert *for* that assigns case to the subject of the embedded clause. This CP blocks the passivization for both verbs.

Figure 2.3 provides a continuum found in English; see Givón (1980) for a slightly different set of complements. The sentences in Figure 2.3 combine two clauses, and, as we go down the list, the verbs that are the core of each clause become more interdependent on the higher

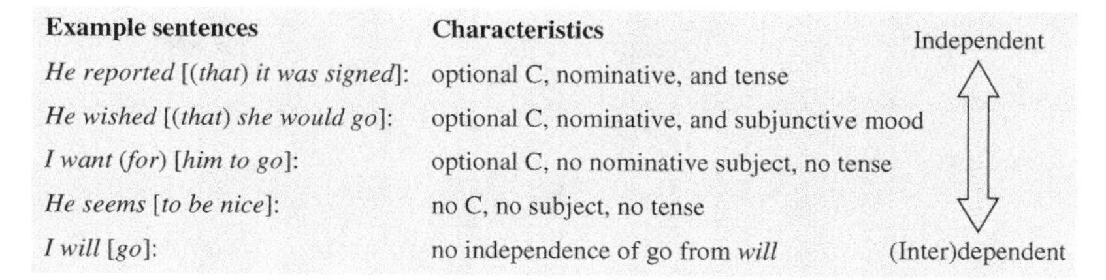

Example sentences	Characteristics	Independent ↕ (Inter)dependent
He reported [(*that*) *it was signed*]:	optional C, nominative, and tense	Independent
He wished [(*that*) *she would go*]:	optional C, nominative, and subjunctive mood	
I want (*for*) [*him to go*]:	optional C, no nominative subject, no tense	
He seems [*to be nice*]:	no C, no subject, no tense	
I will [*go*]:	no independence of go from *will*	(Inter)dependent

Figure 2.3 Degrees of clausal (in)dependence

verb. Take a look at the examples and see if they make sense. The transparency of the complement can be marked in the tree, as in (49), by means of the structure.

(49)

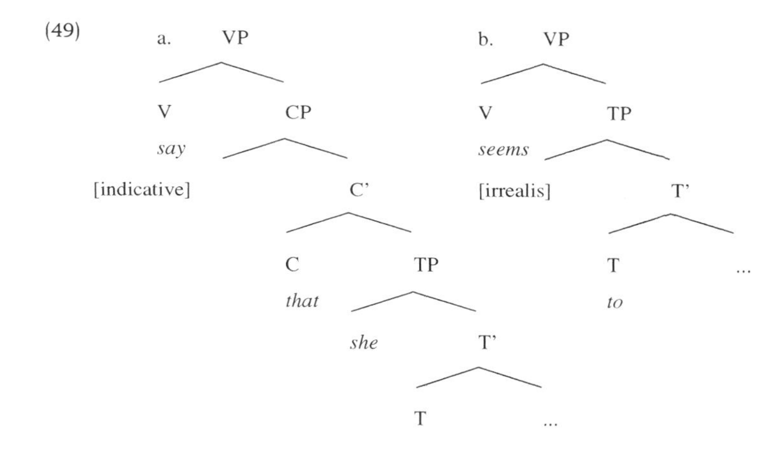

Most verbs, e.g. *want* in (45), have more than one choice, and a continuum can be seen with various complement choices of this verb: the complement in (45c) being the most dependent, and the one in (45a) the more independent. The complement in (45a) is not completely independent because, although it has a subject, it has no independent tense. The same is true of the mood of the embedded clause in (47): It depends on that of the verb of the higher clause.

The descriptive parameters are a +/– C(omplementizer), +/– nominative subject, +/– subject, +/– tense, and +/– realis mood. The minus-value means that the two clauses are more dependent on each other. Another way of putting that is as in Figure 2.4 for the verbs *notice*, *wish*, *want*, and *try* for the sentences in Figure 2.3 (leaving the tense of *wish* unmarked).

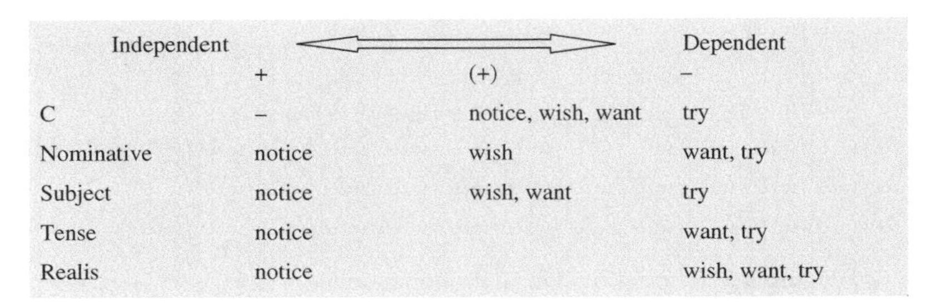

Independent	⟸⟹		Dependent
	+	(+)	–
C	–	notice, wish, want	try
Nominative	notice	wish	want, try
Subject	notice	wish, want	try
Tense	notice		want, try
Realis	notice		wish, want, try

Figure 2.4 Parameters of clausal (in)dependence and some verbs

A lot has been written on the selection of clausal complements. Cross-linguistically, causatives, as in (50), do not seem to have finite complements, whereas verbs of saying, as in (51), typically do.

(50) The odors at work made [them feel bad].
(COCA 2008 *Environmental* magazine)

(51) She said [that Lance had gone crazy].
(COCA 2012 NBC Dateline)

Various researchers have tried to predict the syntactic or semantic properties. Rochette (1988) argues the semantic properties determine the structural ones. She divides predicates into three semantic classes: effective, emotive, and propositional. These select both the semantic (action, event, proposition) and structural type (VP, TP, CP) of the complement. An effective verb, such as *finish* or *dare*, can only have a projection of V as its complement; an emotive verb, such as *like*, has a projection of T as its complement; a propositional verb, such as *say*, *believe*, or *know* has a projection of C. I think this is the direction to go in, but the details remain to be worked out (and not in this book).

We'll now look more at how the verb in the higher clause, the matrix verb, determines its complement, and that will give us more insight into how to represent the various choices. As mentioned, not all languages have the same clausal inventories. For instance, English has what is called **Exceptional Case Marking** (ECM), as in (52), but Dutch, as (53) shows, German, and French do not.

(52) I believe [him to be totally innocent].
(COCA 2007 CBS)

(53) **Ik* *geloof* *hem* *aardig* *te* *zijn* Dutch
I believe him nice to be
'I believe him to be nice.'

ECM clauses are so called because the accusative subject of the infinitive, *him* in (52), doesn't get case from *to be totally innocent*, i.e. the verb it is the subject of, but from the verb in the higher clause. This structure is actually different from (45b), since *want*, unlike *believe*, has an optional *for* that assigns case. Because *believe* lacks *for*, as shown in (54a), it also lacks a CP boundary and can therefore passivize the subject of its embedded clause, as (54d) shows. I have given all the possibilities so as to be able to compare *believe* with *want* in (45) and *try* in (48).

(54) a. *I believe [for her to be innocent].
b. I believe [her to be innocent].
c. *I believe [to be innocent].
d. She is believed [to be still in New Zealand]. (COCA 1995 ABC 20/20)

Not all verbs allow ECM-complements, e.g. *say*, and not all ECMs are the same. The ones with **deontic** verbs, as in (55), have an irrealis/future feature, which is why a *for* complementizer is possible and the verb has to be non-stative; with **epistemic** verbs, as in (56), *for* is not possible, and the embedded verb has to be stative.

(55) Is it too much to **expect for** him to do a long-distance committed relationship for two years? (answers.yahoo.com/question, downloaded August 3, 2011)

(56) We believe (*for) him to have been an honest man.

Apart from the epistemic and deontic distinction, a well-known classification of matrix verbs is that between factive and non-factive verbs and between assertive and non-assertive verbs. I will describe the difference between factive and non-factive, emotive and non-emotive, and assertive and non-assertive, but will ultimately use a variety of features to represent the options.

Factives have several defining characteristics (as explained in Kiparsky and Kiparsky 1970). For instance, they presuppose the truth of the complement clause by the speaker, as in (57), unlike with non-factives, as in (58).

(57) **I forgot** that he left a key. factive
(58) **I believe** that he left a key. non-factive

Non-factive verbs allow what is called **Negative Raising** from an embedded clause such as (59a) to a higher clause, as in (59b), with minimal semantic effects. Negative Raising does not occur with factive verbs because (60a) and (60b) do not mean the same. Both kinds of clause may have an overt complementizer *that*, but only factives block percolation of the negative.

(59) a. I believe that he wo**n't** lift a finger.
b. I do**n't** believe that he'll lift a finger.

(60) a. It bothers me that he wo**n't** lift a finger.
b. It does**n't** bother me that he will lift a finger
(adapted from Kiparsky and Kiparsky 1970: 162).

Kiparsky and Kiparsky (1970: 169–170) further divide verbs into emotives and non-emotives, as in (61). Note that the emotives are different from those of Rochette.

(61) **Emotive:**
factives: regret, resent, deplore, be important
non-factives: intend, prefer, be unlikely
Non-emotive:
factives: forget, be clear, be aware of, know, see, realize, discover
non-factives: say, suppose, conclude, seem, be likely

A *for-to* or subjunctive complement is not well-formed on its own. This means its C is defective and needs to be selected by an emotive or other irrealis higher verb. I have represented that by means of mood features on C that are inherited by T in (62). The verb of the lower clause has to be either subjunctive or infinitive to count as [i-future].

(62)

prefer	C	T	V
[irrealis]	*for*	*to*	infinitive
	[u-mood]	[u-mood]	[i-fut]

The non-emotive C, as in (63), has uninterpretable mood features as well but is also connected to uninterpretable tense features.

(63)

forget	C	T	V
[realis]	*that*		
	[u-mood]	[u-T]	[i-pres/i-past]
	[u-T]		

While I think the classification in (61) gives some insight, it is easier to see the differences between verbs in terms of the transparency of the CP boundary. So, the non-factive emotives are the most transparent, i.e. have the smaller boundary between the two clauses. Verbs that disallow Negative Raising, as in (60), and can have *it* or *the fact that* preceding the complement, as in (64), have a CP with a mood feature, I will argue. This mood feature will be [+realis] for verbs such as *regret* and [-realis] for verbs such as *prefer*.

(64) a. They **regretted** it that Hittite became extinct.
b. Many Americans **regret** the fact that they now discuss sport with the passion that 200 years ago they brought to everyday debates.
(BNC-ABD 752)

Other verbs do not allow this addition to the clause boundary, as shown in (65).

(65) a. *Many Americans **believe** the fact that they now discuss sport.
b. *They **believed** it that Hedwig had brought that message.

Other differences involve ECM, as in (66), the use of *for*, as in (55), raising of the subject from the embedded clause, as in (67a), the possibility of embedded topics, as in (68a), and subjunctives.

(66) a. I believe him to be nice.
b. *I regret him to be nice.

(67) a. He was believed to be pro-French (BNC-CRK 998).
b. *He was regretted to be pro-French.

(68) a. John believes that this book Mary read often.
b. ?John regrets that this book Mary read often.

A possible representation of a factive verb is given in (69). This is a single CP but with no possibility to move through the CP and no independent mood features.[1]

(69)
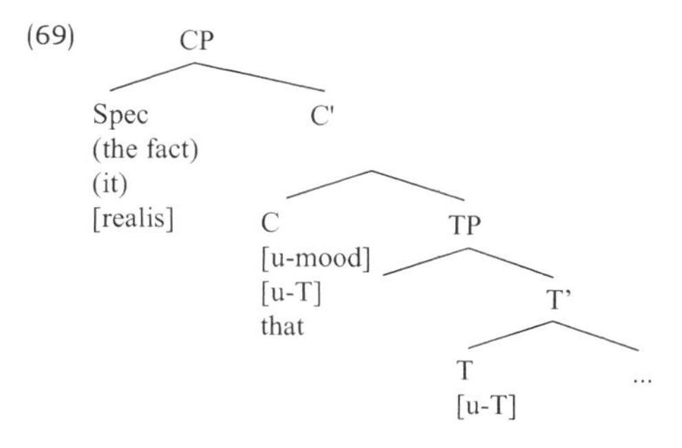

[1] It is possible, as Basse (2008) suggests, that this kind of CP is not a phase and therefore allows no extraction. I will leave that for further work.

Apart from factive and emotive, the term **assertive** is also used. For instance, Hooper and Thompson (1973) have a division, as in (70), where the assertive verb is comparable to the non-emotive and the non-assertive to the emotive verb.

(70)	**Assertive:**	**Non-assertive:**
	saying	emotive factive (resent, regret)
	thinking	negative verbs
	semi-factive	causative
	(forget, discover)	volition

The terminology in this area is daunting, and I have therefore tried to use **transparent** or **intransparent** and some of the features we saw before, namely +/- C(omplementizer), +/- nominative subject, +/- subject, +/- tense, and +/- realis mood. I think that makes more intuitive sense.

This section starts with a continuum of clausal complexity and continues with a classification of some of the types of object clauses. You will see a multitude of terms used in the area of verb classification, since there is no comprehensive system generally agreed upon yet. I have just introduced some of the terms you will see in the literature, but it is more important to focus on structural differences. We'll turn to another frequent type, but one not chosen by the higher verb.

2.3.3 Adverbial clauses

Adverbials function to provide information on how, where, when, and why the action or event took place or to provide information on how true or likely the speaker thinks the event is. These adverbial functions are often realized as PPs or APs, but also as clauses, as in (71) and (72).

(71) a. [After he left] it rained.
  b. It rained [after he left].

(72) a. [When he left] they were relieved.
  b. They were relieved [when he left].

The complementizer specifies the manner (*as*), the time (*before, after, since, when*), the place (*where*), the condition (*if*), or the reason (*because, why, since, in case, lest*) of the embedded sentence in relation to the main clause. The temporal ones are semantically the most complex, as the timelines in (73) and (74) show for (71a–b) and (72a–b).

(73) ———————— left ——————————rain ——————
  tense 1 (after) tense 2

(74) a. ———————— left ———relieved ——
tense 1 (when) tense 2
b. ———————— left/relieved ——
tense 1 (when)/tense 2

The preposition/complementizer *after* has semantic features (e.g. [time, order, later]) and determines the tense interpretation of its clause. The event in the main clause must follow the event in the *after*-clause.

Like the complement that needs a main verb, the [u-time] looks for an [i-pres] or [i-past] in the main clause. The [u-T] on C and T expresses what we've seen before, namely that it needs to probe for present or past tense.

(75)

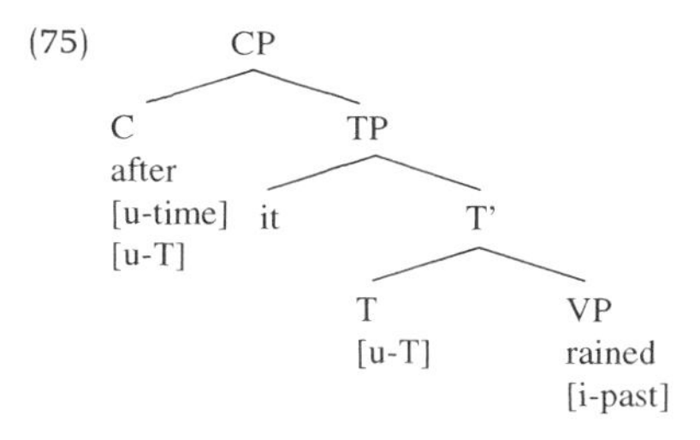

There are many more issues we could bring up here. For instance, when the complementizer is a *wh*-pronoun, as in (76), does this *wh*-pronoun originate as an adverbial as indicated by the copy? Is this a hidden relative clause with a null antecedent "in the place"?

(76) He left the book [where he had found the other one where].

Another question is how to handle the adverbial and object clauses that are non-finite, as in (77) to (79).

(77) [After leaving Greece], she went to Macedonia.

(78) [Kidnapped last week], he was released today.

(79) He insisted on [paying the bill].

Are these nominalizations, and, if so, what is their analysis? I'll leave these issues unaddressed and turn to the description of some other clauses.

2.3.4 Other clauses

In this section, we look at clauses modifying nouns. We'll continue to focus on the various shapes their complementizers have and the features to be checked.

Clauses that modify nouns are called relative clauses because the nouns they modify (*stories* in (80)) have a function in the relative clause, namely direct object of *repeat*, indicated by the relative pronoun *which*.

(80) The stories [which he repeats often] are boring.

Relative pronouns can also have other functions in English, e.g. subject and indirect object.

Complement clauses, as in (81), are quite different from relative clauses because the complementizer *that* in (81a) plays no function inside the clause. A relative pronoun therefore results in an ill-formed sentence, such as (81b).

(81) a. Reports [that he reached Mars] are exaggerated.
b. Reports [which he reached Mars] are exaggerated.

The finite clause following the noun in (81a) is called a complement (and not a relative clause) for other reasons. If we changed (81a) to (82a), we would force the complement to be a relative clause. Now, *reports* (through *that*) is the object of *reached*, but the result is very strange (indicated by the question mark) since *reports* is not an object that you'd expect with *reached*. If we change the verb to *read*, as in (82b), we do get a relative clause because one can read reports.

(82) a. ?Reports [that he reached] are exaggerated.
b. Reports [that he reads] are (always) exaggerated.

Relative clauses need to be predicated of a noun. Since Chomsky (1977), relative clauses have been analyzed using an operator moving to the Spec of CP, as in (83), with either the *which* or the *that*, or neither, surfacing, as (84) shows.

(83)

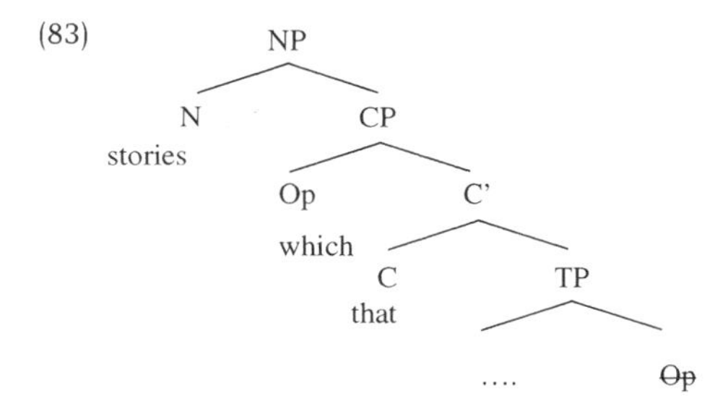

(84) a. The stories [which he repeats often] are boring.
b. The stories [that he repeats often] are boring.
c. The stories [he repeats often] are boring.

In some varieties of English, both *wh*-phrase and complementizer can be spelled out, as shown in (85).

(85) a. This program in **which that** I am involved is designed to help low-income first generation attend a four-year university and many of the resources they and (www.reaksmey.org/JamieTiengEssay.html)
b. it's down to the community **in which that** the people live (BNC-KNF 569).

Children may not yet move the relativized object, as shown in (86), and therefore typically use the complementizer *that* to form an relative clause, not the specifier *which*, which would be moving.

(86) The one that he lifted **it** (Lia, 4;5, Perez-Leroux 1995, from Guasti 2002: 230)

Formulating the exact grammatical rules that govern the choice of a *wh*-word over *that* or *that* over a *wh*-word is not easy, and we'll return to this question after we have looked at a couple of other issues. What we do know, partly thanks to data like (85a–b), is that the *wh*-word has moved to a specifier position, and *that* is base-generated in a head position, as in (87).

(87)

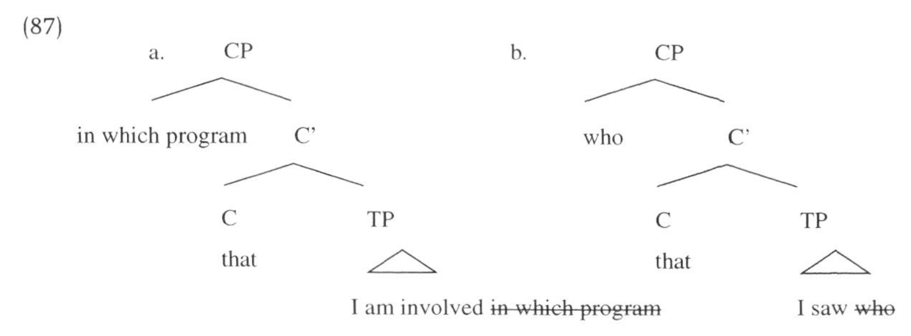

There are many proposals to add features to (87). Adger and Ramchand (2001), for instance, suggest (88), where Λ will insure that the CP is interpreted as a predicate and Var is similar to phi-features (in later work they change the Var, but this is not important for our purposes). The Var features ensure agreement between C and the *wh*-pronoun.

(88) that[Λ, *u*Var] he repeats *pro* [*u*Λ, Var]

I'll stick to the Λ but change the Var into phi-features for simplicity's sake, and I add the finiteness features. This gives the following account for (89).

(89)

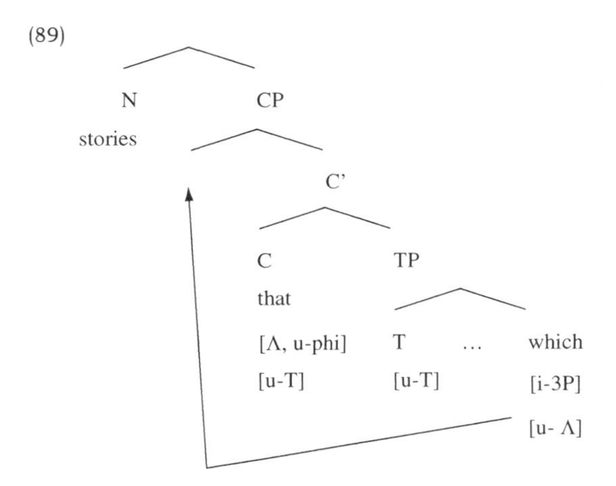

In (89), the Λ in C ensures that the CP is a predicate to the noun, but only if there is a *wh*-element in the clause. The phi-features ensure compatibility between the noun and the relative pronoun.

Apart from the question of the features of the C and *wh*-pronoun, there is a question about the structure. The tree in (89) shows the relative clause as sister to N, and this cannot be correct, since the CP is not the object/complement of the N. If we used N' instead, we'd have trouble with the LCA, because *stories* precedes the words in the relative clause, although the latter asymmetrically c-command *stories*. Kayne (1994) therefore proposes an alternative where a D selects a CP, as in (90a), and the NP moves to the Spec of the lower DP after which the entire DP moves to Spec CP, as in (90b).

(90) a. [DP the [CP C Putin made [DP which [NP decision]]]]
b. [DP the [CP [DP [NP decision]i which ti]j C Putin made tj]]]

If there is no *which* as D, the DP *decision* moves on its own, as between (91a) and (91b).

(91) a. [DP the [CP that [Putin made [DP decision]]]]
b. [DP the [CP [DP decision]j that [Putin made tj]]]]

In this analysis, "[r]elative pronouns are determiners that have lost their associated NP via Raising" (Kayne 2011: 4). I'll draw the tree in (92) for the more complex derivation in (90).

(92)

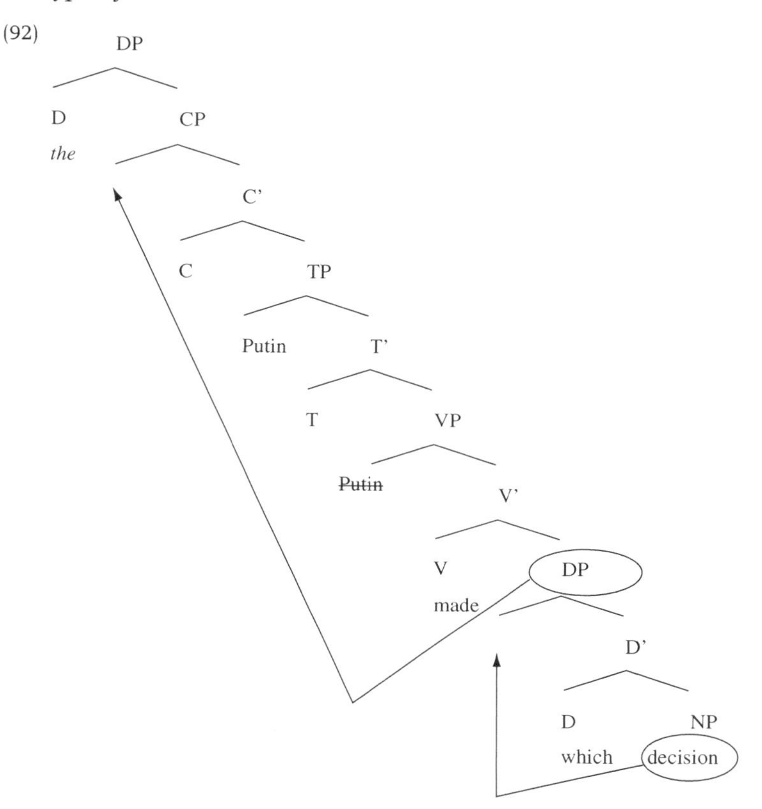

Evidence for the movement of the nominal is given in (93). If *pictures of himself* started out in the higher position, *himself* would not have a c-commanding antecedent. If it starts out in the position indicated by the copy in (93), all is as expected.

(93) The [pictures of himself] that Putin took ~~pictures of himself~~.

The analysis prompted by the LCA allows both complementizer or *wh*-phrase. It is the most accepted analysis of restrictive relative clauses. The features as in (88) are not needed in (92), and this is an advantage. Noun-complements, such as (81a), are straightforward CPs without anything moving, so a *wh*-pronoun is not expected, and this is correct.

There is a special type of relative clause, namely the non-restrictive relative clause. It can go with a nominal, as in (94a), or with a full sentence, as in (94b).

(94) a. Hillary Clinton, who just returned from a trip to Cuba, intends to write a book.
b. The sky is full of chem-trails, which I hate.

Unlike the complement clause or relative clause discussed above, which we will call restrictive, the clauses in (94) can only have *wh*-pronouns, and they have comma-intonation. Kayne (1994: 111) suggests basically the same derivation for restrictive and non-restrictive relative clauses. Let's look at an alternative.

Koster (2000) suggests a "colon-phrase" to account for (94ab), with a colon-head between the DP (or CP) and the non-restrictive CP, as in (95a–b). The colon appears in writing, but in spoken language the colon represents a pause around the phrase.

(95)

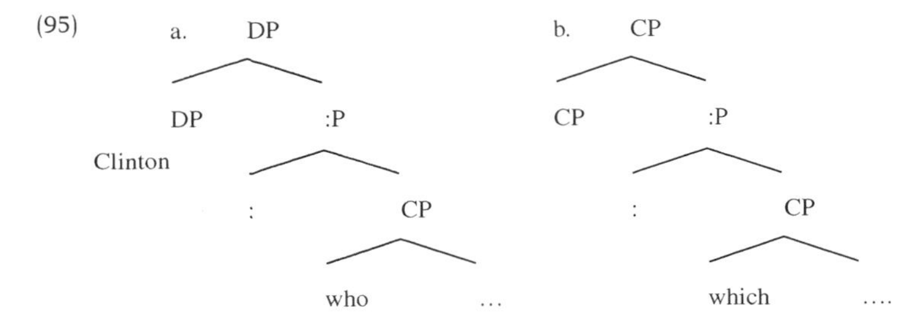

The non-restrictive relative clause in (95) is, correctly, outside the scope of D at LF. The relative pronoun can also be replaced by a full pronoun and then the relative becomes an interjection or a separate clause, as in (96a–b).

(96) a. Hillary Clinton intends to write a book. She just returned from a trip to Cuba.
b. The sky is full of chem-trails. This I hate.

This independence of the noun and the relative clause is the reason *that* is ungrammatical in non-restrictive relative clauses.

Three differences (at least) between restrictive and non-restrictive relative clauses and complement clauses - most of which we have discussed - should be accounted for. They are listed in Table 2.3.

Commas provide grammatical clues in English. They cannot separate a V or N or D from their complements, and they or comma-intonation can therefore not appear in (81) and (92). In non-restrictive relative clauses, the N and CP do not have such as relationship. Instead, we could spell out the colon-phrase in (95) as a comma.

Table 2.3 *Restrictive and non-restrictive relative clauses and noun-complements*

Restrictive	Non-restrictive	Complement
commas cannot surround it	commas may surround it	no commas
wh-pronoun or *that* or zero	only *wh*-pronouns	only *that* or zero
highly relevant information	additional information	may replace the N

As for the choice between the pronoun or the complementizer, complement clauses have no operator moving to the Spec CP, and so have only the *that*-possibility. Restrictive relative clauses can have a *that* or a *wh*-word or nothing, as in (84), although there is a real preference in spoken English for *that*. I think this preference is due to an Economy Principle that favors heads over specifiers (see van Gelderen 2004: 11). In the non-restrictive relative clause (94a), on the other hand, only a *wh*-pronoun occurs, and *that* is not possible, as (97) shows. I would argue that the phi-features have to be overt in structures such as (95). This is due to the independence of the CP from the DP in (95).

(97) *Hillary Clinton, that just returned from a trip to (non-restrictive) Cuba, intends to write a book.

The third difference listed in Table 2.3 is that restrictive relative clauses provide essential information, unlike non-restrictive ones. For instance, in (80), *the stories* is so general that the relative clause restricts and specifies the stories that are meant. In the case of (94a), everyone living in the US at the beginning of the twenty-first century is expected to know who Hillary Clinton is, and therefore the NP *Hillary Clinton* does not need to be restricted. The relative clause just provides background information that is not essential in knowing which noun is meant. That's why it is called non-restrictive relative clause and also explains why splitting the sentence into two clauses is common, as in (96) above.

A nice contrast between restrictive and non-restrictive relative clauses is provided by (98) and (99).

(98) Bankers that are crooks should be fired. (restrictive)

(99) Bankers, who are crooks, work overtime nowadays. (non-restrictive)

Of course, you could substitute *bankers* with *politicians*, *investors*, *house keepers*, *professors*, or *linguists* as well. The choice in the complementizers is crucial here, although that choice is partly stylistic (not grammatical) and partly grammatical. Thus, style guides tell you not to use *that* when the antecedent is human, as in (98); they don't have to tell you to use *who* in (99), because that is automatic.

One last point I'd like to add about relative and complement clauses - since we won't come back to them any more - is **islands**. As we'll see, various CPs are intransparent and cannot have an extraction from the CP. Relative clauses are famous for being islands, as has been noted since Ross (1967). In (100), extraction of the *wh*-pronoun from the CP is possible, because the CP is an object clause, but, in (101) and (102), it is not, because the CP is a complement to a noun and a relative clause respectively.

(100) What did I hear CP[that she said what]?

(101) *What did I hear the rumor CP[that she said what]?

(102) *Who did they meet the man [that knows who]?

Islands have received various explanations. One is that the *wh*-element cannot cross two boundaries, such as the DP, CP, or TP, in one step. I show this for the noun complement in (103), where the first step to the Spec of CP is ok (crossing only on TP), but the second is not (crossing a DP and TP).

(103) *What did TP[I hear DP[the rumor CP[what that TP[she said what]]]]

This way of formulating the constraint on movement is known as **Subjacency**. In the current theory, we account for the ungrammaticality through phases. If only vP and CP are phases, *what* is inaccessible for the probe in the C.

Wrapping up Section 2.3, we have examined embeddings by looking at the role of complementizers, at the dependence of clausal objects on their matrix verbs, at the structure of adverbial clauses, and clauses that are modifiers and complements to nouns. In the next section, we'll divide up the clause into three areas, and this is motivated by e.g. the semantic, grammatical, and pragmatic roles/functions that are marked in different areas in the clause, as we'll briefly explain now before devoting Chapters 3, 4, and 5 to each of these layers.

2.4 THE THREE LAYERS

We have defined a clause as having mood, tense, a grammatical subject, and a lexical verb. Parts of the clause play roles and functions, and indicate the existence of three different clausal spheres. This book emphasizes these three domains, and I will briefly introduce them here before devoting a chapter to each of the three.

The CP is the pragmatic layer and houses the mood of a clause, information on finiteness, and the topicalized and focalized material. Its head, the C(omplementizer), has features of mood and tense and communicates with T(ense) in the TP-Layer. As we've seen in Chapter 1, when I sketched the tension between Minimalism and Cartography, Rizzi (1997: 288) proposes to split the CP into Force, which indicates the mood of the sentence, and the Fin, which marks its finiteness. The Force looks to the "outside" and connects the proposition (what is being asserted about an event at a certain time) to another clause in the case of embedded clauses, or to the discourse event in the case of a main clause. The mood determines the tense, and this is represented on the Fin.

(104) **Splitting the CP into:**

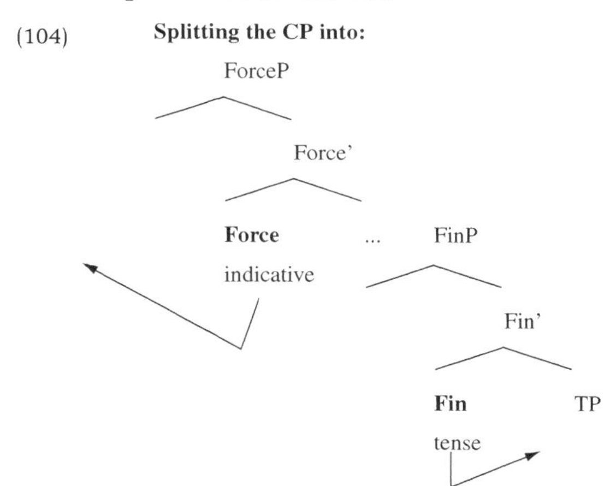

In between Force and Fin, the pragmatic Topic and Focus projections are possible, as well as adverbials that mark the mood of the speaker, as in (105).

(105) Higher adverbs

Mood $_{\text{speech act}}$	Mood $_{\text{evaluative}}$	Mood $_{\text{evidential}}$
frankly	*fortunately*	*allegedly*

(Cinque 1999: 106)

In Chapter 5, we look at how to add the adverbials and the pragmatic roles and the mood together. For now, (106) suffices, where *that book* topicalizes to the specifier of the TopicP.

(106)

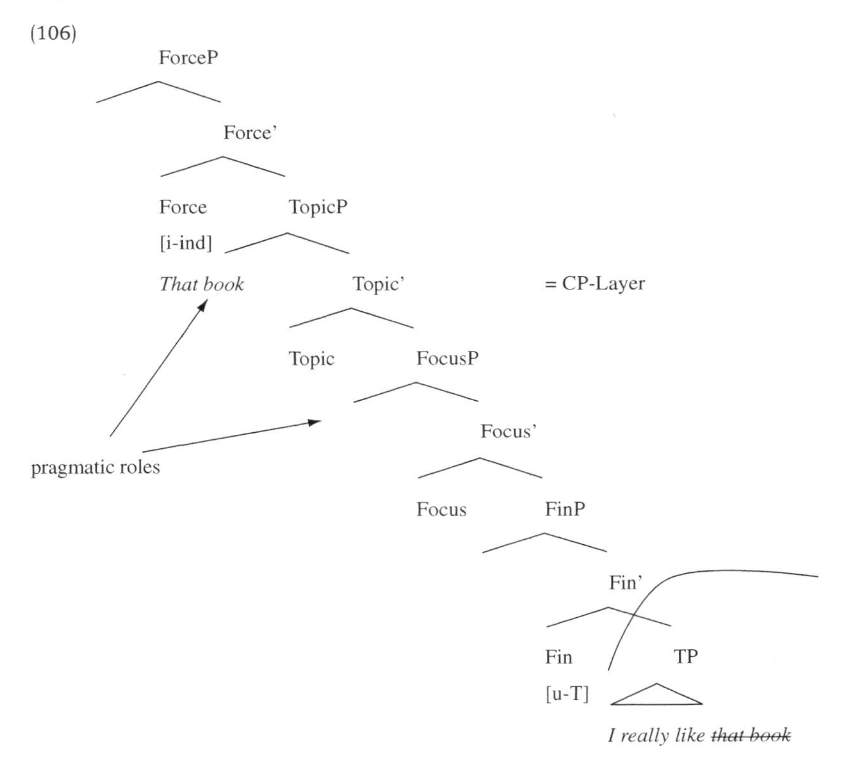

The TP is the grammatical layer and includes tense, (epistemic) mood, aspect, verbal agreement, and grammatical case. It is the area that is cross-linguistically perhaps the most diverse, since not all languages have agreement and case. In English, a TP can be expanded into (107). As we saw in Chapter 1, agreement is represented by [phi]-features, and case by [T] features; I have not represented the Aspect in terms of features but do so in Chapter 4.

(107)

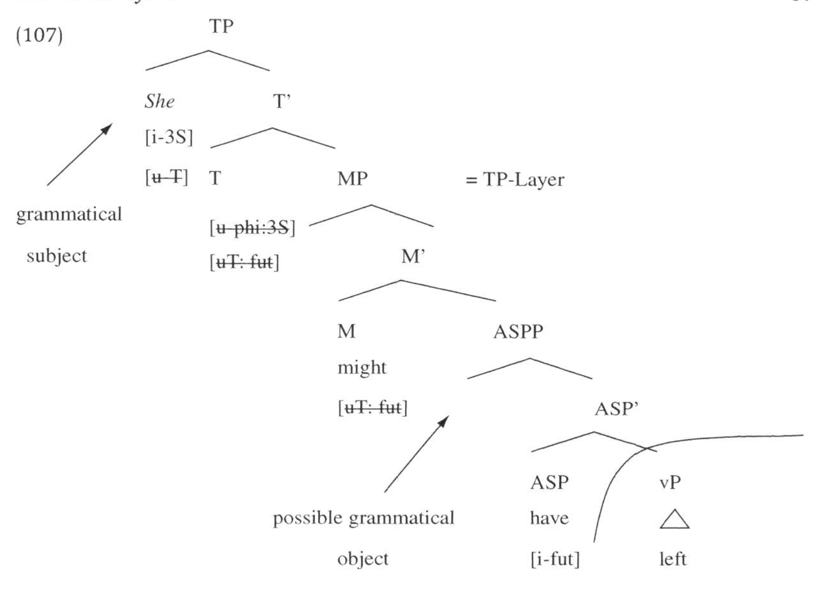

In (108), some of the TP adverbials are listed. Here, too, we'll wait till later to see how they all fit together.

(108)

Tpast	Tfut	Moodir	Modnec	Modpos	ASPhab	ASPrep	ASPfreq
once	*then*	*perhaps*	*necessarily*	*possibly*	*usually*	*again*	*often*

(Cinque 1999: 106)

The vP-Layer is used for information on the argument and event structure. Traditionally, we say it represents argument structure, i.e. "who did what to whom." It has also come to represent the aspectual information directly pertinent to the event (Aktionsart or internal aspect), whereas the aspectual information relevant to viewing the event from the outside (grammatical or external aspect) is in the ASP head in the TP-Layer in (107). The aspect inside the vP relates directly to the verb, e.g. durative verbs are typically imperfective. The vP-Layer houses the lexical verbs and its arguments as well as light verbs. We have introduced the vP in Chapter 1, and the next chapter will have more on this layer. For now, (109) should suffice, with EA marking the highest semantic role, as in Chomsky (2011).

(109)

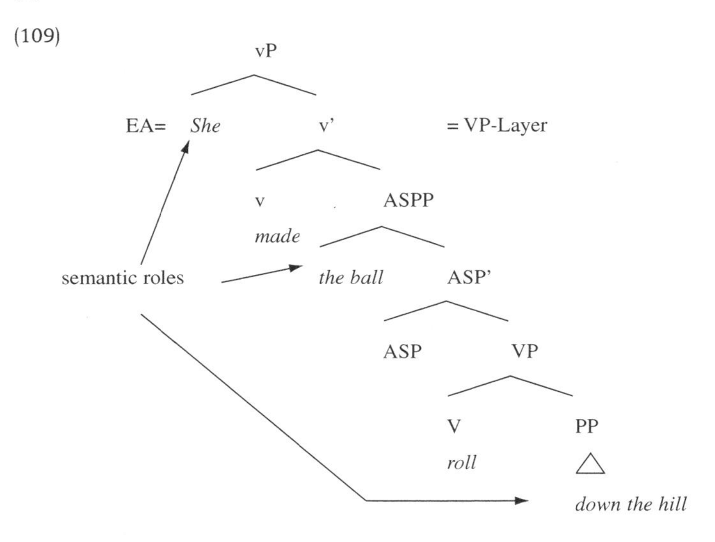

As to the adverbial angle of the vP, Haumann's (2007: 403) list in (110) provides a nice skeleton for aspectual adverbials in the VP, where DegPerf, Freq, Rep, AspPcompl, and Rest stand for Degree of Perfection, Frequency, Repetition, and Completion adverb respectively.

(110) VP adverbs

SpaceP	> AgentP	> DomainP	> MannerP	> DegPerfP >
here	*deliberately*	*universally*	*loudly*	*slightly*
MeansP	> FreqP	> RepP	> AspPcompl	> RestP
manually	*rarely*	*again*	*completely*	*again*

(from Haumann 2007: 403)

Again, we'll wait till later to fit these adverbials in.

This section has introduced the three layers and has also indicated some challenges in keeping them separate. Chapters 3, 4, and 5 will present this material in more detail. First, we'll finish this chapter by looking at a few of the ways clauses may differ cross-linguistically.

2.5 CROSS-LINGUISTIC OBSERVATIONS

In this section, we'll make some brief remarks on the cross-linguistic characteristics of main and embedded clauses: mood/finiteness, the subject function, and the varieties of complex clauses.

Table 2.4 *Yes/no questions (Dryer 2011b)*

Question particle	584
Interrogative verb morphology	164
Mixture of previous two types	15
Interrogative word order	13
Absence of declarative morphemes	4
Interrogative intonation only	173
No interrogative-declarative distinction	1
Total:	954 languages

2.5.1 The main clause

In English, as we've seen, the defining characteristic of a main clause is to have a certain mood; a finite verb, marked for tense and agreement; and a subject. Some languages have very different main clauses from those in English.

Every language has ways to express mood; its expression is not optional, as Table 2.4 shows for interrogatives. The one exception in that table is Chalcatongo Mixtec (Macauley 1996: 126); another variety of Mixtec, however, has a question particle (Daly 1973: 7).

Indicative, interrogative, and other moods are marked in English by word order, namely through the fronting of an auxiliary or a *wh*-element (cf. (2) to (6)). Mood in other languages can be distinguished morphologically on the verb or auxiliary or by means of a particle. For instance, Hindi/Urdu use the particle *kya* to ask a yes/no question.

(111)	***Kya***	*ap*	*jant-e*	*he*	*ke . . .?*	Hindi/Urdu
	Q	you	know-P	AUX	that	

'Do you know that . . .'

The use of a question particle, as in (111), is in fact the most frequent, as the data from WALS in Table 2.4 show. The English strategy is relatively rare, as you can see, represented in this sample by thirteen languages. If you were to look on the WALS map, you'd see the phenomenon is geographically concentrated on Europe.

As for finiteness, there is a lot of debate as to what it means. Many people think it is not a universally definable category. Koptjevska-Tamm (1990: 149) doubts the universality of finiteness: "while it is relatively easy to determine whether a language makes a distinction between independent and dependent verb forms, it is not always easy or reasonable to apply the notion of finiteness."

As we've seen, in English, finiteness involves agreement and tense and nominative case, but that is not so in other languages. Some languages do not mark subjects of finite clauses with nominative or another case, and some languages have verbs not marked for tense or agreement. Chinese is one such language where agreement and case are not marked and aspect, as in (112), only optionally.

(112) *wo* *he* *le* *cha* Chinese
I drink PF tea
'I drank tea.'

There are also languages where what look like typically finite characteristics are used in non-finite clauses. For instance, in the Logudorese-Nuorese variety of Sardinian, infinitives have nominative subjects and the infinitival verb has agreement, as in (113).

(113) *non* *kelj-o* *a* *cantar-**es*** ***tue*** Sardinian
not want-1S to sing-2S 2S.NOM
'I don't want you to sing.' (Jones 1992: 295)

You could ask how (113) is different from an indicative or subjunctive. The answer is that the complementizer is not the indicative *ki* "that," and the subject can only follow the infinitive, whereas indicative subjects can precede. Portuguese and (standard) Sardinian have nominative subjects as well, with Portuguese inflecting the infinitive but having the subject precede the verb. The lesson of this is that embeddedness and dependence can be expressed in many ways.

A last characteristic of the main clause in English is the obligatory expression of a subject, also known as the EPP in Generative Grammar. If you know languages such as Spanish or Italian or Chinese, you know that they need not express a subject, as in (114).

(114) *(Wo)* *chi* *fan* Chinese
1S ate rice
'I ate (rice).'

Polysynthetic languages such as Navajo typically do not express the subject as a separate phrase. There is a debate as to whether the affixes on the verb in (115) count as real pronouns rather than as "just" agreement. If the affix is indeed the subject, the EPP is not relevant in Navajo.

(115) *yiniłtsą* Navajo
yi-ni-*ł-tsą*
it-you-CL-saw
'You have seen it.'

This means that the characteristics of a main clause vary quite a bit. The morphological characteristics of nominative case and agreement may only be valid in languages that are morphologically complex, i.e. in synthetic languages. The syntactic characteristic of expressing an overt subject is quite variable too. Cross-linguistically, languages therefore mark mood but not necessarily tense, and need not move the grammatical subject to a special position or have it at all.

2.5.2 The embedded clause

All languages have complex clauses. Some of the different types of coordination and subordination are briefly mentioned here.

Coordination can be of words, phrases, and clauses. The semantics can be of many types: simple addition (e.g. English *and*) or one but not the other (e.g. English *but not* or *or*) or neither of the two (e.g. English *neither ... nor*). In some languages, the simple addition can be marked without a coordinator. The adversative is always marked, e.g. English *but, although*, German *aber*, and Navajo *ndi*, but the additive need not be. I'll provide a few examples.

In some languages, the coordinator or the verb indicates if the subject remains the same or not. Thus, *nɔ* in (116) indicates that the subject of the one clause is different from that of the other.

(116)	*hegɔ́ kɔ́ygú*	*ét-k'yá:lé:*	***nɔ***	Kiowa
	then Kiowa	3P-invite	and	
	thá:ɔn-hɔ:be:	*ém-k'óp*		
	town-near	3P-camp		

'Then they invited the Kiowas and the latter camped close to town.'
(Watkins 1990: 412)

(The prefixes on the verb also contribute to this interpretation, but I have left that out.) Even though *nɔ* is a coordinator, we could say that the second clause in (116) is embedded in some way.

Languages also differ in the types of subordinate, or embedded, clauses they have. As mentioned in Section 2.3.2, English has various types of infinitival and participial clause, as in (117).

(117) a. Unaccompanied she **began to sing** in the local language.(BNC-H7E 1014)
b. At the bar a group of dossers **began singing** Roaming in the Gloaming. (BNC-BNC 2820)

Purely analytic languages, i.e. with little morphology, lack inflected forms of verbs, and so only have bare forms, as in (118).

(118) *knom* **jɔng** **rian** *pia-saa* *kmae* Cambodian
I want study language Cambodian
'I want to study Cambodian.'

Many such languages have **serial verb** constructions, as in (119). Here, it is hard to see which clause is dependent, and these are often called cosubordinate.

(119) *and ying* **ba** *jian* **kan** Chinese
should hold sword see
'I should take the sword and see it.'
(Tang dynasty poem, Li and Thompson 1974: 202–203)

Heavily inflected languages, also known as polysynthetic languages, such as Navajo, are much more restricted in terms of clausal complements and have frequent nominalizations, as in (120), where the verb with *-nígíí* has been nominalized.

(120) *honeesná-***nígíí** *yoodlá* Navajo
3.win-NMZ 3.believe
'He believes he won/he believes the winner.' (Willie 1991: 178)

In short, all languages indicate mood, although finiteness is a much more language-specific notion. Complex sentences, too, display quite some variation.

2.6 CONCLUSION

In this chapter, we have looked at some ways of differentiating between independent (main) and dependent (embedded) clauses. The presence or absence of a lexical verb, mood, tense, grammatical subject, and complementizer are all relevant. We also discussed different types of complement and how the main verb determines the type of complement, and we'll come back to most of these issues in more detail in Chapter 5.

Complementizers are very important as they give us insight into the clausal mood and clausal selection by a higher verb. Coordinate and non-complement subordinate clauses will not feature in the remainder of this book.

Because the terminology is daunting, Table 2.5 is provided with some synonyms for terms mentioned.

Having stressed that a lexical verb is crucial to a clause and that mood, agreement, and tense render it independent or dependent, we'll turn to this lexical verb and its arguments in the next chapter.

Table 2.5 *Terms for clauses and functions*

sentence = main clause = matrix clause = independent clause = superordinate clause	
Clause	embedded clause/sentence = dependent/subordinate clause = CP
	coordinated clause = coordinated sentence
complementizer = subordinating conjunction = subordinator = C	
coordinator = coordinating conjunction = C	
adverbial = adjunct = modifier	
complement = object	

Keywords

Finite, agreement, subject, tense, mood, aspect, clause, coordination, subordination, embedding, nominalization, relative clause, adverbial, complement clause, CP, TP, vP, layers

DISCUSSION POINTS

1. Circle the finite verbs in the text below and identify the functions of the underlined clauses. Are there any challenges you run into?

   At least 22 families living in the capital's Chamkarmon district say they are being forced to sell their land at below market value to Thailand's Bun Roong Company in order to make way for a housing development. Village representative Chhim Veasna said on Wednesday that the families, living on a parcel of land in Tonle Bassac commune known as T85, had received a notice from the Council of Ministers mandating that they sell their land for US$400 per square metre. The villagers say their land is worth between $2,000 and $2,500 per square metre. "We are very concerned about our houses and living situation because we are being forced to move by the Thai Bun Roong Company," Chhim Veasna said. "They want to expel us from our places by forcing us to sell our houses to them at the lowest prices." (*Phnom Penh Daily*, September 22, 2011)

2. Draw a tree for (1). Would you include the CP? Discuss reasons.

   (1) I expect to leave soon.

3. There is a Baby Blues cartoon where Zoe is asking for a pony and says to her father, "So you're not going to buy me a pony, right?"

and her father answers, "Right." She then proceeds with, "And you're not just saying that to fool me into thinking that you're not going to buy me a pony so I'll be surprised because you really ARE going to buy me a pony which you said your aren't, right?"

> How many main verbs are in that last sentence? Explain the relationships between the verbs in terms of subordination or coordination.

4. Is (2) finite or not; is it a dependent or independent clause? What about (3)?

(2) Me do that? No way.

(3) *En* *of* *ze* *plezier* *hadden!* Dutch
and if they pleasure had
'They were really enjoying themselves.'

5. In the section on relative clauses, we argued that relative clauses are islands. Look at (4) and (5) and identify the relative clauses. Comment on their structure.

(4) Isn't that the song that Paul and Stevie were the only ones who wanted to record?

(5) This is a paper that we really need to find someone who understands. (Chung and McCloskey 1983: 708)

6. Noun-complements have been discussed as nouns with CP-complements. Could they be colon-phrases, as the non-restrictive relative clauses are in (95) above? What are the advantages and diadvantages of such an analysis?

SUGGESTIONS FOR FURTHER READING

For more on clauses, and complement and clause types, read Givón, e.g. (1980), (2006), or (2009), Noonan (1985), and Saddock and Zwicky (1985). Bril (2010) is a collection of typological studies on clause-linking.

Grammatical and other functions of DPs are explored in chapters 4 and 5 of van Gelderen (2010), and Keenan (1976) provides diagnostics for the grammatical subject.

Stewart (2001) has a generative account of serial verbs, and Dixon and Aikhenvald (2006) look at serial verbs from a more typological perspective. Yap et al. (2011) contain information on nominalization.

Kush, Omaki, and Hornstein (in press) discuss a parsing account to islands.

3 The VP-Layer

In this chapter, we examine the layer that represents argument and event structure. The central question is how to map the arguments onto the syntactic structure. When thematic structure is first introduced into generative syntax in the late 1970s, it is projectionist: the lexical item (usually the verb) determines the argument structure of the clause. This is also known as a lexicalist approach. In the early 1990s, the verb is seen as composed of smaller events, and the structure around the verb comes to be seen as playing a major role in thematic/argument structure. This approach is known as constructionist. Structurally, the information on the aspect and the definiteness of the arguments is represented by a double VP, known as the VP-shell.

At the moment, both projectionist and constructionist views are important in the literature. The position argued for in this chapter is that both the information about the verb in the lexicon and structure added from the outside play a role. The crucial problem for both approaches is how we derive the hierarchical order of arguments.

Section 3.1 reviews some of the developments in representing argument structure from the early 1980s to the present. Unergative, unaccusative, and transitive verbs are discussed in Section 3.2. Sections 3.3 and 3.4 discuss alternations, the inchoative/causative alternation and "double object" one, respectively. Section 3.5 looks at aspect and the event structure. Section 3.6 includes some remarks on cross-linguistic variation and on acquisition. In Section 3.7, I end by comparing the lexicalist and constructionist approaches and also by tying argument structure to the main topic of the book, namely how a feature-based approach and constructionist approach work together.

3.1 ARGUMENT STRUCTURE

In this section, valency and voice are briefly introduced. After that, the representation of argument structure is sketched, first via theta-roles, i.e. using a lexical or projectionist approach, and then via the vP, a constructionist approach.

3.1.1 Valency and voice

A simple definition of **valency** involves the number of arguments a verb has. For instance, transitive verbs have two arguments and a valency of two; intransitive verbs have one and a valency of one. Verbs can have from zero to three arguments, as shown in (1), where *it* is an expletive in (1a), i.e. not an argument.

(1) a. rain, snow — 0 arguments, as in 'It rained.'
b. swim, arrive — 1 argument, as in 'They swam.'
c. eat, see — 2 arguments, as in 'He ate an apple.'
d. give, tell — 3 arguments, as in 'They gave us work.'

For now, let's assume that a verb typically has one basic valency. The arguments can be marked on the verb through agreement or via case marking on the arguments (as we have seen in Chapter 1).

Valency, however, is not "either-or," as Hopper and Thompson's (1980) transitivity parameters have shown; see Table 3.1. A verb such as *hit* with an affected object is a highly transitive verb, but *read* with a (hopefully) little affected object is less so; *hit* is also punctual, but *read* is non-punctual. Highly transitive verbs are not likely to drop the object, as (2a) shows for *hit*, but verbs that are not so highly transitive do drop the object more readily, as (2b) shows for *read*.

(2) What did you do yesterday?
a. *I hit.
b. I read.

Table 3.1 *Transitivity parameters (as in Hopper and Thompson 1980: 252)*

	Parameter	High valency	Low valency
A	Participants	2	1
B	Kinesis	action	non-action
C	Aspect	telic	atelic
D	Punctuality	punctual	non-punctual
E	Volitionality	volitional	non-volitional
F	Affirmation	affirmative	negative
G	Mode	realis	irrealis
H	Agency	A high in potency	A low in potency
I	Affectedness of O	O totally affected	O not (totally) affected
J	O individuation	O highly individuated	O non-individuated

Atelic verbs occur more often in the progressive. An informal search in the COCA corpus shows that the verb *hit* is a little less frequent than *read* (61,639 and 86,993 respectively), but the numbers of the auxiliary "be" followed by *hitting* is much less (namely 2,056) than those of "be" followed by *reading* (namely 5,505).

The meaning of a verb is therefore relevant in determining the argument structure as well as its aspect. This is expressed by A to E and H to J in Table 3.1. Factors F and G are not determined by the meaning of the verb but by the properties of the higher CP.

Languages have ways to modify the valency of the verb. The causative and ditransitive constructions will be discussed in Sections 3.3 and 3.4, respectively. A causative construction has an additional argument, namely a Causer, whereas a ditransitive verb has two ways to express its arguments (at least in English). Apart from argument addition and change, we can also reduce the valency, as in passives and middles. This phenomenon is often referred to as passive or middle **voice**, as opposed to the active voice. An example of an active, passive, and middle voice is given in (3), but is not further developed in this chapter.

(3) a. That store sells fake iPods.™ — active
b. Fake iPods™ were sold by that store. — passive
c. Fake iPods™ sell well. — middle

Valency-reduction is a way to promote the lower argument, e.g. *fake iPods™* in (2a) is the grammatical object but is promoted to subject in (2bc). The terms subject and object are confusing here, and this is one of the reasons we add theta-roles, to which we turn next.

3.1.2 Theta-roles

There are many views on how to represent argument/event structure. Based on Gruber (1965), Fillmore (1968), and Jackendoff (1972), Chomsky (1981: 34ff.) introduces theta-roles. Verbs are listed in the lexicon with their theta-roles (theta-grids), and there needs to be a matching number of arguments to theta-roles in the syntax. If *eat* is listed as needing two theta-roles (Agent and Theme), there will need to be two arguments (e.g. DPs), and to each argument a theta-role will have to be assigned. This is known as the Theta-Criterion.

Theta-Criterion

Each argument bears one, and only one, theta-role, and each theta-role is assigned to one, and only one, argument.

Expletive subjects (*it* and *there*) and adjuncts do not bear theta-roles; the infinitival empty subject PRO and the null subject to finite verbs represented as pro in pro-drop languages do have theta-roles.

A list of the typical characteristics of the most common of these roles is given in (4). Not everyone uses exactly the same set or name, e.g. Agent and Theme are also referred to as Actor and Patient respectively.

(4) Agent: an animate entity that deliberately brings about the event.
Causer: entity responsible for (initiating) an event
Experiencer: an animate entity that experiences the event
Theme: person or object affected by the action
Goal: animate entity that the event is done to or for

Williams (1981: 83ff.) has perhaps the clearest (early) representations of argument structure as the "list of its arguments" (p. 86). An example of a theta-grid is given in (5).

(5) a. *hit* (A, Th)
b. *see* (Exp, Th)
c. *give* (A, Th, G)
d. *seem* (Theme, (Exp))

To indicate that one of these arguments may become the grammatical subject, Williams underlines that argument and refers to it as the **External Argument**, earlier abbreviated as EA. Of the verbs in (5), *hit* and *give* have their Agents underlined, since they become the grammatical subject; with *see*, it is the Experiencer that serves as subject. The argument structure of (5a) is given in (6). This is pretty straightforward, as are the ones for *see* and *give* in (5bc) (not provided).

(6) 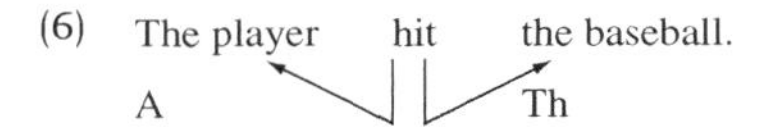

The verb *seem* of (5d) has an optional Experiencer that it assigns to the PP *to me* in (7) and a Theme that it assigns to the CP complement. Neither of these theta-roles are underlined, so neither functions as the grammatical subject. Because English sentences need subjects, a non-argument (expletive) *it* appears in subject position. This expletive does not need, and does not receive, a theta-role, as (7) shows.

(7) 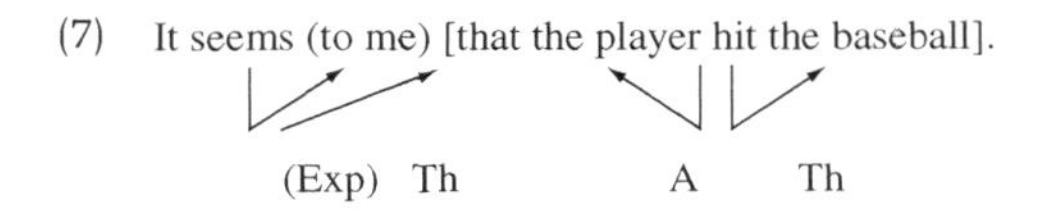

Inside the CP that is the Theme of *seem*, the verb *hit* also assigns theta-roles, namely an Agent and a Theme.

Williams also looks at the realization of the arguments. He includes rules whereby Agents can be realized inside the VP, as in (8a); Goals preceded by the preposition *to*, as in (8b); and where Themes end up as NPs inside a VP, as in (8c).

(8) **Realization rules (a few)**
a. Agent: (NP, PP_{by}) John was seen by Bill
b. Goal: (NP, PP_{to}) to give to John
c. Theme: (NP) hit Bill

(from Williams 1981: 88)

As mentioned, the names of the theta-roles sometimes differ: Actor and Agent are used to refer to the same role, and Patient and Theme as well. In what follows below, I use Agent, Causer, Experiencer, Theme, Goal, and Location/Result; minor roles are Target and Instrument.

A huge refinement of the realization or mapping of arguments onto the syntactic structure comes in terms of thematic hierarchies. This means the lexical entry in (5) no longer needs to idiosyncratically list the EA. Instead, certain thematic roles show up in certain syntactic positions: the Agent is usually the grammatical subject and the Theme the grammatical object, and the Location may be an adjunct. A provisional hierarchy is shown in (9).

(9) (Provisional) **Thematic Hierarchy**
Agent > Theme > Location.

The higher an argument is on the Thematic Hierarchy, the higher it is in the tree and the earlier it is pronounced. One way of ensuring that order is using Baker's (1988: 46) Uniformity of Theta Assignment Hypothesis, or UTAH, given in (10), although the UTAH is not committed to one or other hierarchy.

(10) **Uniformity of Theta Assignment Hypothesis**
Identical thematic relationships between items are represented by identical structural relationships between those items at the level of D-Structure (from Baker 1988: 46).

So, the Theme *fake iPods*™ in (3abc) will have the same underlying position, although it may surface in different positions if higher semantic roles are absent.

Belletti and Rizzi (1988) identify verbs of psychological states, or ***psych*-verbs**, where, in (11ab), the Theme theta-role ends up higher in the syntactic hierarchy than the Experiencer but, in (12ab), the reverse order occurs.

(11) a. That worried me.
TH EXP
b. It pleased me.
TH EXP

(12) a. She was worried about that.
EXP TH
b. She liked it.
EXP TH

If *psych*-verbs sometimes map the Theme higher than the Experiencer and sometimes lower, this means the UTAH is violated.

One possible solution to this mapping problem is to split up the Theme into a **Target** or **Subject Matter** and **Causer**, as Pesetsky (1995) does. In (11), the TH is argued to be a Causer and higher in the Hierarchy than the Experiencer; in (12), the TH is a Subject Matter and lower in the Hierarchy. That saves the Hierarchy, and we can formulate a more precise Hierarchy as (13).

(13) **(Revised) Thematic Hierarchy**
Agent > Causer > Experiencer > Subject Matter > Goal

One of the problems with theta-roles is that they seem so subjective, and, as a result, alternatives have been suggested. More recently, Reinhart (2002), Marelj (2002; 2004), and Haiden (2005) have updated theta-roles and take them as consisting of clusters of binary features, c (for cause) and m (for mental involvement). I will now sketch that system and assume a modified version in the rest of the book.

Reinhart proposes both the fully specified ones on the left side in (14) but also the underspecified ones on the right.

(14) Thematic Feature Clusters

[+c,+m]	Agent	[+c]	Cause
[-c,+m]	Experiencer	[+m]	sentient[1]
[+c,-m]	Instrument	[-c]	Goal
[-c,-m]	Theme	[-m]	Subject Matter

This is a much more restricted set of theta-roles, and it is based on two feature choices that are relevant to argument structure. The fact that theta-roles are not primitives but further decomposable as binary features also allows one to see that there is an overlap, e.g. Agent and Causer have something in common, i.e. [+c], and so do Agent and Experiencer, i.e. [+m], as do the Theme and Subject Matter, i.e. [-m], and the Experiencer and Goal, i.e. [-c].

A transitive verb such as *eat* has [+c,+m] as one of its theta-roles, i.e. an Agent in (15), but *open* has [+c] and is therefore compatible with an Agent, Instrument, and Cause, as in (16).

[1] Reinhart uses [+m] rather than [-c+m] for *love, know*, and *believe*; for the purposes of this chapter (and the book), we will ignore it.

(15) The baby/*the spoon/*hunger ate the soup.
Agent/*Instrument/*Cause = [+c,+m]

(16) Max/the key/the wind opened the door.
Agent/Instrument/Cause = [+c] (from Reinhart 2002: 14–15)

We'll come back to the transitive/intransitive alternation that is possible in (16) with the verb *open* but will first add a little more on the other clusters.

See if you agree with the theta-roles in (17), which I have changed a little from Reinhart (by using [–c+m] in (17b) rather than [+m]).

(17) a. *read* [+c+m] [–c–m]
b. *like, love, know* [–c+m] [–m]
c. *please, worry, frighten* [+c] [–c+m] ([–m])

I think *read* and *like* are pretty obvious, and we'll talk about *please* and others in a minute.

How does this system handle the mapping from the lexicon to the syntax? Based on Williams (1981), Reinhart develops a system that assigns values to verbs that have more than one argument, namely a 1 to a cluster that only has + values and a 2 to a cluster that has – values. The argument with a 2 is first merged with the verb and is therefore the lowest, and the argument with 1 is last merged and is therefore the highest. In English, this highest argument will be moved to the position of the grammatical subject. Clusters with mixed values are not given a number, and if nothing is marked external Merge is preferred.

Let's look at a straightforward example. In (17a), the Agent will be marked 1 and the Theme 2, so the mapping is as predicted by the numbering. In (17b), *like* has an Experiencer and a Subject Matter. The former is not given a number, since it is mixed, but the latter is marked by 2. The Experiencer is therefore free to merge later and to become the grammatical subject, whereas the Subject Matter has to be in a lower position, i.e. merged first.

Example (17c) is the most complex of the three, since it involves the alternating *psych*-verbs discussed in (11a) and (12a). When [+c] and [–c, +m] appear, the result will be a Causer followed by an Experiencer, as in (11a). When [–c, +m] and [–m] occur, the Experiencer will be followed by Subject Matter, as in (12a). The mapping in (11a) follows because the Causer is marked for later Merge, and the Experiencer is thus lower. In (12a), we have a Subject Matter ([–m]) which is first merged, and the Experiencer (the mixed cluster) will be free to merge later.

Reinhart crucially assumes an optional [-m] in (17c), although all three cannot be chosen at the same time, as (18) shows, where the bolded nouns are connected to the theta-roles underneath.

(18) *That **earthquake** worried **me** about the **house**.
[+c] [-c, +m] [-m]

To solve this incompatibility problem, Marelj (2002) invokes an Identity Constraint that bars identical theta-roles. For the combinations in (17c), she argues that the [+c] and [-c, +m] are distinct in the [c]-value, and therefore (11a) is grammatical. The [+c] and [-m] are not distinct, however, and that rules out (18). This non-distinctness between [+c] and [-m] is also the reason that *worry* cannot have a Cause and Subject Matter as its roles, as (19) shows.

(19) *The **wind** worried the **house**.
[+c] [-m]

In conclusion, theta-roles are one way of representing argument structure, and Reinhart's version is the most current instantiation. I personally like the binary way of marking the theta-roles, since they have a simple conceptual basis, namely cause for change for [+c] and mental contribution for [+m]. To be as clear as possible, I will use both the theta-roles and the features in the remainder of the book. The intuition behind Reinhart's mapping that [+c] and [+m] are higher than [-c] and [-m] is sound and similar to that of the Thematic Hierarchy in (13).

I'll end with a speculation as to the origin of the mapping of semantic roles onto syntactic positions. The Hierarchy and the UTAH constitute a principle of the faculty of language. Baker (1997) sees the UTAH as part of the C-I interface, and that would make it a "third factor." If we assume animacy is important semantically, i.e. part of the pre-linguistic stage, we could say that the Hierarchy is the grammaticalization of semantic animacy, i.e. an exaptation of the semantic animacy hierarchy to the Narrow Syntax.

3.1.3 The vP

The theta-approach to argument structure faces a challenge because many factors outside the choice of the verb affect argument structure. The aspect of a sentence, its polarity (affirmative or negative), and individuation of the object affect the argument and event structure as well (as indicated in Table 3.1). The crucial question is which determines which: Does the verb determine which aspect appears, or does the aspect determine the type of verb? In the generative model, Parsons (1990) and Pietroski (2007) have tried to minimize the role of the lexical verb in determining its arguments, and Hale and Keyser (1993; 2002) and Borer (2005a,b) advocate looking at the verb's surrounding shell, and that's what we'll do in this section.

In Chapters 1 and 2, we have seen a basic vP-shell. It initially was introduced to accommodate the three arguments of a ditransitive verb, and we'll see more on ditransitives in Section 3.4. The vP-shell also represents causative structures very well, as we'll see in Section 3.3. Since Hale and Keyser (1993; 2002) it has been used to read off the semantic roles at the C- I interface.

Let's look at one possible vP-shell, namely the structure in (20) with a causative verb *roll* as its core. It is based on ideas by Hale and Keyser (1993; 2002), Tenny (1994), Harley (1995), Pylkkänen (2008), Ramchand (2008), and many others.

(20)

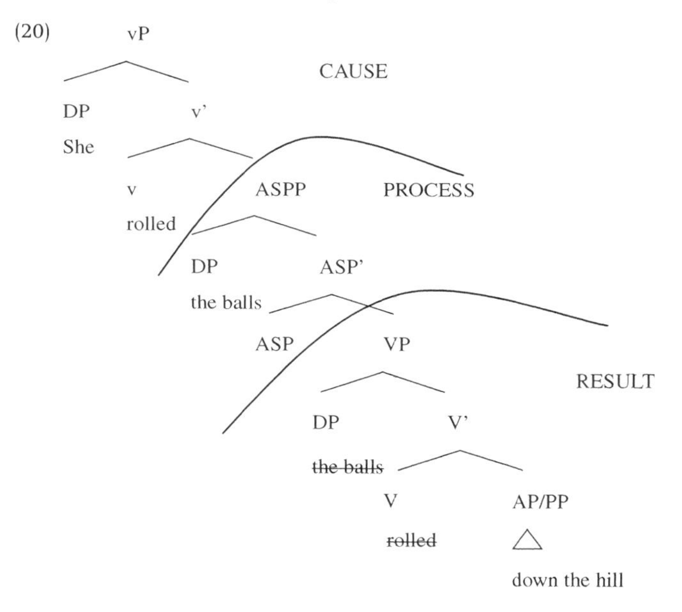

The vP-shell in (20) has three layers representing the event: a Causer/ initiator of the action or result (the vP), a process of the action (the ASPP), and the state or result (the VP).

Folli and Harley (2007) suggest three "flavors" of light verbs to introduce arguments. Depending on the light verb chosen, a different argument appears: The light verb DO introduces an Agent, whereas the light verb CAUSE introduces a Causer, as in (20). Pylkkänen (2008: 7–8) argues that non-core arguments, i.e. everything except the Theme, are introduced by (seven) functional heads, which she takes "to belong to a universal inventory of functional elements from which a particular language must select." Having each light verb (v and ASP in (20)) responsible for the introduction of an argument would mean that all arguments are in specifier position except the arguments of the lexical verb, where there could be an argument in the specifier and one in the complement position, as shown in (20).

The projectionist approach uses the UTAH to ensure that the order of the arguments is correct. The vP-shell approach is one where the child learning the language will have to decide not only on the number of functional heads but also on their order. For most constructionists, the order is a given, and it is therefore a Cartographic approach, even though it is not often put that way. Borer (2005b: 11) assumes that "the properties of functional structure are innate and universal" and that "the order of functional nodes [is] a syntactic given."

As for ASPP in (20), it is not clear to me whether or not the English tree includes this. Definiteness on objects and perfective on verbs does not result in a different position or morphology; we will be using the ASPP when we discuss phrasal verbs, so I will assume it in (20) as well.

The vP-shell accommodates aspect and head positions for the verb to move to. We need both the vP and the lexical information, as Hale and Keyser (2002: 1) suggest. The reason we can't do without the lexical information is that there are verbs that cannot be transitivized, e.g. *arrive* in (21) and *bloom* in (22). This is due to the nature of these verbs, i.e. their conceptual structure that is marked in the lexicon by means of the role [–c,–m].

(21) *I arrived the bus.

(22) *The sun bloomed the sunflowers.

The event of arriving and blooming is internally motivated, unlike events such as boiling and melting that are initiated from the outside.

Another reason that we need an expanded VP is that the inclusion of a certain type of functional head in the vP changes the argument structure and valency of the construction. A good example from Modern English is hard to give, but in Old English (and other languages) examples abound. For instance, as (23) shows in general and (24) in detail, the addition of *ge-* renders an intransitive verb transitive.

(23) *ærnan* 'to run' *geærnan* 'to reach'
feran 'to go' *geferan* 'to reach'
gan 'to go' *gegan* 'to overrun, subdue'
hyran 'to hear' *gehyran* 'to learn about'
restan 'to rest' *gerestan* 'to give rest'

winnan 'to labor, toil' *gewinnan* 'to gain, conquer'
wadan 'to go' *gewadan* 'to traverse'

(24) *ða ferdon þa Pihtas. and* ***ge****ferdon þis land norþanweard*
Then went the Picts and entered this land northward.
(Preface *Peterborough Chronicle*)

Using the vP-shell, one can argue that the functional head ASP determines that a Theme is involved in events that it is part of. There are a number of ways to represent this. Following the spirit of Tenny (1994), I have measure features in ASP that are responsible for the affectedness of the Theme.

(25)

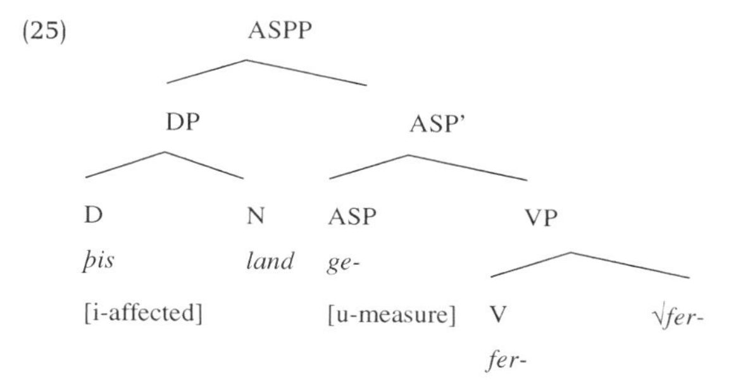

In (25), there is a light verb *ge-* that is responsible for adding a Theme theta-role.

Modern English does add results to activity verbs, such as *sneeze* and *lecture* in (26a) and (27a), and this too is probably determined by the vP-shell: when there is a result, there has to be a Theme, as (26b) and (27b) show.

(26) a. Maybe he sneezed it off the hinges and that was why it fell out of the sky. (Google)
b. *He sneezed it.

(27) a. and they talked themselves to sleep. (COCA 2007 Fiction)
b. *They talked themselves/her.

In addition, Rappaport Hovav and Levin (1998: 97) show that manner verbs such as *sweep*, *whistle*, and *run* have many possibilities that can't all be listed in the lexicon, as exemplified for *sweep*.

(28) a. Terry swept.
b. Terry swept the floor.
c. Terry swept the crumbs into the corner.
d. Terry swept the leaves off the sidewalk.
e. Terry swept the floor clean.

Assume therefore that the lexical entries for *roll* and *melt* minimally have a Theme, a [-c,-m], connected to them, but that it has an optional [+c] connected to it. Verbs such as *arrive* and *bloom* only have the [-c,-m] possibility. Many languages have additional heads that add arguments.

In short, the conceptual structure of the verb and the arguments surrounding it are both necessary. I'll therefore use a tree that has both and that is agnostic as to which determines which.

3.2 UNACCUSATIVE AND UNERGATIVE VERBS

In this section, we examine the theta-roles and vP-shell of unaccusative and unergative verbs. Because many unaccusative verbs can be causativized, we'll discuss that as well before going into causatives more deeply in Section 3.3.

Perlmutter (1978) makes the important distinction between intransitives that have come to be called unergative and those that have come to be called unaccusative (also known as change-of-state verbs). Unergative verbs have Agents, usually animate, and unaccusative verbs have Themes, animate or inanimate. The use with the Agent-compatible adverb *deliberately* in (29) shows this difference.

(29) a. **She** deliberately smiled/coughed.
Agent [+c, +m]
b. ***The ice** deliberately melted/broke.
Theme [-c, -m]

Sorace (2000: 879) puts the distinction in this way: "[t]he single argument of an unaccusative verb is syntactically equivalent to the direct object of a transitive verb, whereas the single argument of an unergative verb is syntactically equivalent to the subject of a transitive verb." Typical unergatives involve willed, volitional, controlled acts, i.e. with an Agent central; typical unaccusatives involve change of location/state. As Rosen (1984), Sorace (2000), and others make clear, this distinction is not a binary one but a continuum.

Some differences between these verbs are provided in Table 3.2. As for (a), the theta-role can be tested through adverbs, as in (29). As for (b), since unergative verbs have an Agent, they can easily be transitivized, as in (30), with a cognate object; unaccusative verbs cannot be transitivized, as (31) shows, except those that participate in the causative alternation, as we'll see. The reason is that unaccusatives already have a Theme.

Table 3.2 *Characteristics of unergative and unaccusative verbs in English*

	Unergative (Agent argument)	**Unaccusative** (Theme argument)
a.	*deliberately* is ok and the argument is human/animate	*deliberately* is not ok and argument can be +/–animate
b.	a Theme can be added	no Theme can be added
c.	V+*er*	*V+*er*
d.	*have* + perfect participle	*be* + perfect participle
e.	*impersonal passive	impersonal passive (Dutch)
f.	no genitive of negation	genitive of negation (Russian)

(30) I sneezed a good sneeze.

(31) a. *The bus arrived me.
b. *The bus arrived a perfect stop.

Characteristics (c) to (f) in Table 3.2 are language-specific. I will just mention them here without critical comment (see e.g. Rosen 1984 and Sorace 2000 for critiques). Characteristic (c) depends on the *-er* suffix in English being used to nominalize unergative verbs with agents such as *swimmer*, *sneezer*, and even *cougher*, but never *arriver* and *comer*.

As for (d), in many Germanic and Romance languages, the choice of the perfect auxiliary depends on the type of verb. Thus, in Italian, French, Dutch, and German, the auxiliary *have* is used when an Agent is involved with transitives and unergatives and *be* when a Theme is involved with unaccusatives. An example of such auxiliary selection from Dutch is given in (32).

(32) a. *Hij* ***heeft*** *gezwommen* Dutch
'He has swum.'

b. Hij ***is*** gekomen
he is arrived
'He has arrived.'

English and Spanish used to select *have/haber* and *be/estar* this way too but have lost it. Using a VP-shell, where functional categories are connected to certain theta-roles, would account for the connection of the auxiliary *hebben* 'have' in (32a) to an Agent. See Kayne (1993) for more.

The impersonal passive mentioned as (e) can be seen in (33). It is typically possible with unergatives but not with unaccusatives.

(33) a. *Er* *werd* *gezwommen* Dutch
there became swum
'There was swimming.'
b. **Er* *werd* *aangekomen*
there became arrived
'There was arriving.'

The reason for this difference is that the Agent in (33a) can be lost (demoted) in a passive but not the Theme in (33b).

There are other differences, but the last one that I'll mention is the genitive case in Russian, optionally present on objects in negative transitive sentences. This genitive can also occur with unaccusative Themes, as (34a) shows, but not with unergative Agents, as (34b) shows.

(34) a. *Ne* *rasstajalo* ***ni*** ***odnoj*** ***snežink-I*** Russian
not melted no single.GEN.S snowflake-GEN.S
'Not a single snowflake melted.'
b. ***Nikak**-ix* ***devoček*** *ne* *tancevalo*
no-GEN.P girl.GEN.P not danced
'No girls danced.' (from Babyonyshev et al. 2001: 12)

The position of the Theme and Agent in (34) is irrelevant. The preverbal unaccusative in (35a) is still grammatical, and the postverbal unergative in (35b) is still ungrammatical.

(35) a. ***ni*** ***odnoj*** ***snezink-I*** *ne* *rasstajalo* Russian
No single. GEN.S snow-GEN.S not melted
'Not a single snowflake melted.'
b. **vcera* *ne* *tancevalo* ***nikak-ix*** ***devocek***
yesterday not danced no-GEN.P girl.GEN.P
'No girls danced yesterday.' (Olena Tsurska, p.c.)

Table 3.3 provides a list of unergative and unaccusative verbs, with the latter subdivided into those that can alternate between intransitives and causatives, a point we come back to in Section 3.3.

As to the structure, with unaccusative verbs the VP is crucial, with a Theme and Result as in (36), with the tree in (37).

(36) It broke into two pieces.

(37)
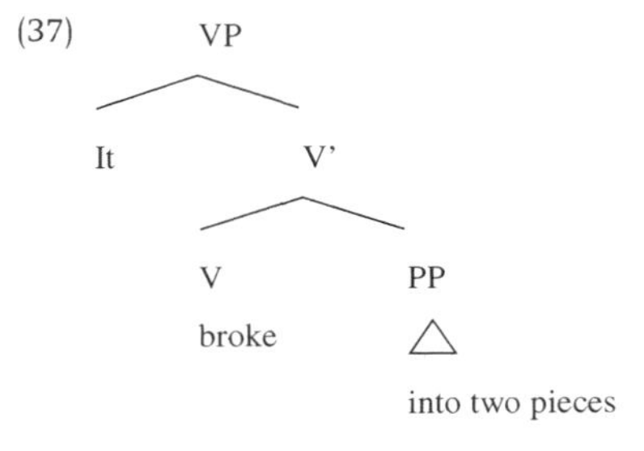

Table 3.3 *Examples of unergative and unaccusative verbs in English*

Unergative	Unaccusative
bicycle, burp, cough, crawl, cry, dance, daydream, frown, grin, hop, jog, kneel, laugh, limp, resign, run, scream, shout, smile, swim, speak, sneeze, sleep, talk, walk, work, yell	**Alternating**: begin, burn, decrease, drop, fall, freeze, grow, increase, melt, reduce, stop, spread, widen
	Non-alternating: appear, arise, arrive, come, depart, emerge, ensue, exist, follow, occur, remain, sit

To the VP-Layer in (37), a Causer can be added, in which case a v and vP appear, as in (38), the tree for (39). The little v introducing the Causer can be seen as an empty light verb with the meaning of 'make.'

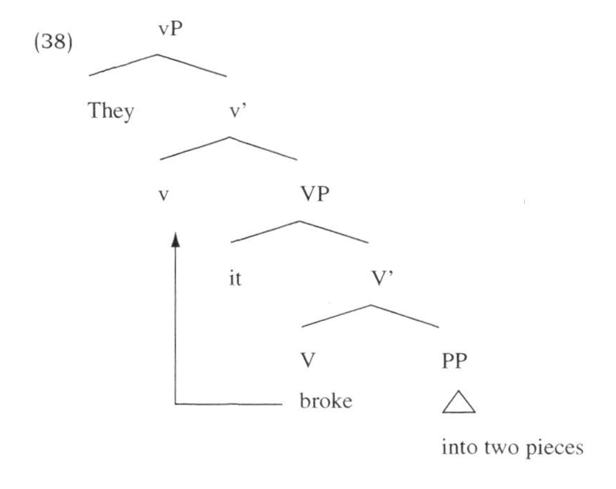

(39) They broke it into two pieces.

This shows that certain unaccusatives can be causativized, not true with unergatives in most languages.

Many alternating unaccusatives are de-adjectival, e.g. *redden, thicken, widen, open*, as Tables 3.4 and 3.5 show. The possible reason for this is that the adjective represents the result and incorporates from the AP to the V. A tree for this is given in (40), adapted from Hale and Keyser (2002: 31).

Table 3.4 *The causative suffix* -en *for adjective–verb pairs (from Levin and Rappaport Hovav 1995: 96)*

awaken, blacken, brighten, broaden, cheapen, coarsen, dampen, darken, deafen, deepen, fasten, fatten, flatten, freshen, frighten, gladden, harden, hasten, hearten, heighten, lengthen, lessen, lighten, loosen, madden, moisten, neaten, quicken, quieten, redden, ripen, roughen, sadden, sharpen, shorten, sicken, slacken, smarten, soften, stiffen, straighten, strengthen, sweeten, tauten, tighten, toughen, waken, weaken, whiten, widen, worsen

Table 3.5 *A zero-affix with adjective–verb pairs (from Levin and Rappaport Hovav 1995: 95)*

brown, clean, clear, cool, crisp, dim, dirty, dry, dull, empty, even, firm, level, loose, mellow, muddy, narrow, open, pale, quiet, round, shut, slack, slim, slow, smooth, sober, sour, steady, tame, tan, tense, thin, warm, yellow

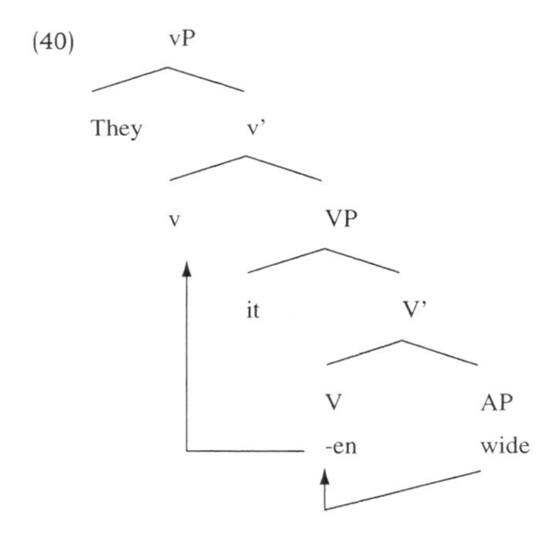

Unergatives are frequently denominal, so we could argue, as in Hale and Keyser (2002: 63), that there is a VP with the N incorporated into the V and moving to v to merge with an Agent DP, e.g. (41) with a structure as in (42). This light verb has the meaning of 'do' (as argued in Folli and Harley 2007 and mentioned above).

(41) They laughed.

(42)

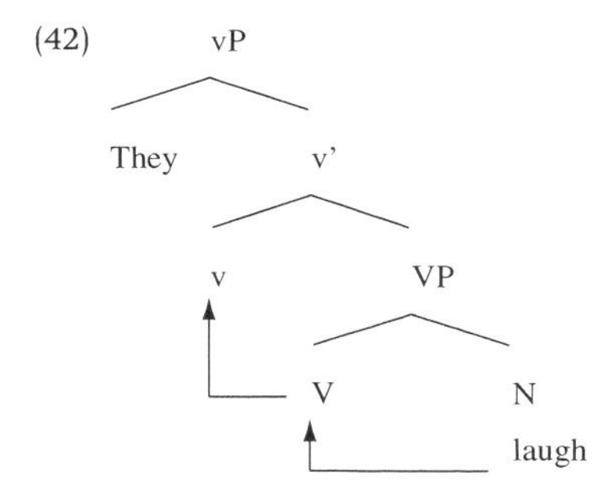

A number of linguists, including Chomsky, use v* for verbs with an Agent and v for verbs with only a Theme. In (37) above, I suggested there is no vP-Layer with unaccusative verbs; Chomsky assumes there is a defective one, marked as v. I will not mark the difference between v and v* in this book.

In sentences with transitive verbs, the Theme (externally) merges with the V (order doesn't matter before spell-out, and I have merged it on the left). If the action is telic and the object definite, the Theme will (internally) merge with the V that has internally merged with ASP. After a Merge with v and the Agent DP, the vP is complete, as in (43), with a tree as in (44).

(43) They ate the apples.

(44)

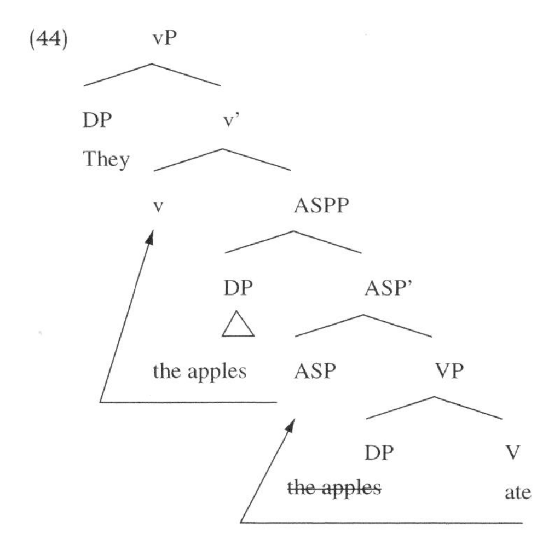

In this section, I have reviewed the well-known distinction between unaccusatives and unergatives. Unaccusatives can be causativized if they are compatible with being externally caused. We'll turn to causatives next.

3.3 THE CAUSATIVE

Causatives were among the first to be used in a vP-shell and are a perfect fit for it, as we saw in (22) of Chapter 1. In most languages (English included), causatives can be derived from unaccusatives (although some people derive unaccusatives from causatives).

Verbs, such as *roll* and *burn*, that can be accompanied by a Theme, as in (45a), or by a Theme and an Agent, as in (45b), are called **labile verbs**. Many causatives in English are labile.

(45) a. The ball **rolled** down the hill.
Theme
b. I **rolled** the ball down the hill
Agent Theme

An additional light verb can be added, as in (46).

(46) **I** made **him** roll **the ball.**
Causer Agent Theme

In the literature, (45a) is referred to as anti-causative or inchoative (change of state), (45b) and (46) as **causative**. Unaccusatives often have the possibility to be causative, as in (45b). However, there are those who don't typically have that possibility (*arrive, appear, bloom*), as was mentioned.

Unergative verbs, with just an Agent, cannot be causativized except when the light verb *make* is added. This is shown in (47ab) and holds in most languages. Note that they do appear with cognate objects, as in (47c), usually to express aspect.

(47) a. *I laughed my neighbor.
b. I made my neighbor laugh.
c. he laughed the light laugh that's not about something funny.
(*COCA* 2002 Fiction)

As Hale and Keyser (2002) show, many other languages have an inchoative causative alternation, as in (45ab), and similar restrictions, although English is more wont to use labile verbs.

Haspelmath (1993) looks at thirty-one alternating verbs, given in Table 3.6, and sees a split between spontaneous action and externally caused action. The ranking is based on percentages of causativizing strategies in the different languages. *Boil*, for instance, is typically

Table 3.6 *Alternating verbs in Haspelmath (1993: 97, 104)*

Spontaneous, or freeze-type:
boil, freeze, dry, wake up, go/put out, sink, learn/teach, melt, stop, turn, dissolve, burn, destroy, fill, finish

Outside force, or break-type:
begin, spread, roll, develop, get lost/lose, rise/raise, improve, rock, connect, change, gather, open, break, close, split, die/kill

intransitive and is causativized in 96 percent of the languages, whereas *split* is only causativized in 4 percent (these figures are from Cysouw 2008: 382).

That *boil* prefers causativization is shown in the history of English. The first use of *boil* in English is as an intransitive; its first transitive use has a light verb, as in (48).

(48) *þei filled a leed of picche and oile / And fast* ***duden*** *hit to boile*
they filled a kettle of pitch and oil and fast made it to boil
'they filled a . . . of pitch and oil and made it boil fast.'
(1300 *Cursor Mundi* 11886 (Trinity), from the *OED*)

Haspelmath formulates the universal in (49) that describes the difference between the verbs.

(49) Verbs of the "freeze"-type tend to be transitivizing whereas verbs of the "break"-type tend to be detransitivizing.

There is another set of internally caused events that resist causativization. They are verbs such as *flower*, *bloom*, and *blossom*, as shown in (50).

(50) a. The saguaro bloomed.
b. *The sun bloomed the saguaro.

These verbs are restricted to a [−c,−m] Theme argument and are not compatible with a [+c] Causer augmentation. Similarly, certain verbs tend not to be intransitive, as (51) shows.

(51) a. The knife cut the cloth.
b. *The cloth cut.

Haspelmath's (1993: 94) explanation for the data in (51) is as follows: "A verb meaning that refers to a change of state . . . may appear in an inchoative/causative alternation unless the verb contains Agent-oriented meaning components or other highly specific meaning components that make the spontaneous occurrence of the event extremely unlikely." So, *cut* has as part of its meaning the use of scissors/knife and is therefore agentive. Thus, semantic properties of verbs are crucially important to determining an event.

Morphologically, causatives can be divided into lexical (e.g. *kill*), synthetic (e.g. *soften*), and analytic (*make*) causatives. I'll consider labile verbs (e.g. *break*) as morphologically derived via a zero-morpheme. The alternation between intransitive and causative for these types is given in (52) to (54).

(52) He died - The disease killed him.

(53) a. It broke - The wind broke it. (= labile)
b. It softened - The washer softened it.

(54) He laughed - I made him laugh.

Lexical causatives bring about direct causation that can be seen by comparing (55) with an analytic causative in (56).

(55) The disease killed him.

(56) The disease caused him to die.

The reason for that is that in (55) there is one TP and one event, whereas in (56) there are two events, indicated by the marker *to*.

In conclusion, (lexical and synthetic) causatives are interesting in that they fit the vP-shell but show that inherent semantic properties determine the argument alternations. Verbs such as *freeze* have a lexical representation with a [-c,-m] argument and may have a little v with a [+c] Causer. Verbs such as *arrive* just have [-c,-m] Theme, and those like *split* have [+c] Causer, [-c,-m] Theme.

3.4 DITRANSITIVES

Ditransitives can be defined in terms of semantic roles, namely as verbs that have an Agent, Theme, and Goal (or Recipient). The grammatical functions of these arguments are subject, and direct and indirect object. In English, these verbs show an alternation between two DP objects and a DP and PP set. Two approaches to this alternation are given. First, an analysis is given that derives one from the other, and then an alternative is discussed whereby the two options are base generated.

3.4.1 The ditransitive alternation

Ditransitive verbs have three arguments. In English, they occur either as (57a) or (57b) with the supposed theta-roles marked.

(57) a. I gave Louise the article. =DP DP
Agent Goal Theme
[+c,+m] [-c] [-c,-m]
b. I gave the article to Louise. =DP PP
Agent Theme Goal
[+c,+m] [-c,-m] [-c]

Right away, a problem for a Thematic Hierarchy appears: How can the Goal be higher than the Theme in the one and the Theme higher than the Goal in the other? One answer is that one derives from the other through movement, and that the UTAH works on the base structure, to be discussed in Section 4.2; the other answer is that there are different theta-roles in (57ab), to be discussed in Section 4.3. First a little more on the alternation.

All three nominals are arguments in (57ab) because they are obligatory, as the awkward (58) shows, where *give* appears with only two arguments.

(58) a. #I gave Louise.
b. #I gave the article.

The sentences in (58) would be grammatical only under very specific pragmatic circumstances, e.g. if someone asks if you are going to give money to charity, you could say "I gave Doctors without Borders," and if they know you are giving to the Salvation Army, you could answer "I gave furniture." (58) could only occur as cases of direct and indirect object pro-drop.

Other evidence that *Louise* and *the article* are arguments is that they both can be passivized, e.g. in (59) and (60). In some varieties of English, (61) is grammatical as well.

(59) Louise was given the article.

(60) The article was given to Louise.

(61) The article was given Louise.

Among the ditransitive verbs, there are very clear instances, such as *give*, and less obvious ones, such as *buy*. Table 3.7 provides examples of verbs that never have three arguments, verbs that typically do, and verbs that optionally do.

Table 3.7 *Verbs with direct and indirect objects (from van Gelderen 2010: 70)*

With only direct objects	With direct and mostly obligatory indirect objects	With direct and less obligatory indirect objects
see, eat, love, hit, hear	give, teach, offer, tell, show, ask, provide, send, hand, promise, grant, award, begrudge, mail, throw	buy, bring, bake, read, pay, build, cook, knit, prepare, earn

It is often argued that "original English" words, e.g. *give, show*, and *teach*, can have DP DP (as well as DP PP), but that verbs that are borrowed from French or Latin can't have two DPs, e.g. *donate* and *narrate*. There are also a few verbs that have only the double DP pattern of (57a), e.g. *owe*, which verb is of course "original" to English.

As mentioned, there are basically two kinds of analysis for (57ab). Some people argue that one of the two is basic and the other derived. Others argue that the two patterns have different underlying structures with different theta-roles. Larson (1988) and Baker (1997) argue that the dative alternation is a result of movement and that (57a) is derived from (57b), whereas Aoun and Li (1989) argue that (57b) is derived from (57a) in English. Oehrle (1976) believes the two are base generated separately. Arguments can be presented for all of these. In Section 3.4.2, I present the analysis that seems the most widely accepted if we assume one derives from the other and, in Section 3.4.3, there is some discussion on having two separate lexical entries.

3.4.2 Larson's tree and Baker's changes to it

Adapting an analysis by Chomsky (1955), Larson (1988: 342) proposes the structure as in (62), where I have kept Larson's notation.

(62)

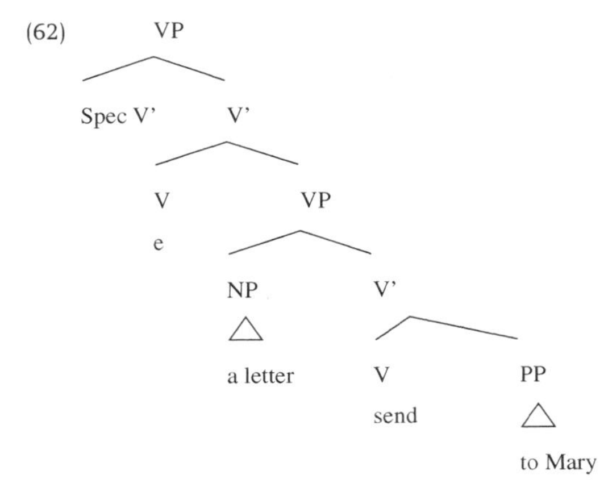

In (62), the verb *send* moves to the higher V to be able to assign case to *a letter*. Evidence for this movement provided by Larson is that the grammaticality of (63a) receives a straightforward analysis as the conjunction of the lower VP (which I think is easier to see in (63b)).

(63) a. John sent [a letter to Mary] and [a book to Sue]. (Larson 1988: 345)
b. John sent [a letter ~~sent~~ to Mary] and [a book ~~sent~~ to Sue].

This analysis of the double verb structure is still very accepted. However, Larson's derivation of (64), the double object construction, is quite dated. I'll provide it here but will then suggest an alternative.

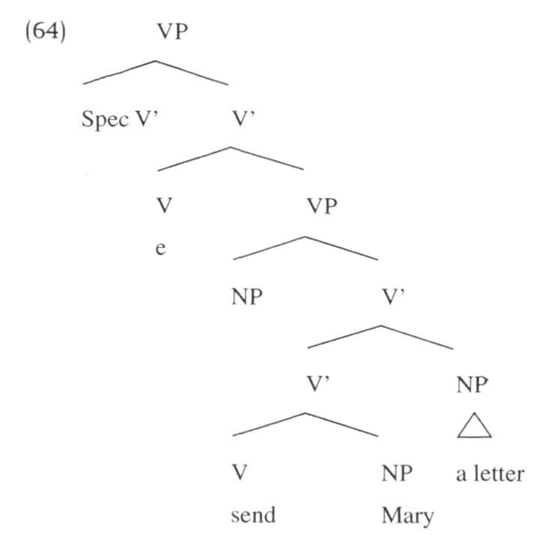

Larson argues that (64) is derived from (62) in the same way a passive is. The case to the indirect object is absorbed (hence no *to*) as well as the theta-role of the direct object *a letter* (hence its adjunct status). The indirect object *Mary* moves to the higher NP position and the verb *send* to the higher V to assign case to *Mary*. Case assignment to *a letter* is done by the reanalysis of the lower V' as a V which can then assign case to *a letter*.

An alternative for (64) is provided by Baker (1997), who agrees with Larson that the indirect object moves to a higher position. For Baker this is the specifier of an inner Aspect Phrase, and the preposition *to* incorporates into the verb, as indicated in (65).

(65)

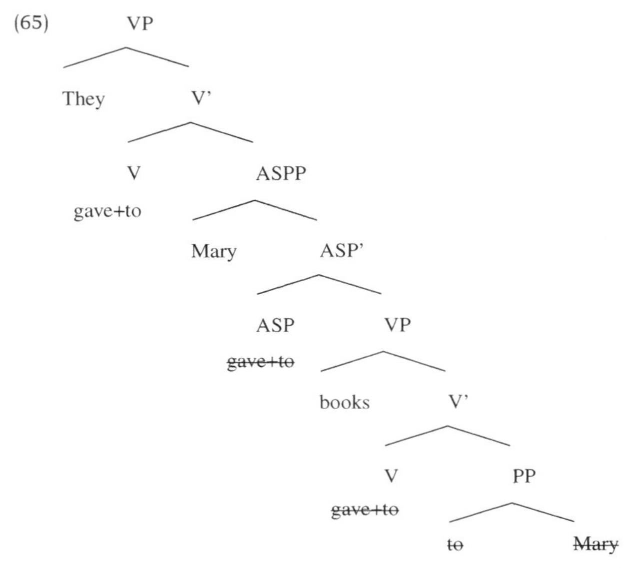

This has the advantage (not mentioned by Baker) that the object in Spec ASPP is predicted to be affected, and this is correct, as the difference between (66) and (67) shows.

(66) Ivy taught James Chinese.

(67) Ivy taught Chinese to James.

In (66), *James* actually learns some Chinese, but in (67) he probably did not. The case marking of *Mary* in (65) is still not terribly satisfying, and it also is not clear why *to* incorporates into the verb.

In closing Section 3.4.2, the ditransitive alternation can be accounted for by assuming one underlying structure, as in (62). The analysis for the DP PP-complements is straightforward, but the one for the DP DP-complements is not. We now turn to an alternative account.

3.4.3 Different structures

There is a second way to account for the ditransitive alternation, one that was originally suggested in Oehrle (1976). With some verbs, e.g. *send* and *teach*, there is a meaning difference between the DP DP and DP PP constructions, as (66) and (67) above show in terms of the affectedness of the Goal with the verb *teach*. Another such instance is shown for the verb *send* in (68). The DP PP version is grammatical, but the DP DP one is not, because *Phoenix* is marked as more affected than a city can be.

(68) a. I **sent** a package to Phoenix.
b. *I **sent** Phoenix a package. (where *Phoenix* is the city)

Passivization is possible in (69ab) but not in (69c). This suggests that the city to which a package is sent is less of an argument than a person to which something is sent.

(69) a. The package was sent to Phoenix.
b. Bill was sent a/the package.
c. *Phoenix was sent a/the package. (where *Phoenix* is the city)

Not all ditransitive verbs are susceptible to that distinction. For instance, *tell*, *give*, and *show* do not really have different meanings with DP PP- and DP DP-complements.

Based on verbs like *teach* and *send*, we could argue that the theta-roles in (66) and (68b) are different from those in (67) and (68a). This is indicated in (70). In (70a), the Goal is an Experiencer and therefore higher than the Theme, whereas the Theme is higher than the Goal in (70b). The two structures are represented for the verb *teach*.

(70)
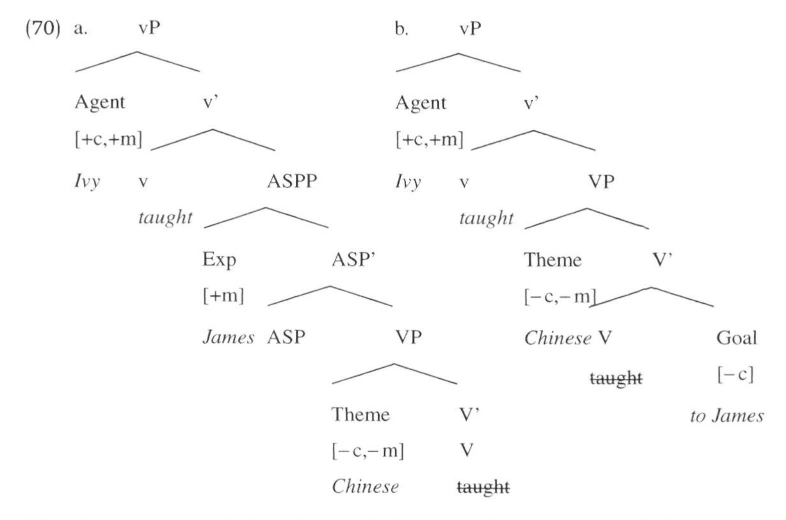

The Experiencer in (70a) could also remain a Goal, and the PP could be a Location/Result. That too would satisfy the UTAH.

A very interesting proposal is given by Harley (2002: 33–34) in terms of different flavors of P. In the DP PP version, Harley assumes an abstract locative P_{LOC}, and, in the DP DP one, she assumes an abstract P_{HAVE}.

Recently, work by McGinnis (2001; 2004), Jeong (2007), Pylkkänen (2008), and others use an Applicative Phrase, ApplP, where some languages place the applicative higher and some lower, and some, like English, can do both. I will not go into this here.

Sections 3.3 and 3.4 have used the vP-shell to accommodate the causative and ditransitive verbs. We'll turn to other possible uses of the vP-shell, some briefly mentioned in Section 3.1.3.

3.5 ASPECT, DEFINITENESS, AND ADVERBIALS

In this section, I start by sketching the lexical aspect connected to the meaning of a verb. I'll make a brief connection to grammatical aspect, although more on this will come in Chapters 4 and 6. I then look at definiteness and VP adverbs.

3.5.1 Lexical aspect

Aspect is concerned with how an action proceeds. The meaning of certain predicates implies duration or change of state, i.e. aspect. It is often put as a four-way distinction, e.g. in Vendler (1967) and Verkuyl (1972) and others, and this is shown in Table 3.8. The two distinguishing features are **telicity** and **durativity**.

This aspect is also known as **Aktionsart**, inner aspect, or situation aspect, since it has to do with the meaning of the verb. As you can see, the accomplishment verb is an activity verb with an object that renders the predicate telic. So, accomplishments depend on the construction, not just on the verb.

There are well-known diagnostics for these categories, and a few are provided in (71).

(71) a. states are typically incompatible with the imperative
b. states are typically incompatible with the progressive
c. durative non-telic predicates can be modified by a *for*-NP adverbial
d. telic predicates can be modified by an *in*-NP adverbial

For instance, an (atelic non-durative) state, such as *be tall*, cannot occur as a progressive or an imperative, as (72) shows, and cannot be

Table 3.8 *Lexical aspect or Aktionsart*

	+durative	-durative
+telic	build a house (=accomplishment)	recognize (=achievement)
-telic	swim (=activity)	know, be tall (=state)

modified by either a *for*-NP or *in*-NP, as (73) and (74) show. Living in a Harry Potter universe, these are all perfectly possible, of course.

(72) *You aren't **being tall**. **Be tall**!

(73) *He was tall **for an hour**.

(74) *He was tall **in an hour**.

The diagnostics in (71) depend on the meaning of the verb, but this meaning becomes evident by using outer aspect: Something outside of the verb reinforces the Aktionsart, e.g. a certain PP or the progressive.

Let's look at some examples. The verb *look* is durative and atelic, as (75) shows, whereas the verb *recognize* in (76) is non-durative and telic.

(75) She was **looking** at the stars for a long time (*in an hour).

(76) She **recognized** the dog in a second (*for an hour).

Verbs have a lexical aspect that depends on their durativity and telicity characteristics. This aspect is part of the verb's meaning but is relevant to the outer or grammatical aspect. I have represented the interpretable affix *-ing* in (77) as the head of an Aspect Phrase. More on this in Chapter 4.

(77)

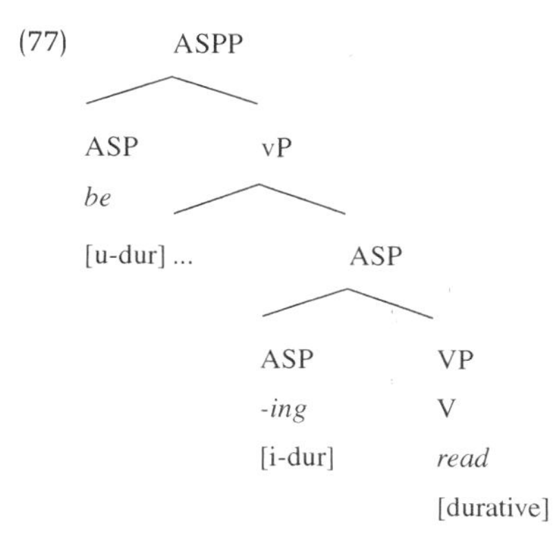

We'll now turn to how the environment of the verb can coerce the lexical aspect.

3.5.2 Aspect, definiteness, Goal: coercion

There is a lot of evidence that aspect and argument structure are related, and a huge literature exists on it. For instance, if an object or goal is added, as between (78) and (79), the interpretation changes from durative to telic. We use **coercion** to refer to how some verbs change their lexical aspect.

(78) He **ran** for hours/*in five minutes. (durative, a-telic)

(79) a. He **ran** the mile in five minutes. (telic)
b. He **ran** to the store in five minutes. (telic)

If the object is indefinite, the telicity is less strong, as in (80), and if the progressive is used, the same is true, as (81) shows.

(80) He ate (of) **a turkey** for hours. (durative, atelic)

(81) He was **eating** the turkey for hours. (durative, atelic)

While definite objects are just as frequent with the imperfective *eating* as with the perfective *ate* (806 and 802 respectively in COCA), the indefinite objects are more frequent with *eating* than with *ate* (1357 and 792 respectively).

How is the lexical aspect seen in Table 3.8 connected to theta-structure? We can see how lexical aspect can be modified by the construction around it. Telic verbs need a Goal, so transitive verbs or verbs with a location are good candidates. Unaccusative verbs are typically telic, since they are verbs of change of state, whereas unergative verbs are often durative, although criticism of such a connection has been voiced. If the relation holds, we could argue in a very projectionist way that the [-c,-m] Theme triggers the inclusion of a Result in the tree and that the [+c,+m] Agent triggers the inclusion of a durative ASPP.

We'll discuss **phrasal verbs** next. Here, the connection between definiteness and movement to the specifier of an ASPP is evident. In English, the definite object of a phrasal verb often precedes the particle, e.g. *down* in (82a), whereas indefinites most often follow it. When the object is a pronoun, it obligatorily precedes the particle.

(82) a. She turned **it/that great job offer** down.
b. She turned down **a great job offer**.

The particle indicates perfectivity, as (83) to (85) show, where the particle is added for emphasis.

(83) Up to a half-ton of water per cord will evaporate **out**.
(COCA 1994 *Mother Earth* magazine).

(84) But it's going to take some time for this process to issue this money **out**.
(COCA 2006 Fox, interview)

(85) Boost **up** his lecture fees. (COCA 2008 NBC *Meet the Press*)

Table 3.9 *The phrasal verb* turn down *and its objects in COCA*

	turn down obj		*turn* obj *down*		Total
obj is "*a* N/*an* N"	496/176 = 672	(99%)	7/0 = 7	(1%)	679
obj is "*the* N"	510	(70%)	216	(30%)	726
obj is *it*	7	(1.5%)	469	(98.5%)	476

Indefinite objects are rarely placed before the particle, but definite objects do appear after the particle. The reason for the latter is that the word order with the verb and the particle together has become more frequent in the recent period, according to Davies and Gardner (2007), even with definite nominals. The use of pronominal objects, typical for the first order, with these verbs has gone down too. That being said, we still see a huge difference between definite and indefinite nouns for the phrasal verb *turn down* in Table 3.9.

An account for the differences in position is complicated by the fact that the particle can be a head as well as a full phrase. When the adverb is a full phrase, it can be modified, e.g. by *right* as in (86a); when it is the head of ASP, it cannot, as in (86b).

(86) a. He got that package **right back**.
b. *He got **right back** that package.

Because of this difference in modification, I will assume that *down* in (82a) and *back* in (86a) are adverbials in the VP, but that *down* in (82b) and *back* in (86b) are ASP heads.

In (87), a possible representation for the various positions is given, with perfective aspect represented by means of an internal ASP head. The order in (82a) is derived by merging the head *away* with the VP and moving the verb *put* to (merging internally with) the ASP and then the v. This is shown in (87a) and is most common with indefinites.

To check perfective aspect, it is also possible for the nominal object to move to the specifier of the ASPP (i.e. internally merge in that position). This is typical for definite objects, as in (82b). In this case, the adverb is in the VP, as shown in (87b).

If the object is pronominal, it can (internally) merge with the head of the ASPP to check definiteness and perfective aspect, and the verb will left-adjoin to it on its way to v. This is shown in (87c).

(87)

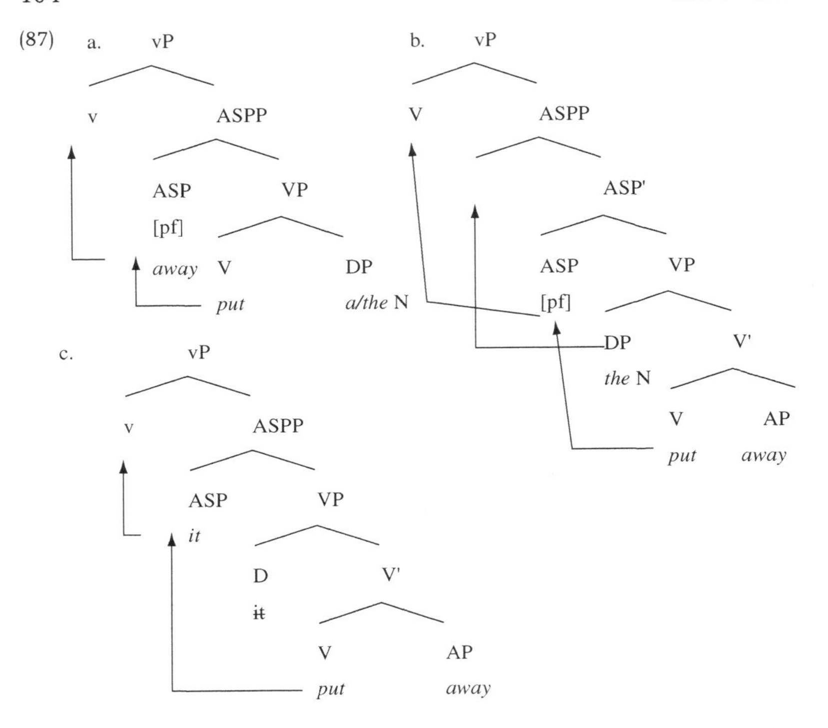

In (87), I have left the [pf]-features unspecified for interpretable or uninterpretable. These features depend on the status of the erstwhile adverb *away*, something I ignore here.

We see that the vP-shell is very flexible. It is not only used to accommodate various arguments but also definiteness and perfective aspect. As a last point, we look at how to represent VP adverbials.

3.5.3 Adding VP adverbs

Cinque's (1999) Functional Hierarchy involves the entire clause, and of the thirty-two functional categories, I take the lower nine heads to clearly be part of the VP-shell: eight aspect heads and one voice head, as in (88).

(88) VP adverbs as in Cinque

ASPgeneric/progressive ASPprospective ASPsg.completive(I)
characteristically *almost* *completely*
ASPpl.completive Voice ASPcelerative(II) ASPrepetetive(II)
tutto *well* *fast/early* *again*
ASPfrequentative(II) ASPsg.completive(II)
often *completely* (Cinque 1999: 106)

Haumann (2007) modifies this and argues for the following ten functional categories, many of which are of course aspectual.

(89) VP adverbs as in Haumann

SpaceP	> AgentP	> DomainP	> MannerP	> DegPerfP >
here	*deliberately*	*universally*	*loudly*	*slightly*
MeansP	> FreqP	> RepP	> AspPcompl	> RestP
manually	*rarely*	*again*	*completely*	*again*

(from Haumann 2007: 403)

Modern English adverbials in e.g. (90) and (91) of course show broad patterns of agreement with the Functional Hierarchy. In (90), *again* is the repetitive aspectual and *completely* the completive; in (91), *rarely* is the frequentive and *again* the repetitive.

(90) until the Sun is once **again completely** uncovered.
(http://csep10.phys.utk.edu/astr161/lect/time/eclipses.html)

(91) I will **rarely again** be so privileged. (www.earthfoot.org/lit_zone/seals.htm)

There is some overlap between (88) and (89), e.g. *again*, *often/rarely*, and *completely*, but there are some differences, suggesting the hierarchy is still somewhat controversial. A second problem is that there are possibly 4,000 adverbs in English alone, and there is obviously some leeway as to which to assign a structural position. A third problem with the hierarchies in (88) and (89) is that some combinations are frequently units, even though they appear quite far apart in the hierarchies. For instance, *once again* occurs as a combination 3,580 times in the BNC, and this occurs about 10 percent of the time when *once* appears.

A fourth problem is an old one, and one I'll spend some time on, namely what to do with PP adverbials, as in (92).

(92) I read the book [in the garden] [for a while] [with pleasure].

Cinque (1999: 28) refers to these PPs as circumstantial adverbials and considers them different from the adverbs in (88), in that they are not rigidly ordered and can be in each other's scope. He therefore doesn't include them in the hierarchy. Schweikert (2005: 132) proposes a PP hierarchy, which I will adapt using a Dutch example.

(93) *Ik denk dat ik* *[in alle waarschijnlijkheid]* *[in de ochtend]* *[met die twee]*
Evidential Temporal Comitative
I think that I in all probability in the morning with those two
[vanuit Geertruidenberg] [via Utrecht] [naar Groningen] [met de auto] zal komen.
Source Path Goal Manner
from Geertruidenberg via Utrecht to Groningen with the car will come
'I think I will probably go by car from Geertruidenberg to Groningen via Utrecht with those two in the morning.'

The Dutch sentence is quite reasonable, but the English translation is difficult to do. It is also likely that the evidential is not part of the VP but outside, so I will ignore that below.

Note, however, as argued by Koster (1974; 2000), that there is a mirror effect between PP adverbials that occur before the verb, as in the Dutch original, and those that occur after the verb, as in the English translation. I have provided all adverbials as PPs in (94) (except the evidential). See if you agree with the order in the English (94).

(94) I think I'll drive [by car] [from Geertruidenberg] [via Utrecht] [to Groningen]
Manner Source Path Goal
[with the two of them] [in the morning]
Comitative Temporal

The only PPs that are not the mirror of (93) are the Path and Goal PPs, but I think this sequence has become fossilized in English.

If there exists an adverbial PP hierarchy, we'd probably have to take either the Dutch or the English order as basic. If we consider scope (with the temporal PP having high scope) and assume the LCA, the Dutch PP-order in (93) is basic. The English order would have to be derived by taking the VP and moving it before the Manner PP and then taking this constituent and moving it before the Source, and so on. The Dutch V-final order is a result of movement as well. I think there are still a number of issues that haven't been understood, so I will refrain from a definite analysis.

In conclusion, the vP-shell accommodates the argument structure as well as the aspect and definiteness. Adverbs appear in a hierarchy, as in (88), and so do PPs, though it is harder to provide a structure for the latter.

3.6 CROSS-LINGUISTIC OBSERVATIONS AND ACQUISITION

The vP is the most cross-linguistically uniform layer because the argument structure of languages is similar. Most languages will express Agents, Themes, Goals, have telic and atelic verbs, and affected and non-affected arguments. The vP-shell can therefore be used across languages. In Section 3.6.1, I focus on something that has been raised in the typological literature, namely whether or not certain languages have a particular basic valency. Languages do differ in causative and ditransitive structures, and in how their aspect and definiteness is marked. Because this is important for argument structure, I'll discuss these issues briefly in Sections 3.6.2 and 3.6.3.

3.6.1 Basic valency

Haspelmath (1993: 91–92) distinguishes causatives (C), anti-causatives (A), and non-directives (labile L, equipollent E, and suppletive S), where a C means that something is added to make a causative, as in English *laugh* and *make laugh*; an A means something is added to detransitivize, as in Russian *katat'sja* from *katat* 'to roll'; an E means we can't tell which form is derived, as in Japanese *atumaru* and *atumeru* 'gather'; an L that the same form is used, as in *roll* and *roll*; and an S if the two forms have no relation to each other, as in *die* and *kill*. As mentioned earlier, Haspelmath looks at thirty-one sets of verbs in twenty-one languages; his findings for four languages are given in Table 3.10.

The numbers in the table show that some languages have more transitivizing morphology than detransitivizing. Nichols et al.'s (2004) data for a slightly different set of languages similarly show that augmented forms are the most frequent cross-linguistically and throughout the lexicon. The inanimates in Haspelmath's data (cf. Table 3.6) can be divided into two types of verb and here the spontaneous ones are more causativizing. This particular fact must have to do with the semantic features of the verb. I think Haspelmath's and Nichols et al.'s data show that languages do not have a basic valency but that there are two cross-linguistic tendencies: causativizing and the influence of verb semantics.

Can data from acquisition shed light on basic valency? Tomasello's (1992) data from an English-learning child between 1 and 2 years of age show that verbs expressing outside force, such as *open*, are very common (forty-seven instances of one-word and combinations), and almost all of those express the [+c, +m] Theme, as in (95), with the [+c] Causer implied; only three have an overt Causer, as in (96) to (98).

Table 3.10 *Russian, German, English, and Indonesian (from Haspelmath 1993: 101)*

	A	C	E	L	S
Russian	23	0	5	0	3
German	15.5	1	4	9.5	1
English	2	0	1	25	3
Indonesian	0	14	17	0	0

(95) open door (Tomasello 1992: 333, T. 1;5.27)

(96) snake open (Tomasello 1992: 333, T. 1;6.21)

(97) daddy open daddy on daddy open this top (Tomasello 1992: 334, T. 1;7.22)

(98) watch me open doors (Tomasello 1992: 334, T. 1;7.30)

Some more explanation on (95) and (96) is perhaps needed. Tomasello's comments (1992) reveal that the child wants to open the door in (95), i.e. *the door* is a Theme, and that it wants the keychain, the "snake," to open the door in (96), i.e. the snake is a Causer or instrument.

Close is a verb of the same type and is used sixteen times, many with an *it* object, as in (99); again the Causer is mostly implied.

(99) Close it this door (Tomasello 1992: 334, T. 1;7.23)

Drop and *break/broke(n)* are also verbs that are more often externally caused. The former appears seventeen times in the expected context, as in (100). *Break* appears only three times, but all with causers (implied), as in (101); *broke(n)* occurs eight times with a Theme.

(100) drop it ice (Tomasello 1992: 336, T. 1;7.13)

(101) Weezer break my mirror (Tomasello 1992: 337, T. 1;8.19)

These data confirm the causativizing tendency. If externally caused ones occur with a Theme and not a Causer, the Theme seems to be primary.

There are overgeneralizations of intransitives used transitively, as in (102). These are very understandable if the child has the Theme as basic and adds a Causer.

(102) How come you had a little trouble going it? (Bowerman 1974, C. 3:5)

Concluding, it is hard to argue that languages have a basic valency. There are a few cross-linguistically frequent tendencies, and some that depend on the semantics of the verb.

3.6.2 Causatives and ditransitives

Causatives are present in all languages, as far as I know. As mentioned in Section 3.3, causatives can be lexical (e.g. *kill*), synthetic or morphological (e.g. *soften*), and analytic (*make*). Comrie (1981: 160) notes that "pure analytic causatives are relatively rare." Morphological causatives are much more common. For instance, in Sanskrit, there is a suffix *-ay*, that makes *khad-* 'to eat' into *khād-ay-* 'make eat,' as in (103).

(103) khād-ay-āmi
eat-CAUSE-1S
'I feed.'

Old Germanic transitive verbs are often derived from intransitive verbs by means of a *-j-* suffix. This suffix surfaces as *-i-* in Old English and has, among other things, a fronting/Raising effect on the vowel. This is the reason Modern English has a confusing set of alternations left, e.g. *fall* and *fell*, *sit* and *set*, *lie* and *lay*, and *rise* and *raise*. English lost the *-i* affix and instead has labile verbs with a zero-morpheme.

This preference for morphological causatives can even be seen in analytic languages such as Cambodian, in which Haiman (2010: 58) distinguishes four causative morphemes, an infix *-am(n)-*, and the prefixes *baN-*, *paN-* (where the N indicates an assimilating nasal), and *p-*. Examples are given in (104).

(104) a. *ho*: 'flow' *bang-ho*: 'irrigate'
b. *bat* 'disappear' *nam-bat* 'eliminate' (Haiman 2010: 59)

Lexical causatives occur in all languages, and suppletive forms such as *die* and *kill* are common.

I mentioned above that unaccusatives are the easiest to causativize, and that is true across languages. Rice (2000: 171) shows that Navajo is like English, but that the related Athabascan language Ahtna can causativize unergatives as well. This is shown in (105), where the affix *ł-* is the transitivizer; the English translation has to make use of the analytic *make*.

(105) a. *ghi-tsaex* Ahtna
3-cry
'He was crying.'
b. *i-ghi* **-ł**-*tsaex*
3-3-CAUSE-cry
'He is making her cry.' (Rice 2000: 173, from Kari 1990: 274)

Ditransitives have been defined as having Agent, Theme, and Goal arguments, and, again, all languages have ways to express these three arguments. Haspelmath (2010) distinguishes three types: the indirect object one (the Theme is marked like a transitive Theme, but the Goal is marked differently); the double object one (the Theme and Goal are marked like the transitive object); and the secondary object construction (the Goal is marked like the transitive Theme, and the Theme is marked differently).

English has both the indirect construction (the DP PP one) and the double object construction (the DP DP one), as we've seen in (57b) and

Table 3.11 *The verb 'give' (from Haspelmath 2010)*

Indirect object construction	189
Double object construction	83
Secondary object construction	66
Mixed	40
Total	378

(57a) above respectively. It is therefore of a fourth kind, namely mixed. Languages that only have the indirect object type include Persian, Sami, Yukaghir, and Slave, and those that only have the double object one are Zulu, Wolof, Ket, and Lakhota. Chamorro has a secondary object, where the indirect object *i patgon* 'the child' in (106a) has the same marking as the direct object *i kannastra* 'the basket' in (106b). Somali, Hausa, Ojibwa, and Ainu are other such languages.

(106) a. *Ha na'i i patgon ni leche* Chamorro
he.ERG give ABS child OBL milk
'He gave the milk to the child.'
b. *Ha tuge' i kannastra*
he.ERG weave ABS basket
'He wove the basket.'
(Topping 1973: 241, 251, from Haspelmath 2010)

Haspelmath's data are given in Table 3.11 and show that the indirect object strategy is the most common.

3.6.3 Aspect and definiteness

Unlike English, many languages link aspect and definiteness by a special morphological marking or syntactic position. In (20) above, an ASP was included in the vP-shell, but I mentioned that there wasn't much evidence for a special position, except perhaps in the case of phrasal verbs. In this section, we'll see examples where certain objects have special markings and positions, evidence for a separate ASP. However, whether this ASPP is inside or outside the vP-shell is a difficult question.

Perfective aspect in Russian is expressed through a verbal prefix, *ras-*, as the perfective–imperfective alternation in (107) shows, and the perfective also makes the object definite.

(107) a. *On* ***ras**-kolo-l* *drova* Russian
He PF-split-PST wood
'He split **the wood**.'

b. *On* *kolo-l* *drova*
he split-PST wood
'He was splitting **wood**.' (from Leiss 2000: 12)

Aspect and definiteness both indicate how the action/event and the nominal are measured and seen as complete or incomplete.

In other languages, the definite object occupies a special position that is also associated with a specific aspectual interpretation. In (108a), when the object *dat boek* 'that book' is inside the VP, either the book was read completely or parts of it were. This would also be the position of indefinite objects. In (108b), however, where the object moves out of the VP (considering the adverb to indicate the left-boundary of the VP), the book has been read completely a number of times. In this position, an indefinite object would be ungrammatical.

(108) a. *omdat* *ik vaak* ***dat boek*** *gelezen heb* Dutch
Because I often that book read have
'because I've read that book often.'
b. *omdat* *ik* ***dat boek*** *vaak* *gelezen heb*
because I that book often read have

The reason for the difference between these readings is that the DP in (108b) moves to a higher position, where a certain aspect is checked (as well as specificity and boundedness) and the action must be complete. The DP inside the VP, as in (108a), on the other hand, can be partitive.

In this section, I have pointed out a few cross-linguistic differences regarding valency, valency-alternations, and aspect and definiteness. They do not give a systematic cross-linguistic overview, of course.

3.7 CONCLUSION AND A TIE TO FEATURES

In this chapter, we have considered how to represent the argument structure of a sentence. One of the major questions posed in this book is how a Minimalist derivation of the clause proceeds. As far as the basic argument structure is concerned, this question becomes how much we attribute to the lexical characteristics of the verb and how much to the functional heads. Gruber (1965), Jackendoff (1972), and Chomsky (1981), among others, are projectionist. The verb has theta-roles, and these are projected onto the syntax. Hale and Keyser (1993), Borer (1994; 2005a,b), and Harley (1995), among others, are constructionist to varying degrees, where light verbs determine the argument structure. Borer uses the terms Endo-skeletal for the projectionist and

Exo-skeletal for the constructionist approaches. A big issue with both approaches is the mapping, the UTAH for the projectionist, and a shell-Cartography for the constructionist approach.

Rather than select one of the two approaches, I have argued that both factors are important: the verb itself and its surroundings, such as aspect and definiteness. The evidence for the verb's importance is that certain verbs can never be transitive, e.g. *arrive* or *laugh*. In addition, we see cross-linguistically that such verbs as *freeze* have a different argument structure from such verbs as *break*. The former (*freeze*) is more often linked to one argument and the latter (*break*) to two arguments, as argued for in Haspelmath. Evidence for the importance of the surroundings has been given throughout, e.g. the role of aspect in determining the argument structure. I have referred to this sometimes as coercion.

A last point not yet discussed in the chapter is how the theta-roles drive the derivation. As we've seen in Chapter 1, uninterpretable features drive Internal Merge; it would be interesting if such features could also be responsible for External Merge. I would like to suggest here (in the spirit of Hornstein 1999) that the verb's [+/–c] and [+/–m] are uninterpretable and are probes looking for the nominals that have the appropriate semantic/interpretable features. The reason I have not brought it up in the text is that this suggestion is quite radical and needs refinement. I will leave it for future work.

Keywords

Argument structure, event structure, theta-roles, vP, projectionist, constructionist, unaccusative, unergative, transitive, causative, ditransitive, valency, voice, mapping, definiteness, lexical and grammatical aspect, telicity and durativity, coercion

DISCUSSION POINTS

1. Put the following verbs in sentences and determine the theta-role of each. Then, try to use Reinhart's system. Are there problems you encounter?

   (1) see, ruin, watch

2. Draw trees for (2) to (3) and discuss the derivation.

   (2) The leaves reddened.

   (3) They sent packages to Haiti.

3. Work by Schein (1993), Kratzer (1996), and others has suggested that the Agent is not represented on the verb but is introduced by an independent functional head, i.e. little v or Voice. Recently, similar arguments have started to appear about the Theme, e.g. Bowers (2010). Having read the chapter, can you come up with empirical challenges for these positions?
4. Why can (English) unergatives not be used as causatives, e.g. **laugh a baby*, unlike the unaccusatives *burn* and *boil*? Why do unergatives need *make*?
5. There is a locative alternation in English, exemplified in (4). How would you account for this?

   (4) a. I loaded the truck with hay.
   b. I loaded hay onto the truck.

6. There are many types of causative. Discuss the difference between direct and indirect causation, as in Shibatani and Pardeshi (2001).
7. Anne Walton-Ramirez reports that her daughter uttered (5). Can you explain why?

   (5) I can't pick up you.
   'I can't pick you up.' (Layla, age 3)

8. Activity verbs that express manner are quite versatile in their complement structure. For instance, as we've seen, *sweep* can have (6a) to (6c).

   (6) a. They swept.
   b. They swept the floor.
   c. They swept the crumbs off the floor into the yard.

   Try to see if other verbs have these possibilities and come up with an account.
9. In the chapter, I have suggested that the expletives *it* and *there* both lack theta-roles. There is evidence that *it* has a pseudo theta-role (e.g. Chomsky 1981). For instance, what would it mean if you could reflexivize an expletive?

SUGGESTIONS FOR FURTHER READING

Hale and Keyser (1993; 2002) were among the first to advocate the vP-shell and to refine it. You might read them or Rappaport Hovav and Levin (1998) for more on argument structure.

Pesetsky (1995) has more on *psych*-verbs, as does I. Landau (2012), and Hale and Keyser (2002) write on locatum verbs. Malchukov et al. (2010) write on the typology of ditransitives.

Postal (2010) shows how not all objects are equally affected and transitive verbs are therefore not uniform. Read Tenny (1994; 2000) for more on affectedness.

If you are intrigued about the use of [−m] and [+m], read Marelj (2002). If you are interested in models that do not use theta-roles, read Bowers (2010) on a complete eradication of theta-roles or Lohndal (2012).

For a view that Themes are acquired first, read Ryan (2012).

4 The TP-Layer

This chapter examines the layer where tense, mood, and aspect, as well as the grammatical functions of subject and object, are indicated. Of the three layers, the TP-Layer is perhaps the one that shows the most cross-linguistic variation, not only in TMA but also in agreement and grammatical case. We've seen some of this variation in Chapter 2 when we discussed the finite clause.

Roles and functions can be marked by position or morphology. In English, the grammatical roles are marked through their position and through some agreement on the verb. Case on the noun can mark the grammatical and semantic roles, but, because English lost most overt case marking in its 1500-year history, case is hard to use as a criterion for deciding the grammatical function.

In Section 4.1, we'll look at how the TP was first introduced and then justify the attempts to expand and restrict it. In Section 4.2, we'll describe a Cartographic approach to tense, mood, aspect involving both auxiliaries and adverbials. In Section 4.3, we'll look at the positions of the subject and object and at displacement, mainly by discussing the EPP. Section 4.4 deals with case and agreement. In Section 4.5, some cross-linguistic observations are made. Section 4.6 is a conclusion that revisits all the features of the TP-Layer needed in a probe-goal approach.

4.1 EXPANDING TP

In this section, we'll examine in depth the functional categories that are included in the middle layer. We explore how this layer was initially thought of as having INFL as its main component but is now seen as being centered around T. We'll discuss the phenomenon of affix-hop and how features are relevant.

In Chapter 1, I have provided some background on how the TP emerged from a 1950s structure with AUX (not shown) to an early

1980s structure with INFL, as in (1), to a mid 1980s tree that is in accordance with X-bar in (2), to a late 1980s tree with an expanded middle that splits INFL into T and AGR in (3).

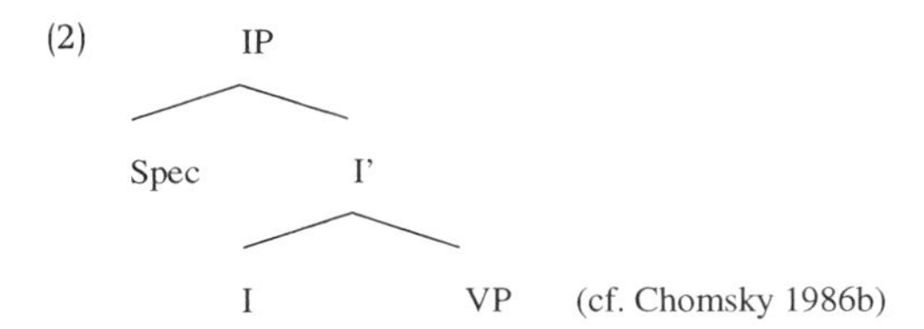

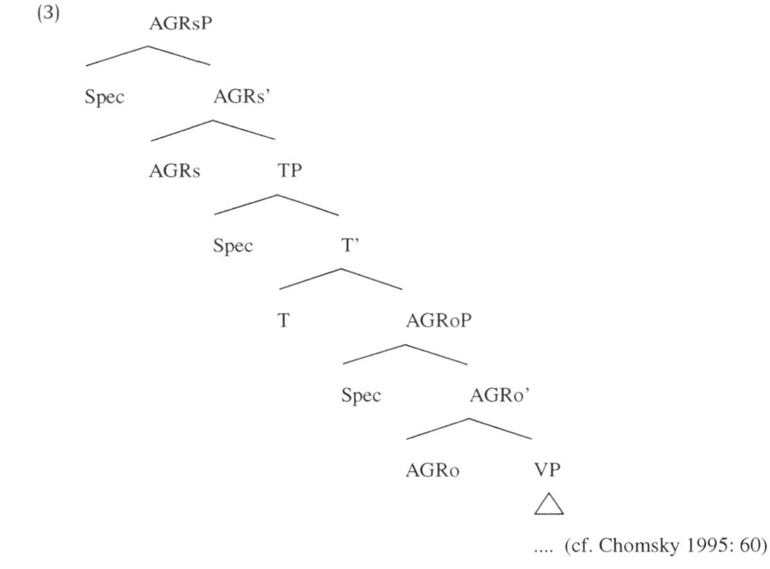

The advantage of (3) is that each feature has its own position, and the checking relation is between Spec and H. AGRs and AGRo are rejected by Chomsky (1995: 355), however, because he claims there is no semantic contribution and no empirical evidence for the AGR heads, i.e. there is no language that has a particle or auxiliary expressing agreement.

With AGR eliminated from the tree, the tree is reduced to TP, as in (4), and of course CP, which is not included in (4). The Spec-Head agreement of (3) is abandoned in (4) in favor of checking by a probe with uninterpretable features in T (and also in v) looking down the tree for a goal, indicated by an arrow.

(4)
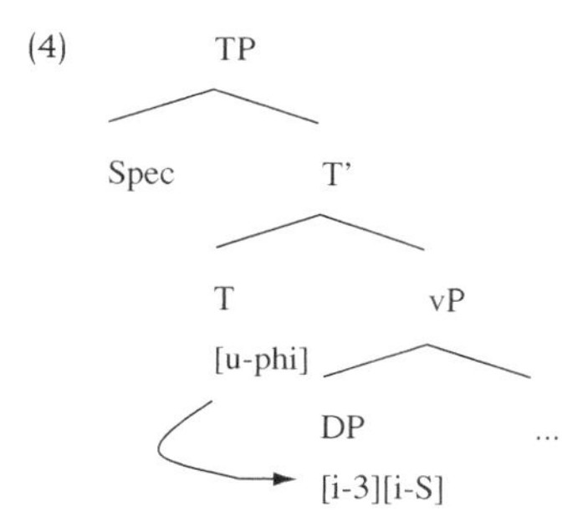

Because agreement and nominative case are linked (at least in English), the T probe in (4) is responsible for checking both case and agreement and does the work that AGR and T had earlier done separately. In (4), the EPP feature triggers the subject DP to move to the specifier of the TP position rather than through last resort to check case in a specifier position, as in earlier models. I haven't shown this movement of the subject in (4).

We know that (4) is not specific enough. There are other categories connected to the middle layer: modal auxiliaries, the *to*-infinitive marker, and perfect and progressive aspect. Tense is the grammatical expression of time that can be thought of as points on a time line, e.g. past precedes a point that is speech time. Aspect is the expression of how the event progresses and if it has boundaries. As we have seen in the previous chapter, aspect can be lexical or grammatical, i.e. it can express duration or completion of the lexical verb, or it can be made durative through external means, e.g. by the progressive *-ing* marker. Mood relates to how the speaker understands the event, how possible or likely s/he thinks it is likely to occur, and if it occurs in our world (indicative) or in some other world (subjunctive).

Tense, mood, and aspect are marked through adverbs, as in (5), or by auxiliaries, as in (6), or by affixes, as in (7), or by preverbs/particles, as in (8), from Old English.

(5) I [possibly] saw him [quickly] [some time ago].
Mood aspect tense

(6) I [may] [have] seen him before.
mood tense + aspect

(7) I walk[ed] around.
tense

(8) *leofes* *mannes* *lic* *eall* *for-swealg*
dear man's body all up-swallowed
aspect

'He swallowed up the entire body.' (*Beowulf* 2080)

I am listing the sequence of these elements as TMA, but nothing hinges on that. There are other ordering possibilities, as (5) and (6) show. Not all types of TMA markers are grammaticalized; the ones in (5) are fairly lexical.

If we pay attention just to the auxiliary elements for now, we see that English poses quite a challenge, having sentences such as (9).

(9) He **might have** **be-en** **be-ing** see-n (committing that crime).
modal perfect progressive passive

The phenomenon is known as **affix-hop**, because the affix belonging to the auxiliary moves to the next verb. The modal needs an infinitive to its right, the perfect a participle, the progressive an *-ing*, and the passive a participle.

Chomsky (1957) accounts for sequences such as this by means of the phrase structure rules in (10). The verb contains an AUX position and a verb, and the AUX position minimally hase a T(ense).

(10) a. Verb → Aux + V
b. Aux → Tense (M) (have + en) (be + ing) (be + en)
(adapted from Chomsky 1957: 39)

If the auxiliaries are added to the phrase structure, a transformation accounts for the order, namely as in (11). The *Af* stands for any of the affixes of tense and agreement (past, *en*, *ing*, *s*, etc.), and (11) ensures that the affix will be attached to the verb or auxiliary following it.

(11) **Auxiliary transformation - obligatory**
SD:X - *Af* - *v* - Y
SC:1 - 2 - 3 - 4 → 1 - 3 - 2# - 4
(where *Af* is any *T* or is *en* or *ing*; *v* is any *M* or *V*, or *have* or *be*; adapted from Chomsky 1957: 113)

In the early 1980s, there is a debate triggered by an article by Akmajian, Steele, and Wasow (1979) as to whether or not AUX exists as a designated category and what it includes. The argument is that English has a special position where a modal or infinitival *to* are situated, but that other languages might not. *To*, *do*, and modals also occupy this AUX position but are in complementary distribution. Akmajian, Steele and Wasow's (1979: 22) structure is as in (12).

(12)

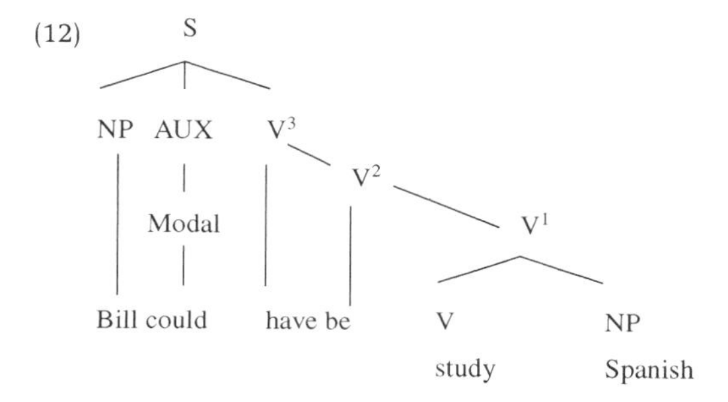

They argue that each of the numbered Vs has a special set of characteristics connected to it. For instance, V^3 cannot form an imperative, but V^1 and V^2 can, as (13) shows.

(13) a. *Have done your homework when I come home.
b. Be studying when I get home.
c. Study Spanish!

(adapted from Akmajian, Steele and Wasow's 1979: 37)

This approach is remarkably "modern" and quite Cartographic.

In the Government and Binding approach (Chomsky 1981), the AUX of (10a) and (12) is replaced by INFL, as in (1) above. Here, INFL can be [+/– Tense], and if [+Tense], an AGR element appears that is "basically nominal in character" and "identical to PRO" (Chomsky 1981: 52), with person, number, and gender features. This AGR then becomes responsible for assigning nominative case, and the emphasis shifts to other duties of INFL. After Chomsky (1981, e.g. p. 140), not much is said about auxiliaries and affix-hop (no entries in Chomsky 1986a,b or 1995 for either), and the focus is no longer on the auxiliaries but on the position T and on verb movement to T (e.g. Chomsky 1995; Lasnik 1999). Thus, *have* and *be* move to T, but main verbs do not in English, and this is attributed to the strength of the features in T.

There is nothing that stops us from adding the auxiliaries of (12), however, and updating them through features. Using TMA, the tree could be as in (14). Apart from tense in T (inherited from C), other features marked in (9) are the mood and the aspect. I have also shown the values of the uninterpretable features.

(14)

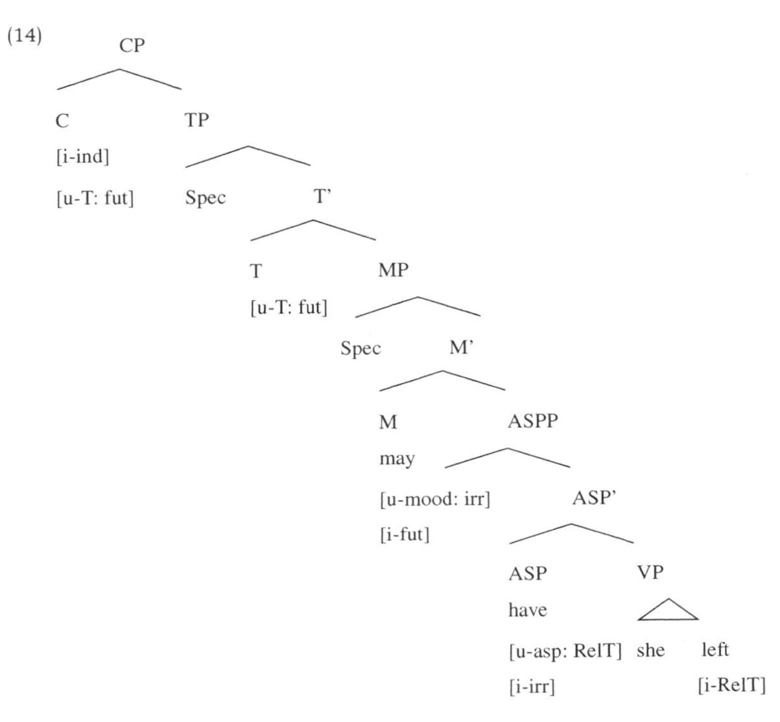

In (14), I have left out agreement and case marking, and the subject has not moved to Spec of TP. I will add those features in Sections 4.3 and 4.4.

As mentioned, affix-hop in English describes the phenomenon that modals have infinitives following them, the perfect auxiliary *have* has a participle following it, and the progressive auxiliary *be* has a present participle. In (14), I have represented this phenomenon as checking by the functional head, e.g. *have*, directly with the lexical item, here *left*. This means that the participle ending on *left* is responsible for the (present) perfect meaning and the infinitival form of *have* for the irrealis meaning.

I have followed Solà (1996: 227) and Haumann (2007) in using Relative tense (RelT) to represent the present perfect. It expresses that the event time precedes the reference time, as in a present or past perfect, unlike in a simple present or past where the event time and the reference time are the same. Anterior is an alternative term.

There are other ways of representing affix-hop. Haumann (2007: 191) uses two functional heads, as in (15), to check the perfect and the progressive (and the passive, but I haven't shown that). The verb complex in (13) is for *have been swimming*.

(15)

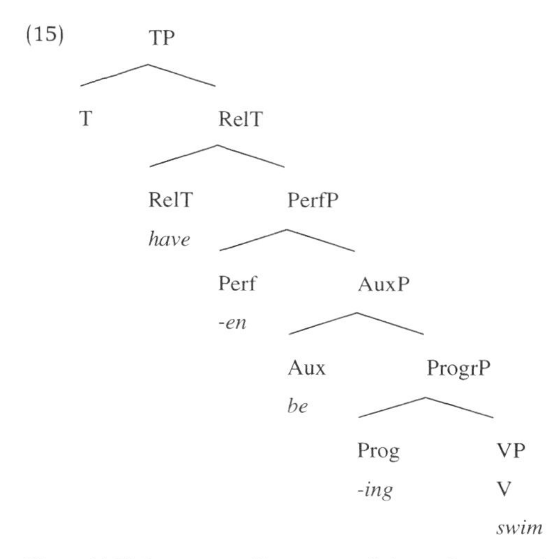

Tree (15) is more Cartographic, whereas (14) claims features are central. I prefer the minimalist character of (14).

Negatives in English also belong in the TP-Layer. We'll add a NegP which, in English, is below the TP, but will wait till Chapter 6 to examine that question because negatives are relevant for all three layers. We'll turn next to a suggestion for a more elaborate TP-Layer.

4.2 CARTOGRAPHY OF THE TP

Cinque's (1999) classification of the various TMA heads is well known and will first be outlined. The Hierarchy is more elaborate for the TP than for the VP or CP, as (16) shows. Several problems with such an elaborate hierarchy present themselves, and a more modified structure will be suggested.

Cinque's (1999: 106) Hierarchy has thirty TMA heads distributed throughout the sentence but concentrated in the TP (having eighteen of the thirty). Mood is the highest category, modals and tense are in the middle, and aspect is lowest. The distribution is four Mood, four

Mod, three T, and eighteen ASP heads. Mood is in the CP (except for the irrealis) and Mod is in the TP, and the ASP heads only involve grammatical (external) aspect, not lexical (internal). Voice, which I will mainly ignore, is represented by the adverb *well* and on its own in the middle of aspectual VP adverbs.

(16) The Universal Hierarchy of Clausal Functional Projections

[Moodspeech-act	*frankly*	
[Moodevaluative	*fortunately*	CP adverbs
[Moodevidential	*allegedly*	
[Modepistemic	*probably*	
[Tpast	*once*	
[Tfuture	*then*	
[Moodirrealis	*perhaps*	
[Modnecessity	*necessarily*	
[Modpossibility	*possibly*	
[ASPhabitual	*usually*	
[ASPrepetetive	*again*	
[ASPfrequentative(I)	*often*	TP adverbs
[Modvolitional	*intentionally*	
[ASPcelerative(I)	*quickly*	
[Tanterior	*already*	
[ASPterminative	*no longer*	
[ASPcontinuative	*still*	
[ASPperfect(?)	*always*	
[ASPretrospective	*just*	
[ASPproximative	*soon*	
[ASPdurative	*briefly*	
[ASPgeneric/progressive	*characteristically*	
[ASPprospective	*almost*	
[ASPsg.completive(I)	*completely*	
[ASPpl.completive	*tutto*	(Italian)
[Voice	*well*	VP adverbs
[ASPcelerative(II)	*fast/early*	
[ASPrepetetive(II)	*again*	
[ASPfrequentative(II)	*often*	
[ASPsg.completive(II)	*completely*]]]]]]]]]]]]]]]]]]]]]]]]]]]]]]	

(Cinque 1999: 106)

A little later in the book (1999: 130), Cinque adds two Mod categories under Mod-volitional, Mod-obligation, and Mod-ability, and the heads of the ModPhrases accommodate the modals in his model. I have put a few modals in, as shown in (17), but, as with some other categories, I think it is fairly subjective and would have to be tested in languages that can have multiple modals.

(17)

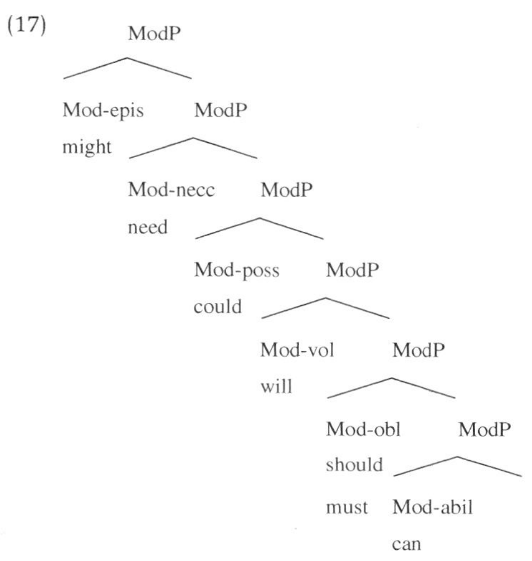

The adverbials in (16) are in the specifier positions. In addition, the English auxiliaries would be in head positions, as we've seen before. The tree in (18) represents (19), a sentence with a variety of adverbs and auxiliaries but with M and ASP phrases unspecified for the flavor of these in a Cinque-like sequence. The initial *I guess* might also be a separate clause, but I have represented it as a CP adverb, but, for reasons of space, have left C out.

(18)

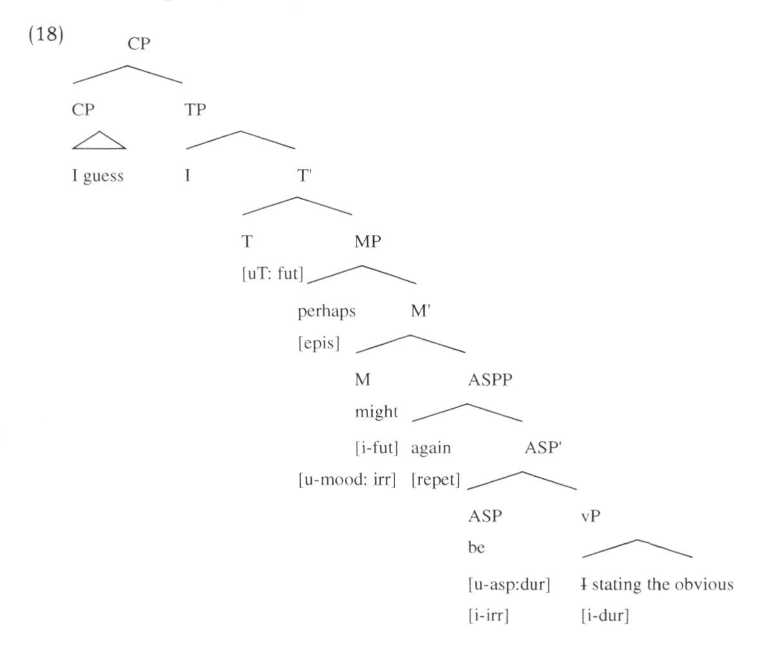

(19) I guess I **might perhaps again be** "stating the obvious" and I apologise to FTers who feel annoyed by this.
(http://flyertalk.com/forum/archive/index.php/t-63529.html)

The features on the auxiliaries are as we've seen in (14) before. As for the question if adverbials participate in feature checking, Laenzlinger (2004: 208–209) argues their features are interpretable and checked by Merge. That would mean the uninterpretable features in the head would no longer be probes for the features lower down. Since this issue is not clear to me, I have not marked them as [i-F] or [u-F] but as semantic features.

Cinque's categories are hard to decide on sometimes. For instance, is *probably* evidential or epistemic? Is *again* repetitive or habitual, or both? As I mentioned in the previous chapter, there are over 4,000 adverbs, and they could all be argued to need accommodation in the Functional Hierarchy. Haumann (2007: 232) happens to have the same eighteen as TP-adverbs as Cinque does, but the inclusion of others is possible, e.g. *sometimes* and *finally*. With *finally*, one could argue it is in the ASPterminative position, occupied by *no longer* in (16). However, we can have both of those adverbs in a sentence, as (20) shows.

(20) when she **finally no longer** feels guilty (Google)

That indicates (16) would need to include another position.

We have two positions for *again* and *often*, and this doubling is necessary since there are two meanings, one in the higher domain, as in (21a) and (22a), and one in the lower domain, as in (21b) and (22b).

(21) a. He **again** opened the door. (means that he had opened it before)
b. He opened the door **again**. (means that the door had been opened before)

(22) a. Gianni **often** dates the same person.
b. Gianni dates the same person **often**. (adapted from Cinque 1999: 92)

Both uses of *again* and *often* date back a long time, according to the *OED* (to Middle English at least), and this stability is unexpected, with two separate positions in (16). When elements grammaticalize, they are realized higher up the tree (van Gelderen 2004). In this process, we see frequent "jumps," e.g. from manner adverb to sentence adverb and from deontic modal to an epistemic one, but the path never goes through every step in (16).

My main reason for worrying about (16), however, is the possible number of adverbs to incorporate, i.e. in the thousands. Therefore, rather than have a rigid order of all of these and possibly more, I suggest (as in Butler 2003) that certain areas in the TP (and the other domains) are typical for certain moods, tenses, or aspects. I will suggest (23) instead of (16).

(23)

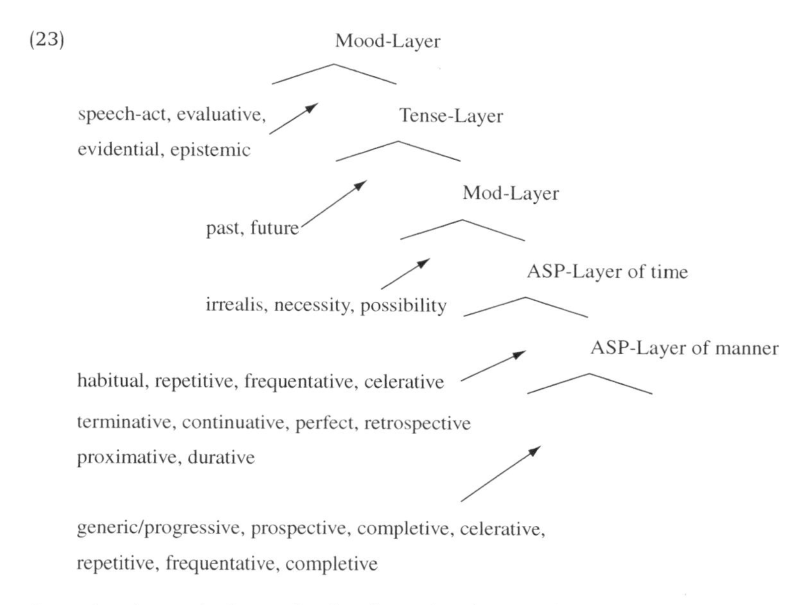

A major issue is how the basic order is acquired, and there are two answers that are compatible with Minimalism: (a) the order is due to a third-factor effect, namely the relative scope of these categories; (b) the order and the categories themselves are innate, i.e. provided by Universal Grammar.

A third factor approach might be to think about scope. For instance, Bybee (1985: 15) formulates the notion of semantic relevance: "a category is relevant to the verb to the extent that the meaning of the category directly affects the lexical content of the verb stem." A verb stem describes an action or state, so aspect is very relevant to it and will be merged closer to it than mood. Zagona's work (e.g. 2007) argues that the interpretation of modals depends on what they merge with. Hacquard (2010: 109), similarly, argues in connection with modal auxiliaries that the same modal verb can have a high and low meaning, i.e. epistemic or deontic, depending on how it relates to an event: "[A]n epistemic modal base needs to be bound by a contentful event, which both attitude and speech events are, but regular VP-events aren't." To put it in simpler terms, an epistemic modal expresses the likelihood of an assertion (and need not occur in an actual world), but a deontic modal modifies an actual event (and needs to occur in an actual world). One example of such ordering is that a "[p]erfective takes a predicate of events (VP) and returns a predicate of times, which then combines with tense" (Hacquard 2009: 294), and this determines the order.

The other possibility, namely that the order is given by Universal Grammar, is avoided as much as possible in current Minimalism (although I think Chomsky's main worry that there was not enough evolutionary time for Universal Grammar to develop a lot of detail is not warranted if non-humans already have a lot of semantics; see Jackendoff 2002). The semantic features which make up the auxiliaries can be argued to be determined by Universal Grammar, as I have mentioned in Chapter 1. The order could be third factor, although Universal Grammar could also be involved, as Chomsky (2001: 12) suggests: "[a]ssume that substantive categories are selected by functional categories. V by a light verb, T by C."

Various syntacticians have worried about (16), in particular Ernst (2002). In the spirit of Jackendoff (1972), Ernst argues that the base positions of adverbs are determined by zones, as in (23), partly determined by the lexical entry and partly by compositional rules (2002: 10, 37). Attractive about Ernst's proposal is that the position is in principle free but that interface requirements play a significant role. Interpretability at the LF interface, for instance, rules out (24), because *cleverly* must take an event to form another event, and that is not happening.

(24) *Theo **cleverly probably** bought flowers.
(Ernst 2002: 19)

Ernst's scope relations will not be spelled out here. See Ernst (2002, e.g. pp. 143–144) for more. What I wanted to emphasize is that adverbs are more zone-sensitive, as shown in (23), than that they fit in a precise hierarchy.

Another possible problem for (16) is Haider's (2000) point that adverbials of the same type can stack in the Spec of CP in German. I have given a Dutch example in (25a). Since Dutch is a verb-second (V2) language, the preverbal adverbials in (25) must be lumped together in some way, and this is easier to account for in (23) than in (16). If the adverbials are not of the same type, e.g. temporal and spatial in (25b), the result is ungrammatical.

(25) a. *[Morgen]* *[in de middag]* *[om ongeveer half zes]* *ga ik* *dat* *doen.* Dutch
Tomorrow in the afternoon at about half six go I that do
'I'll do that tomorrow around half past five in the afternoon.'

b. *[*Morgen*] [*naar Canada*] *ga ik vertrekken*
Tomorrow to Canada go I leave
'I leave for Canada tomorrow.'

Biskup (2011) is perhaps the most recent critic of (16). Using English data from Abels (2003) but also lots of his own from Czech, Biskup argues that Adverbial Hierarchies of various clauses interact, unexpected in the model of (16). For instance, *already* has scope over *no longer* and can only appear in the higher clause, as (26) shows.

(26) a. It is **already** the case that he **no longer** goes to school.
b. *It is **no longer** the case that he **already** goes to school.
(Biskup 2011: 132, from Abels 2003)

Cinque classifies only *once* and *then* as tense adverbials (i.e. past and future in (16) above). Compared with the number of aspectual and modal adverbs, that is meager indeed. Haumann (2007: 263) explains that there are many other temporal adverbs, such as *afterwards*, *before*, *now*, *since*, *today*, *tomorrow*, and *yesterday*, but that for a variety of reasons many are not grammatical in the area between the subject and the VP. For instance, the calendar-adverbials (*Sunday*, *last week*, and *next year*) can occur to the right side of the V, as in (27a), and in the left-periphery, as in (27b), but are barred from an internal position, as (27c) shows.

(27) a. They were very happy **last week**.
b. **Last week**, they were very happy last week.
c. *They were **last week** very happy.

These adverbials are much more like the circumstantial adverbials we have seen in Chapter 3, because they are PP-like. Hence, they are assumed to have moved from a VP internal position to the left-periphery. The temporal adverbials of the TP-Layer occur in most positions (with the right intonation), as (28) shows.

(28) a. She said that **once**.
b. **Once**, she said that.
c. She **once** said that.

Table 4.1 presents some temporal adverbials and their positions.

The position of the aspectual adverbials in the clause is flexible. As Haumann (2007: 232) writes, the positioning is "vitually free: they may occur between the subject and the finite lexical verb ... between a modal and the bare infinitive ... between any finite auxiliary and the participle ... after non-finite auxiliaries." In addition, they can also occur at the beginning and end of a sentence. Some of these positions

Table 4.1 *Temporal adverbials (based on Haumann 2007: 263–267)*

Inside TP	Outside TP
now, once, (long) since, then, long ago, after(wards), before	today, tomorrow, yesterday, last year, on Monday, next year, etc.

are provided in (29) for the frequency adverb, i.e. ASPfrequentative in (16), *rarely* (adapted from Haumann 2007: 233 and Google).

(29) a. She **rarely** goes out.
 b. She could **rarely** find those colors.
 c. She has **rarely** been in the same boat.
 d. She has been **rarely** seen on stage.
 e. **Rarely** will she get angry.
 f. They do that **rarely**.

This freedom of position does present a problem for a strict sequence, as in (16), but less so for (23).

The mood and modal adverbials in the TP (16) involve *probably*, *perhaps*, *necessarily*, *possibly*, and *intentionally*. They too are quite free in position, as I show for *possibly* (adapted from Google).

(30) a. They **possibly** murdered the butler.
 b. They could **possibly** be the worst thing to happen all week.
 c. They could be **possibly** going to give a news report that they have struck oil somewhere else.
 d. **Possibly**, this is going nowhere.

In short, adverbials in the TP-Layer are said to fit as specifiers in a very specific universal hierarchy, and auxiliaries are heads of the corresponding phrases. Some of the challenges come with asking how many adverbials can be grammatically marked, and if their features are checked. I have suggested a less strict approach than Cinque, basically with areas of tense, mood, and aspect throughout the clause. The ultimate order should be determined by a third factor, as suggested by Ernst, Hacquard, and others.

4.3 DISPLACEMENT IN THE TP

Nouns and pronouns can be marked for each of the three roles/functions they play. In Chapter 3, we discussed the semantic or thematic roles; in this section and the next, we look at the grammatical functions of subject and object; and in the next chapter, the pragmatic roles of topic and focus are examined. In English, grammatical subjects and objects are mainly marked through position, as will be discussed more in Section 4.3.1. It is the EPP that is said to be responsible for getting a DP from the VP to the subject position in Spec TP, and the object is said to remain in its postverbal position. This will be shown in Section 3.2. As mentioned, we'll suggest some ways to make the EPP less ad-hoc and also discuss V to T movement in Section 3.3.

4.3.1 More on the subject

How do we recognize a grammatical subject? Keenan (1976) distinguishes how they are coded from how they behave in controlling other parts of the sentence. As for the **coding**, I mentioned in Chapter 2 that there is limited marking of the nominative on the subject in English, and there is, again limited, agreement between the subject and the finite verb. A very reliable criterion to find the subject is through its position, namely before the finite auxiliary or verb (in an indicative sentence). This position is supposed to be the Spec of TP. The exact label doesn't matter so much, although its position relative to other parts of the sentence does matter, following C and preceding T.

Subjects also **control** infinitival null subjects, represented by PRO in (31), and reflexives, as in (32). They also control the subject of an elided coordinate, as in (33). These properties are probably due to the structurally high position of the subject.

(31) **We** want [PRO to eat frybread].

(32) **I** saw myself.

(33) **I** ate frybread and (I) enjoyed myself.

There are languages where only subjects can control the subject of an infinitive and be the antecedent for a reflexive. In English, however, grammatical objects can also control PRO and serve as antecedents for reflexives, as (34) and (35) show.

(34) I persuaded him PRO to eat frybread.

(35) They showed Bill to himself (using a picture).

Using the vP-shell for double object constructions, this could still be an issue of the object being higher, at least in English (36).

(36)

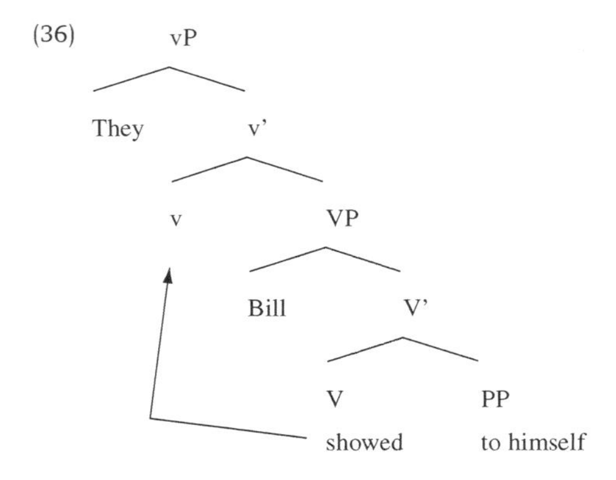

Subjects are different from objects in being able to control coordinate-elided subjects, which objects cannot. Thus, the elided subject has to be the same as the earlier subject, as (37a) shows, and could never be interpreted as the object in English in (37b).

(37) a. I want to visit them and (Subject = I) have fun.
b. *I want to visit them and (Subject = they) have fun.

Although grammatical subjects are often Agents, in terms of semantic roles, they can also be Themes, as in (38), or Experiencers, as in (39), or Goals, as in (40), or have no thematic roles, as in (41). That's the reason we need to distinguish grammatical and semantic role.

(38) a. **The books** were destroyed.
b. **That** irritated me.

(39) **They** saw the beauty in the landscape.

(40) **We** were given four choices.

(41) **There**'s five unicorns in the room.

The subject position we have identified in English is Spec TP. What is the reason that the subject moves to this position? Under the probe-goal system of checking the features between the T and the subject in Spec vP, there is no reason due to checking for it to move. This is where the EPP comes in, to which we turn in Section 4.3.2.

4.3.2 The EPP and movement of the DP

The EPP is based on the **Projection Principle**, which is used in Chomsky (1981: 29) to ensure that the argument structure from the lexicon is kept the same (is "projected") throughout the derivation. This is a mapping problem, similar to the one we saw in Chapter 3, namely how to map the arguments to the syntax. The E in EPP stands for "extended" and helps create a subject position if the verb has none, as in the case of passives. The EPP is later used more broadly than just to trigger movement to the subject position, as we'll see.

In the early 1980s, most subjects are directly base generated in the higher position because the phrase structure rules are as in (42), and movement to the subject position is not needed.

(42) (a) S → NP VP (=Subject and Predicate)
(b) VP → V NP (NP) (PP) (=Verb and Objects)

This base generation of the subject outside of the VP changes, of course, around 1988 with the VPISH. Even before that, there is an attempt to reduce redundancy between the lexicon and the phrase structure rules. If the lexicon specifies that a verb has an NP, the phrase structure rules shouldn't do this as well. The Projection Principle allows (42b) to be rewritten as in (43), and that was seen as a reduction of redundancy.

(43) a. XP → YP X'
b. X' → X ZP

Reducing the phrase structure rules to (43) introduces X-bar theory. Doing that means there has to be a special rule for the subject. As Chomsky (1982: 9–10) writes, "it might be thought that this [fact that each sentence has a subject] follows from the Projection Principle, since . . . verbs θ-mark their subjects, but this is not quite correct." The reason is that verbs mark agents and themes but not subjects and objects, so we have to specify that English has a special position for subjects. Chomsky goes on to give two reasons: Passives have no theta-marked subjects (i.e. they only have a Theme), and there are expletives that appear in subject position. Not being theta-marked, expletives fall outside the Projection Principle.

Because "the Projection Principle and the requirement that clauses have subjects are conceptually quite closely related," Chomsky refers to both as the EPP (Chomsky 1982: 10). He doesn't say much about the actual position of the subject in 1982, except that it is Subject-VP. A subject requirement ensures that each sentence has a subject, but that it is situated in the Spec of TP is a later addition.

As mentioned, expletives, such as *it* and *there*, are not relevant to the argument structure but are used to satisfy the EPP in (44) if the *five unicorns* fail to raise to the subject position from a postverbal base structure.

(44) a. There were five unicorns in the parking lot.
b. Five unicorns were in the parking lot.

The two DPs *five unicorns* in (44ab) differ in interpretation, namely indefinite and specific respectively. This is known as the Definiteness Effect and explains why (45) is ungrammatical.

(45) *There were the/those/my five unicorns in the parking lot.

The Definiteness Effect will become important as a way of rephrasing the EPP as a less ad-hoc principle.

After the change in the late 1980s to base generate the Agent theta-roles in the Spec of VP, i.e. what typically moves to the position of the grammatical subject, the EPP becomes important for all subjects, not just subjects of passives and expletives. However, it is a language-specific principle, because not all languages require grammatical subjects in a higher position, e.g. *twee boeken* 'two books' in Dutch (46).

(46)	*Gisteren*	*werd-en*	*mij*	*heel goedkoop*	*twee*	*boek-en*	*aangeboden*	Dutch
	Yesterday	became-P	me	very cheaply	two	book-P	offered	

'Yesterday, two books were offered to me very cheaply.'

This variation prompts van Gelderen (1993) and others to argue that the Spec TP position is optional in some languages. Seeing the subject consistently in Spec TP in addition to elements that are clearly in the T is an indication for the child to include the T and TP as part of its set of functional items. Since Dutch subjects are often in Spec CP as well, there is no reason to assume a Spec TP, and this makes the EPP even more stipulative.

Currently, there are moves to think of the EPP either in terms of pragmatic roles or structural requirements. A representative of the pragmatic view is Rosengren (2002). Subjects are always specific, if not definite, and the Spec TP is argued to be the position in which DPs are interpreted as specific (see Diesing 1992). Such a formulation is less stipulative, since there is direct evidence to the language learner of a connection between position and specificity. The expletive constructions in (44) above show the same connection. The DP in (44b) is specific, but the DP in (44a) non-specific. (In (44a), we'd have to argue that *there* can check definiteness/specificity by being a spatio-temporal topic, as in e.g. Kiss 1996.) Even Chomsky (2000: 102) admits that "EPP features are uninterpretable ... though the configuration they establish has effects for interpretation" (of course, this is contrary to the notion of uninterpretable features, but we'll ignore that). Bošković (2002) goes back to the idea that case is behind the EPP.

Chomsky (2011) accounts for the EPP in a structural way. He argues that constituents need to get labels in order to be interpreted. If the subject remains in the Spec of vP, he argues that this subject and the rest of the vP do not form a syntactic object and cannot be labeled. Therefore, the subject must move out of the vP. Medeiros (2011) justifies a model where phrasal movement is forced by complexities of the derivation. With this multitude of possibilities, let's thus assume that we can find a more motivated reason why Spec TP is occupied in some languages, either a specific interpretation or a last resort due to structural problems. In many languages, there is an EPP for object positions, to which we turn now.

In some languages, the object can occupy a position outside of the VP as well. This position is reserved for definite objects (as we've seen for Dutch in Chapter 3, Section 3.6.3) and that makes the process similar to the subject moving to the Spec TP, since that is a position for specific subjects. For instance, in Yiddish, a nominal object that moves out of the VP, as in (47a), has to be definite; indefinite nominals moving to that position result in ungrammaticality, as in (47b). This movement is called **scrambling**, after Ross (1967).

(47) a. *Maks hot* ***dos*** *bukh mistome/nekhtn/keyn mol nit geleyent* Yiddish
Max has the book probably/yesterday/no time not read
'Max has probably/never read the book(/yesterday).'
b. **Maks hot* ***a*** *bukh mistome/nekhtn/keyn mol nit geleyent*
Max has a book probably/yesterday/no time not read
'Max has probably/never read a book(/yesterday).' (Diesing 1997: 389–390)

Based on Holmberg's (1986) analysis, Chomsky (2001) examines Scandinavian **object shift**, as in (48), where the pronominal object moves out of the VP only if the lexical verb also moves out of the VP.

(48) *Han köpte den inte* ~~*köpte*~~ ~~*den*~~ Swedish
He bought it not
'He didn't buy to'

In Icelandic, it is also possible to move a full DP. Chomsky (2001: 33) argues that the position to which the nominal moves is just above the vP, and that this movement is due to an EPP feature of v, a feature named Int for "Interpretation." The Swedish verb *köpte* 'bought' would be moving to its regular position in a V2 language, namely to the C. We'll now turn to the movement of the V to v and to T and C.

4.3.3 Verb movement

I'll first briefly talk about V to v and then V to T and C movement.

English lexical verbs stay inside the VP-shell, as we'll see in a minute. Assuming a VP-shell with the lexical verb base generated as V, there is the possibility of V to v movement. Is there evidence that a lexical verb moves to v in English? There is with phrasal verbs, such as (49), and especially with causatives, as in (50).

(49) a. I **turned off** the light.
b. I **turned** the light **off**.

(50) I gently **rolled** the ball quickly down the hill. (adapted from Radford 2009)

The trees for phrasal verbs and causatives were given in Chapter 3, and there I used V to v movement. I have added the adverbs in (50) to show the adverbial modifications of the different verbs, the light verb and the full verb. Because *the ball* does the rolling, we assume the verb *rolled* has moved to the left of *the ball*.

How about V to v movement in sentences such as (51)?

(51) I ate the apple.

We don't have much evidence in fact, but we assume that, if it does in (49) and (50), it will move in (51) as well.

Turning to movement of the verb into the higher layers, as with the movement of the subject to the Spec of TP, it is still an open question what determines movement of V to T in (52), in languages such as French, as opposed to languages such as English (53).

(52) *Elle* ***va*** ***souvent*** *à* ***Tucson*** French
She goes often to Tucson
'She often goes to Tucson.'

(53) *She **goes** often to Tucson.

We know the verb *va* has moved because if there is an auxiliary the lexical verb stays behind the adverb, as in (54).

(54) *Elle* *est* *souvent* ***allée*** *à* ***Tucson*** French
She is often gone to Tucson
'She has often been to Tucson.'

Turning to V to T to C movement, this is limited in English. It only happens in interrogatives, not in topicalizations, imperatives, and exclamatives. German, Dutch, Swedish, and others move the verb to C in all main clauses. We'll assume that the reason is that there is an EPP in the Fin head, which, as in the case of all EPP-accounts, is pretty stipulative.

Some people see a connection between verbal movement and overt morphological features on the verb. For instance, English lost its overt agreement around 1600 when the verb stopped moving to T and C. This relationship between movement and inflection can't completely be the right approach, since many languages have verb movement with very little inflection on the verb, e.g. Afrikaans and the Scandinavian languages. So, verbs are pronounced in positions that suggest Raising, but it is not clear why.

Another unresolved question is whether head movement takes place in the syntax or at PF as Chomsky (1995) suggests. This was mentioned in footnote 4 in Chapter 1. If the V moves to T and C after the derivation splits up into a phonological and semantic component, one would not expect any semantic effects. We'll consider some evidence that there are such effects and that head movement is in the syntax. The evidence comes from the licensing of Negative Polarity Items (see next paragraph).

As I said before, we won't introduce the NegP until Chapter 6, but most of you have probably heard of Negative Polarity Items (NPIs). Such items need to occur in a special position (Giannikidou 1997 calls this environment anti-veridical), e.g. being c-commanded by a negative or an interrogative marker. In (55a), *n't* c-commands *anyone* because the NegP is higher than the object; in (55b), there is no negative to c-command the NPI; in (55c), the negative doesn't c-command the NPI; and in (55d), *anyone* is c-commanded by an interrogative.

(55) a. I did**n't** see **anyone**.
b. *I saw **anyone**.
c. ***Anyone** didn't see.
d. Did I see anyone?

As Roberts (2010: 8) explains, the licensing of *anyone* is a semantic question, and, with (55d) grammatical, we have evidence that verb movement in fact occurs before the derivation splits up into a phonological and semantic part.

In Turkish, similar constructions provide evidence that verb movement must happen before the sentence is interpreted, as shown in Kural (1993). In (56a), the verb moves to Neg and then to T, and this movement licenses the polarity item *kimse*. If the verb stayed in the VP and only moved just before spell-out, both (56ab) would be similarly ungrammatical.

(56) a. ***kimse*** *gel-**me**-di* Turkish
nobody come-NEG-PST
'Nobody came.'

b. ***kimse** gel-di
nobody come-PST
(Kural 1993: 84)

This is evidence for verb movement before the C-I interface.

In this section, we have identified characteristics of subjects and objects and have looked at movement of DPs and Vs to positions in the TP, and a little bit at movement to the CP. In the next section, we examine morphological phenomena connected to the TP.

4.4 CASE AND AGREEMENT

As is well known, (pronominal) subjects and objects are recognizable by the case they carry and the agreement they cause on the verb. In Section 4.4.1, we discuss case and the model of case and agreement checking that we introduced in Chapter 1; in Section 4.4.2, we look at agreement in more detail.

4.4.1 Case

In Chapter 1, the famous Case Filter attributed to Vergnaud was mentioned. Vergnaud's observation had been that certain NPs, now DPs, are ungrammatical in certain environments, e.g. in (57a), where the pronoun cannot be case-marked by the non-finite *to be* or by the passive *supposed*. Instead, the pronoun has to raise to get nominative case, as in (57b).

(57) a. *It is supposed he/him to be nice.
b. He is supposed to be nice.

Case has remained a constant concern since the 1980s. In recent Minimalism, structural cases such as the nominative and accusative are seen as assigned by finiteness (the T) and transitive verb (little v) respectively. Structural case is assigned in certain positions and has no thematic meaning connected to it. There is also inherent case which is connected to a specific semantic role (see Chomsky 1986a). If structural case is uninterpretable both on the verb and the noun, it is a very different feature from the phi- and T features.

In English, it is hard to see any case at all (either structural or inherent) except on pronouns. It may, however, be true that the distinction between *I* and *me* and *s/he* and *him/her* is one between head and phrase and not of case: the "nominative" may be a head and the "accusative" a full phrase (as argued in e.g. van Gelderen 2011).

Since that position is controversial, I will stick to the idea that both subject and object are licensed in some way and continue to call that nominative and accusative case.

Nominative and accusative case, according to Pesetsky and Torrego (2004), involve an uninterpretable/unvalued T on the nominal which is valued by a finite T or transitive v, at least in English (but other languages may differ). Pesetsky and Torrego connect case, finiteness, and agreement by having a tense feature in T and v look down the tree for a feature on the DP. My adaptation of this is as in (58).

(58)

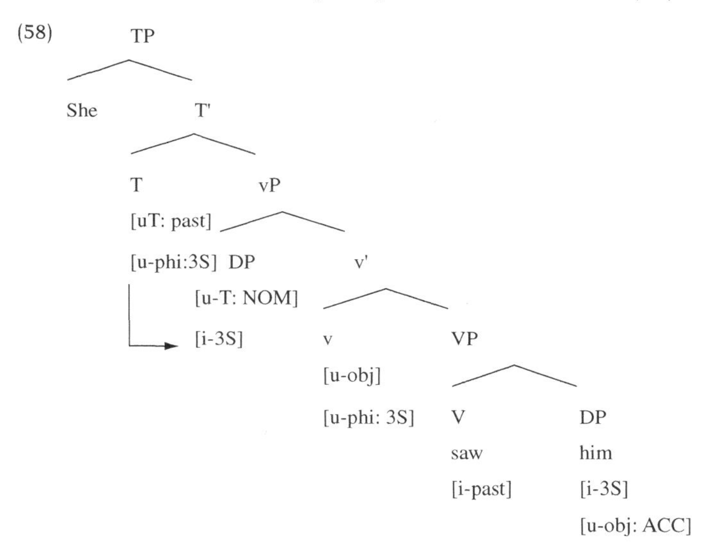

In (58), the [u-phi] features in v act as the probe to value these [u-phi]. The latter agreement is visible in languages with object agreement on the verb. The same valuation happens with the T, where the [u-phi-] features act as a probe. The proposal in (58) thus represents structural case as valued by tense and an object value.

As was mentioned in Chapter 1, there are languages without case, and (58) would therefore have to be adapted; there are also languages without overt tense. The dependence of case on tense could be severed by having [u-phi] first look for valued phi-features and then have the DP move to look for case. Such "delayed valuation" is suggested in e.g. Carstens (2012) and would require that we allow DPs to act as probes. I won't pursue this possibility further.

There are other problems with the picture in (58), namely, Greenberg's Universal in (59) has been known for a long time, and it implies that orders where the V is first will have less agreement than when the nominal is before the V. We have seen some Arabic sentences in Chapter 1 that show this asymmetry between SV and VS.

(59) **Universal 33**

> When number agreement between the noun and verb is suspended and the rule is based on order, the case is always one in which the verb precedes and the verb is in the singular. (Greenberg 1963: 94)

This indicates that agreement as in (58) is too simplistic. I turn to agreement next, looking at the different agreement features first before tackling the word order issue of (59).

4.4.2 Agreement

In (58), I use a generic [phi-] feature, representing number, person, and gender. There are theoretical and empirical issues connected with that, and in this section I look at some other possibilities and suggest an account for the universal in (59).

First, there are general issues with phi-features. Kayne (2011: 1) notes that "allowing lexical items to have any number of features is akin to allowing n-ary branching for any n." For about twenty years, there has been a debate on whether feature bundling is allowed or if each feature F has its own projection. If we disallow feature bundles, we could have the following DP with interpretable features spread out (in the spirit of Ritter 1995).

(60)

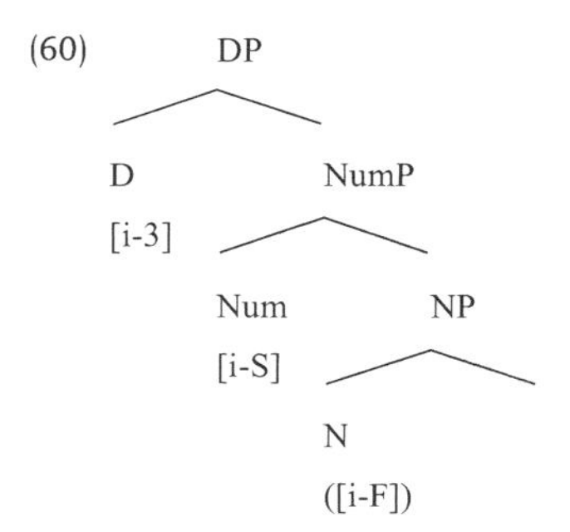

We could argue the D is essential for an NP, and that would fit with Forchheimer's (1953) observation that almost all languages have person expressed overtly in their pronoun system, but not all have number and gender. See also Richards (2007) and Harley and Ritter (2002).

The features on the T and v would have to be split as well, perhaps as in (61a) and (61b), respectively. Languages would select the features.

(61)

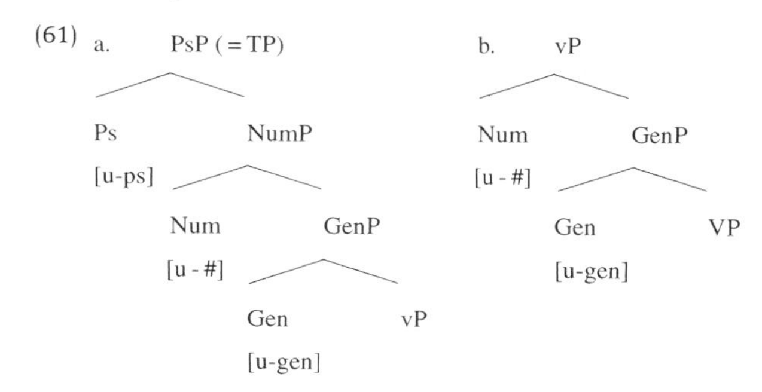

Person features are crucial to the T but not to the v; at the moment, this is a stipulation.

A second question with phi-features and AGREE in (58) is why SV orders result in more agreement than VS orders, as we've seen with Arabic in Chapter 1, and the same with OV and VO orders, as we'll see in Section 4.5. The interesting part is that number is lost, not person! Some examples are given in (62) to (65), from various stages and varieties of English.

(62) *On ðæm selfan hrægle* ... ***wæs*** eac awriten ða naman ðara twelf heahfædra
'On the same robe ... was also written the names of the twelve patriarchs.' (Ælfred, *CP* 6, 15)

(63) In that cytee **was** the sittynges of the .xij. tribes of Israel.
(*Mandeville's Travels*, 71, 17–18)

(64) **Is** all things ready for that Royall time? (Shakespeare, *Richard III*, III, 4, 5)

(65) **Is** Decius Brutus and Trebonius here?
(Shakespeare, *Julius Caesar*, I, 3, 148)

This suggests a role for Spec-Head agreement in addition to just AGREE.

If it is typically the number feature that disappears, the probe in T might only be looking for person (and gender). Possibly a tree as in (66) is feasible.

(66)

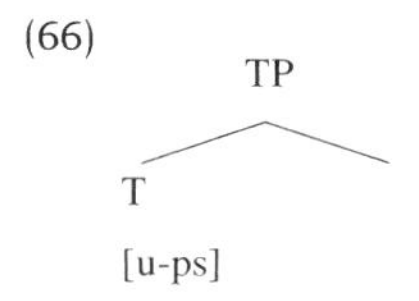

As we've seen in Chapter 1 (Table 1.2), languages either have case or agreement, or both, or neither. Baker (2008a: 155) therefore suggests the macroparameter in (67). He also suggests (68), which is a way of accounting for Spec-Head agreement.

(67) The Case Dependence of Agreement Parameter (CDAP)
F agrees with DP/NP only if F values the case feature of DP/NP (or vice versa).
(No: most Bantu languages; Yes: most Indo-European languages)

(68) The Direction of Agreement Parameter (DAP)
F agrees with DP only if DP asymmetrically c-commands F.
(Yes: most Bantu languages; No: most Indo-European languages)

The parameters can be stated in a simplified form as (69) and (70).

(69) Cluster [u-T] and [u-phi] or not, i.e. case and agreement depend on each other or not.

(70) Spec-Head or AGREE.

It would be good if the DAP and CDAP could be generalized, e.g. to *wh*-movement, and I'll show that now.

Person is definitely checked through probing, and number may be checked in a Spec-Head relationship. The latter is confirmed by some seemingly unrelated cases of movement through the CP-Layer. Kimball and Aissen (1971) describe a variety of English that allows relative clauses as in (71ab) but not as in (72).

(71) a. The people $_{\text{CP}}$[who the boy **think** $_{\text{CP}}$[~~who~~ are in the garden]].
b. The people $_{\text{CP}}$[who the boy **think** $_{\text{CP}}$[~~who~~ the girl **know** [~~who~~ are in the garden]]].

(72) *The people $_{\text{CP}}$[who ~~who~~ think $_{\text{CP}}$[that John **know** the answer]].
(Kimball and Aissen 1971)

In (71ab), the nominative plural *wh*-element agrees with the verb of a higher clause in number if that *wh*-element has cyclically moved through the Spec of the higher CP as in (71). Sentence (72) shows that this type of agreement takes place only if the *wh*-element indeed moves through the relevant Spec CP. In keeping with Chomsky (1995: 59ff.), I assume there is a strong Q feature that triggers the *wh*-element. This variety is more widespread and appears regularly in the history of English, as (73) and (74) show.

(73) **What cares** these roarers for the name of King? (Shakespeare, *Tempest*, I, 1, 17, van Gelderen 1997a: 67)

(74) Overheard: What you already knows.

There are other languages with similar phenomena. When the *wh*-element precedes the auxiliary in C in Tohono O'odham, as in (75), the auxiliary is different in shape from when it follows C, as in (76). In addition, the morphology on the auxiliary is different.

(75) **Do:** **'o** *kuḍut* *g* *'ali?* Tohono O'odham
who AUX.3 bother.IMPF the baby
'Who is/was bothering the baby?' (Zepeda [1983] 1994: 53)

(76) **k** **heḍai** *ṣoak?* Tohono O'odham
AUX.3 who cry.S.IMPF
'Who is/was crying?' (Zepeda [1983] 1994: 55)

In conclusion, the tree in (58) is a way of connecting agreement, case, and tense/aspect in English. There are a number of issues unresolved, however. First, not all languages make the connection between tense, case, and agreement; second, the issue of the bundling of the phi-features is up in the air; and third, Spec-Head agreement still plays a role in checking phi-features, unaccounted for in (58). I have therefore suggested a few modifications, although these remain stipulative.

4.5 CROSS-LINGUISTIC OBSERVATIONS

In this chapter, we have looked at the relatively rich auxiliary structure indicating TMA in English and the substantial number of adverbials. We have also examined the ways the subject and object are marked and the movement by the verb. Since the TP is cross-linguistically so variable, we have already seen examples from many languages. In this section, I add a few more facts and examples.

4.5.1 TMA auxiliaries and adverbials

Do auxiliaries and adverbials appear in the order of (16) in all languages? Cinque (1999) argues that the functional order is universal, and I will follow that, even though I have suggested fewer positions. In this section, I will indicate a few areas where languages differ: (a) having TMA affixes rather than auxiliaries; and (b) not selecting all the categories from the Functional Hierarchy.

In principle, each of the functional phrases in (16) can be filled by a full phrase in the specifier position (adverbial), and a word (auxiliary) or an affix in the head position. Throughout each language's history, there are many changes, and one of these is the change from phrase to word to affix. For instance, in Navajo, there is a *-d-* future on the verb that could be related to *doo(leeł)*, the future auxiliary; in Melanesian Pidgin, the future auxiliary *bai* 'will' can cliticize as *b-*; and in Greek *tha* 'will' is an affix originating from *thelo* 'to want.' (77) is an instance of a future affix.

(77) *b-em* *i* *go* Melanesian Pidgin
FUT-3S PART go
'S/he will go.' (Crowley and Bowern 2010: 222)

It is well known that not all languages select the same set, but let's look at an intriguing example where aspect is much more elaborate than in English. Mithun (2000) shows that Central Pomo, spoken in Northern California, contains a very rich system of aspectual marking. She notes that the markers are drawn from a restricted set and that they repeat themselves, so to speak. In (78), you see three imperfective and two perfective markers; in (79) you see the fuller forms.

(78) *Wá.ymin-wa* *ma* *ʔé.y-yo-h-du-w-a-d-anʔ* Central Pomo
Often-Q you away-go-PF-IMPF-PF-IMPF-IMPF
'Do you go away a lot?' (Mithun 2000: 273)

(79) IMPF *-an*; PF *–w*; PROGR *–wan*; Continuative *-(h)duw*;
Habitual IMPF *-adan*; Habitual PF *-(h)duwan*;
Frequentative *-(h)duwandan*

When a native speaker was asked about the difference between the habitual perfective and the frequentative, she said "not much difference" (Mithun 2000: 276). So Pomo uses affixes where other languages might use auxiliaries. However, even if we might find places for these in (16), it is not clear that that would be the right analysis.

4.5.2 Subject and object and agreement and case

We'll first look at how languages other than English mark subjects and objects through position and then at agreement and case. I'll also add a little on so-called **free word order** languages.

As we've seen, English subjects and objects are marked through position and possibly through agreement and case. Closely related languages such as German have a freer word order and show more case and agreement to mark the subject and object. This is true in (80), where the accusative-marked object precedes the nominative-marked subject. Special intonation is needed, however.

(80) *Den* *Jungen* *hat* *der* *Hund* *gebissen.* German
the.ACC boy has.3S the.NOM dog bitten
'The dog bit the boy.'

There are a few languages where it has been argued that only semantic and pragmatic roles are marked; see Keenan (1976), Schachter (1976), and Mithun (2008). This suggests that not all languages have the grammatical role of subject. A very helpful observation in this respect comes from Donohue (1999: chapter 20), who says that in some languages the pivot (or the grammatical role) is directly tied to the semantic role - he mentions the languages Archi and Aceh - but that in others it is tied to pragmatic or syntactic roles. In Tukang Besi, an Austronesian language, the system is mixed, e.g. the addressee of an imperative always has to be a semantic Agent, the pronominal indexing on the verb is tied to the grammatical role (S or A), and cases are tied to the pragmatic roles.

Turning to cross-linguistic variation in agreement, it is relevant to note Givón (1971; 1978), who, arguing that agreement markers arise from pronouns, says "agreement and pronominalization ... are fundamentally one and the same phenomenon" (1978: 151). Therefore, it is cross-linguistically interesting to see how pronominal an agreement marker still is. If agreement and pronouns are the same thing, we expect either pronouns or agreement, as Table 4.2 shows.

This means that most languages in the sample use agreement and not so many a pronominal subject. This difference can be expressed by using interpretable and uninterpretable phi-features. Languages with an overt pronoun and agreement make use of uninterpretable phi-features in T to probe the interpretable features of the subject, whereas those without a pronoun have interpretable features on T.

Agreement with the object on the verb is quite frequent as well, again not something we'd expect just looking at English.

Table 4.2 *The marking of subjects (from Dryer 2011a)*

Pronominal subjects are expressed by pronouns in subject position	82 (11.5%)
Pronominal subjects are expressed by affixes on verbs	437 (62%)
Pronominal subjects are expressed by clitics with variable host	32 (4.5 %)
Pronominal subjects are expressed by pronouns in a different syntactic position from full noun phrase subjects	67 (9.4%)
Pronominal subjects are expressed only by pronouns in subject position, but these pronouns are often left out	61 (8.6%)
More than one of the above types, with none dominant	32 (4.5%)
Total	711

Table 4.3 *Marking on the verb (from Siewierska 2011)*

No person marking of any argument	82 (22%)
Person marking of only the A argument	73 (19%)
Person marking of only the P argument	24 (6%)
Person marking of the A or P argument	6 (1.6%)
Person marking of both the A and P arguments	193 (51%)
Total	378

Examples of marking of the object on the verb are given in (81) from Tohono O'odham and in (82) from French. Note, however, that in the latter most agreement is only present in the written language.

(81) a. *Gogs 'o* ***ha**-huhu'id hegam* Tohono O'odham
dog AUX.3S P-chasing them/those
'The dog is chasing them.'
b. *Gogs 'o hegam* ***ha**-huhu'id*
dog AUX.3S them/those P-chasing
'The dog is chasing them.'
c. *Ceoj 'o 'añi:* ***ñ**-ceggia*
boy AUX.3S me 1S-fighting
'The boy is/was fighting me.' (Zepeda [1983] 1994: 34–35)

(82) a. *Les chais-**es** sont repeint-**es*** French
the chairs-FP AUX.P repainted-FP
'The chairs are repainted.'
b. *Il* ***les*** *a repeint-**es***
he them AUX.3S repainted-FP
'He has repainted them'.

Tohono O'odham has agreement in VO (81a) and OV (81bc). French follows Universal 33, and the participle agrees only if the object appears before it, as in (82), as the absence of agreement in the VO (83) also shows.

(83) *Il a repein-**t*** ***les chaises*** French
he AUX.3S repainted-MS the chairs (FP)
'He has repainted the chairs.'

An analysis of (82) and (83) would be one where the object has to move through a particular specifier in order to trigger agreement. As was said in connection to (58), there is no good account for that in a purely probe-goal approach, but I will suggest an account for it below.

Table 4.4 *Navajo subject agreement and independent pronouns (fourth person, indefinite, and areal left out)*

	Agreement			Pronouns		
	S	Dual	P	S	Dual	P
1	-sh-	-iid-	da + iid	shi	nihi	danihi
2	-ni-	-oh-	da + oh	ni	nihi	danihi
3	-0-	-0-	da	bi	bi	daabi

Table 4.5 *Variability of case (adapted from Iggesen 2011)*

No morphological case marking	100 languages
2 cases	23 languages
3–4 cases	18 languages
5 cases	12 languages
6–7 cases	37 languages
8–9 cases	23 languages
10 or more cases	24 languages
Total	237

Apart from differences in agreement and position, there are also differences in features selected. As is known from the work of Forchheimer, Ingram (1978), and Cysouw (2003), pronominal paradigms vary quite a lot across languages. To give just one example, there are languages with a dual number, as Table 4.4 shows for the markings on the verb on the left and the independent pronouns on the right.

Turning to case, it is very variable. Siewierska and Bakker (2009: 299) say that "case marking of arguments is overall considerably less common cross-linguistically than agreement marking." Table 4.5 shows this. The numbers of cases also vary enormously, as the table also shows, where high numbers represent inherent case.

Case often indicates grammatical roles such as subject and object, but also signals specific or definite, e.g. the Russian negative genitive that we've seen in (34) of Chapter 3. This means a language can grammaticalize pragmatic information through its structural case system.

A question that often comes up is "What about free word order languages?" Australian languages, such as Warlpiri and languages such as Latin are often mentioned as examples. It turns out that when one looks at these carefully, the word order is pragmatically determined. Swartz (1988) and Hale (1992) thus argue for Warlpiri that the sentence topic comes first.

4.5.3 Movement in the TP by the DP, V, and VP

In this section, I will give further examples of various movements in languages that are richer in movement than English.

As we've seen above, in languages such as French, the (main) verb moves to T if there is no auxiliary; in other languages it is even moving to C, as (84) shows.

(84) *Dat* ***weet*** *ik jammergenoeg niet meer* Dutch
that know I unfortunately not more
'Unfortunately, I don't remember any more.'

In French, as in English, the subject moves to the Spec of TP, but this is not necessary in languages such as Russian, Spanish, or Irish (85).

(85) *Tá an bóthad díreach* Irish
is the road straight
'The road is straight.' (Dillon and ó Cróinín 1961: 27)

VS languages provide evidence for V to T movement; other languages, as we've seen in Chapter 1, have VP movement or object movement to derive a diversity of word orders. The triggers for these are tricky, of course. Table 4.6 provides a list of all movement possibilities.

As for Germanic scrambling, we have seen an example in (47) of Section 4.3.2; we've also seen an example of Scandinavian object shift in (48). Chocano (2007) argues that the two phenomena are the same. In both, a definite topic is moved outside of the VP. Both scrambling and object shift constructions pose problems for checking by a higher T because the (shifted) object would be in between the probe and goal.

Table 4.6 *Types of movement*

X movement: French V movement; T-to-C in English interrogatives
XP movement: Subject to Spec TP; *wh*-element to Spec CP; VP to Spec CP in VOS languages; scrambling of the object; object shift
Remnant movement: VP movement after the V or DP have moved out

Sentence (48), repeated here as (86), has a structure as in (87), which shows the derivation at the moment that the T has been merged and before the subject *han* 'he' and the verb move higher. The problem is that the probe in T would see the features of the object first! I won't go into this more.

(86) *Han* *köpte* ***den*** *inte* Swedish
He bought it not
'He didn't buy it.'

(87)

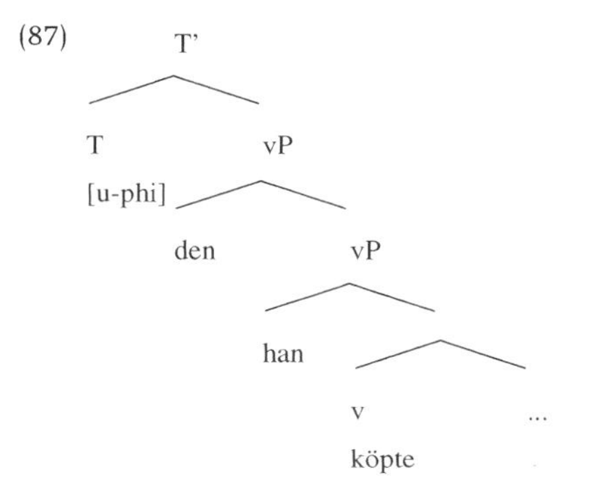

In Section 4.5, as in all cross-linguistic sections in this book, we have just scratched the surface of all the types of variation that is around.

4.6 CONCLUSION

In this chapter, we have discussed the grammatical layer which includes temporal, modal, and aspectual information in the shape of auxiliaries and adverbials. The former are heads and the latter specifiers. The TP-Layer houses the subject in most languages and accommodates the finiteness (or non-finiteness) by marking e.g. a nominative subject and agreement on the verb. The grammatical object can be marked by agreement or case as well, although not in English.

As I have tried to make clear, a purely Cartographic approach is perhaps too rich. I have suggested a modified tree and will finish with a tree with all features of the TP (except progressive and lexical aspect).

(88)

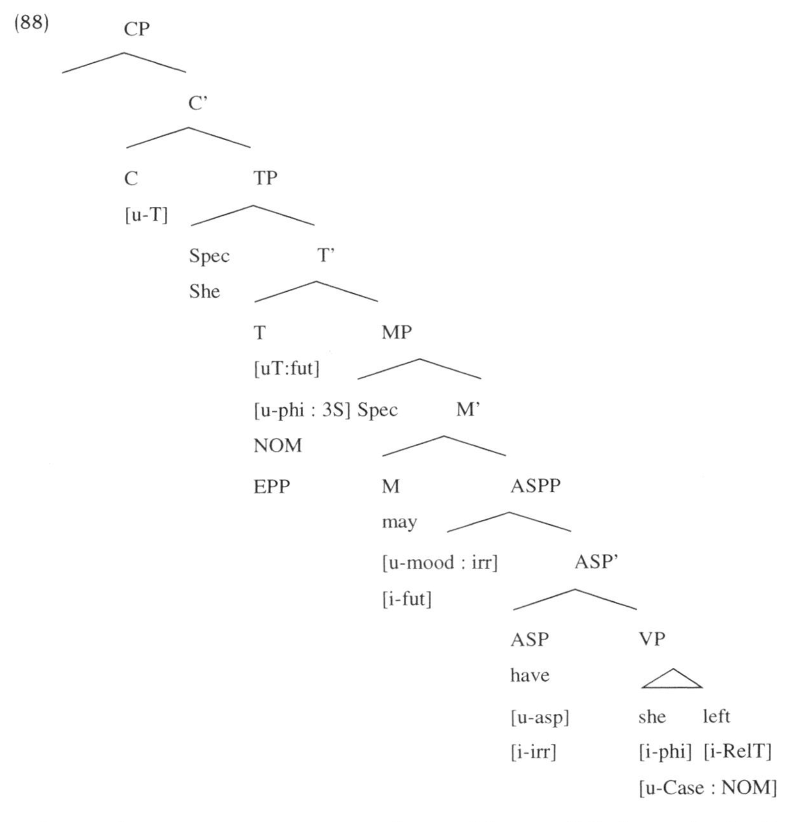

A bare phrase structure approach would start (88) from the bottom and not label where the branches come together. Even though I think a label-less tree is on the right track, I continue to use the labels in (88) for expository purposes. In this tree, I ignore the formation of the VP, but, assuming it has been merged, the merging of ASP triggers the checking of the aspectual auxiliary *have*, for which I use RelT. The next Merge may be the subject *she* in the Spec of ASPP, and then the modal auxiliary *may*, after which checking takes place. The next Merge is T, which values its uninterpretable phi-features with *she*, after which *she* moves to the Spec of TP.

Keywords

TMA, adverbs/adverbials, auxiliaries, grammatical subject and object, agreement, EPP, nominative and accusative case, inherent and structural case, V to T movement, scrambling, object shift

DISCUSSION POINTS

1. What distinguishes an item as lexical or grammatical? Think of adverbs such as *then*, *soon*, etc.
2. Discuss a tree for (1) and justify your choices.
   (1) They may have all left early.
3. Think of adding features to the tree of (1).
4. Jespersen ([1922] 1959: 335) remarks that verbal agreement is a superfluity, and that languages would do well to get rid of it: "By getting rid of this [agreement] superfluity, Danish has got the start of the more archaic of its Aryan sister-tongues." If agreement were lost, what ramifications would that have for the tree in (58)?
5. Provide a derivation for (2).
   (2) Five monkeys were assumed to have been in the parking lot.

SUGGESTIONS FOR FURTHER READING

Pollock (1989) is a classic on the splitting of I into T and AGR; his comparison of French and English verb movement is elaborate.

See Hegarty (2005) for feature-based functional categories. Lyons (1977) is helpful on the semantics of mood and aspect, and Ernst (2002) provides semantic alternatives to adverbial Cartography.

For more insight into the EPP, see Lasnik (2001), Richards and Biberauer (2005), Chomsky (2011), and Medeiros (2011). The latter two have structural approaches to the EPP.

Baker (2008a) keeps Spec-Head agreement in his model, and Moro (1997) and Hazout (2004) provide more theoretical background to expletives.

5 The CP-Layer

After looking at the thematic layer in Chapter 3 and the grammatical layer in Chapter 4, we reach the last and highest layer, the pragmatic one. This is the layer that looks "outside" the clause. If the CP is a main clause, its C indicates the mood (indicative, interrogative, imperative, etc.); finiteness, and the topic and focus are all part of the expanded CP. If the CP is an embedded clause, it links itself to another clause by means of a complementizer, and hence the name Complementizer Phrase. Embedded CPs are typically less expanded and also are subject to much cross-linguistic variation. English is actually rather restricted in its use of the matrix CP for topic and focus.

In Section 5.1, I first provide some background on the history of the CP before going into the expanded CP. Section 5.2 looks at complementizers, and Section 5.3 at mood and CP adverbials that are also candidates for inclusion in this layer. Section 5.4 provides evidence for topic and focus positions as part of the CP-Layer, and Section 5.5 provides some cross-linguistic observations. As in the case of the TP-Layer, the chapter argues that languages differ in the categories that are included in this layer. It also provides an alternative to the strict Cartographic approach, suggesting there is a requirement of pragmatic interpretation at the C-I interface.

5.1 THE EXPANDED CP

In this section, I sketch how the representation of the simple clause changes from S' (pronounced as "S-bar") in the 1970s to CP in the 1990s and then to an expanded or split CP in the late 1990s.

Although recursion is an important topic in early Generative Grammar, clausal embeddings do not appear in the phrase structure rules of e.g. Chomsky (1957: 111). They do in Chomsky (1965: 100, 102), in the form of S' as complements to N and V. The TP and CP are relatively "recent" innovations, results of the extension of the X-bar schema to functional categories in Chomsky (1986b) and Fukui and Speas (1986). This additional structure had been emerging for many years (e.g. in the work of Bresnan 1972, Rosenbaum 1976, Stowell 1981, etc.). The S', as in (1), is replaced by a CP in the mid 1980s, as in (2).

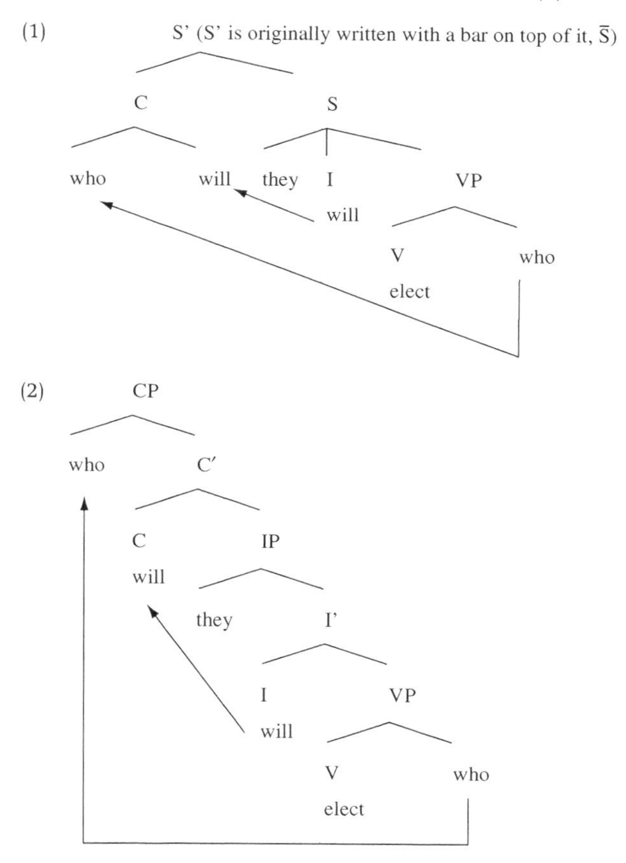

The advantage of (2) is that it can accommodate a head and a specifier. The representation of *wh*-questions in (1) is awkward because of the two constituents in C but receives a natural analysis in (2). Note that I have left the I-position, which was used in the 1980s, rather than change it to the more current T-position.

In addition to an intuitively pleasing account for *wh*-movement in English, (2) works very well for V2 languages, which den Besten (1983) is one of the first to note. He advocates that the finite verb in V2 languages moves to C in main clauses, as in (3), and is therefore in complementary distribution with an overt complementizer, as in (4).

(3) *Gisteren* ***heeft*** *Hans* *dat* *gedaan* Dutch
Yesterday has Hans that done
'Yesterday, Hans did that.'

(4) **a.** . . . **dat** Hans dat heeft gedaan Dutch
that Hans that has done
'that Hans has done that.'

b. *. . . ***dat*** *heeft* *Hans* *dat* *gedaan*
that has Hans that done
'that Hans has done that.'

This shows the parallel between Germanic V2 and auxiliary-fronting in English interrogatives. In what follows below, we will fine-tune where exactly the verb goes.

The tree with a single CP, as in (2), is very familiar by now, and it clarifies certain word orders in languages across the world. It also accounts for the order of [*wh* – that], where the *wh*-element can be a phrase, as in (5) and (6), which occurs in varieties of English, as well as in many other languages.

(5) she doesn't know **where that** she runs, but she runs . . . (www.adriandenning.co.uk/ooberman.html)

(6) We know **when that** she has to be scooped up immediately upon exiting her crate in the morning . . . (www.vegaskelly.com/?cat=4)

A tree for (6) is given in (7).

(7)
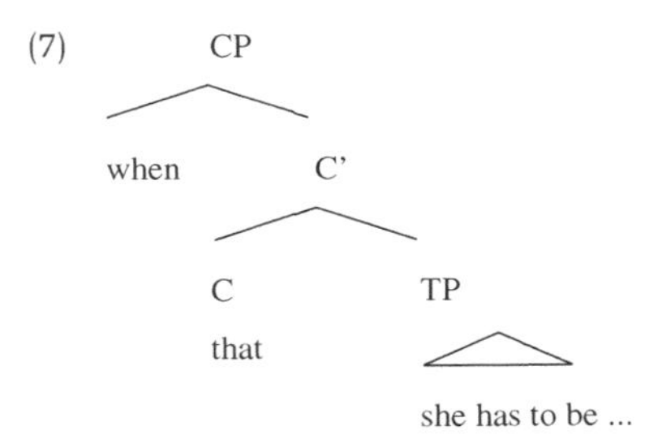

Topics do not trigger V-movement in English, as (8ab) shows, but they do in the other Germanic languages, e.g. (9) from Swedish.

(8) a. **Instructions** we always avoid.
b. ***Instructions** avoid we always.

(9) ***Föröisk fotboll*** *har jag ingen aning om* Swedish
Faroese soccer have I no idea about
'I don't know anything about Faroese soccer.' (adapted from Google)

This difference suggests that the verbs in (8a) and (9) are in different positions and that the CP is more complex than the one presented in (2). We come back to the precise position of topics in Section 5.4.

Let me note that, for instance, Chomsky (1977: 91) distinguishes topicalization, as in (8a), from left dislocation, as in (10).

(10) **Instructions**, we always avoid **them**.

Chomsky argues the former comes about through movement and the latter by base generation. He adds a rule for a topic position, and that tree, i.e. the one in (11), points towards the split in the CP we currently have, namely with an area for topic and one for questions.

(11)
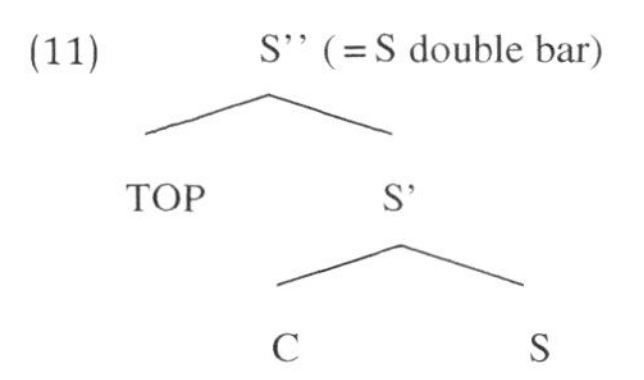

Apart from topics, Focus elements appear in the CP, as in (12) from English. Note that the verb moves to second position. English is not a very CP-heavy language, and many speakers do not like (12ab).

(12) a. **No mountain lion** do I ever need to encounter again!
b. **Only five of the questions** did she answer correctly.

Since languages accommodate topic and focus elements at the same time, as (13) shows, we need to expand the CP. Again, most English speakers are not crazy about these, but there is evidence from other languages, as in (14).

(13) [As for Leonard] [what] should we give (him) on his birthday?

(14) *[János]* *[MARIVAL]* *veszett* *össze* Hungarian
János Marival fell out
'It is stated about John that it was Mary that he fell out with.' (from Olsway 2004, as reported in Kiss 2007)

Topics (and sentence adverbials) are sometimes seen as adjoined to the main clause, e.g. McCloskey (1991), Lasnik and Saito (1992), and Ernst (2002). However, adjunction is not very restrained unless it is done in terms of scope (see the discussion in Chapter 4). Therefore the Cartographic approach thinks of the "adjoined" topicalized and focused elements as occupying separate functional categories. The disadvantage of this approach is that we create a lot of extra structure, but the advantage is that it creates clarity as to the structure of the projection.

Expanding the CP starts in the early 1990s, e.g. Authier (1992) and Hoekstra (1993), and culminates in the influential Cartography of Rizzi (1997). Rizzi's more expanded functional projection to accommodate the complementizer and other material appearing on the left edge of the sentence is given in (15).

(15) ... Force ... (Topic) ... (Focus) ... Fin ... TP (adapted from Rizzi 1997: 288)

In (15), Force looks outside of the clause and indicates the mood, whereas Fin looks inside the clause and marks the tense.

After (15), many alternative formulations follow, e.g. (16), where 'Int' is interrogative and * means the Topic can be repeated. These many alternatives, some others of which we will see in Section 5.4, will prompt me to suggest a layer approach.

(16) Force (Topic*) Int (Topic*) Focus (Topic*) Fin TP ... (adapted from Rizzi 2001: 289)

In short, the expanded CP is very helpful for all the heads and phrases in the **left-periphery**, i.e. the complementizer, interrogatives, topics, and focus. The main problem, as in the rest of this book, is to decide how much of this structure is determined by Universal Grammar and how much derives from third factors. Perhaps the most obvious evidence for the CP and the expanded CP is the complementizer, as we'll go into now.

5.2 THE FEATURES, POSITION, AND TRANSPARENCY OF COMPLEMENTIZERS

In this section, I first look at complementizer types and their features, and include those introducing argument, as well as adverbial clauses. Many of the complementizers indicate the mood of the clause, the finiteness, and various temporal distinctions. We also look at complementizer doubling and the position of complementizers with respect to topics, focused elements, and adverbials. Lastly, we return to the topic of clausal transparency, also known as "deficiency."

Table 5.1 *A few English complementizers*

C	Example of C use	Other use	Example of other use
after	**After** she left, it rained.	P	**after** him
as	**As** I said, this can be done	degree Adv	**as** nice
because	**Because** he left, it is better.	-	
before	**Before** it snowed, it rained.	P	**before** me
for	I expect **for** you to do that.	P	**for** Santa
if	**If** she wins, that will be great.	-	
once	**Once** you listen, you hear a lot.	Adv	I went **once**
since	**Since** he left, it is better.	Adv and P	**since** yesterday
so	He was tired, **so** he went to sleep.	Adv	**so** tired
that	I know **that** the earth is round.	D	**that** book
though	**Though** she left early . . .	Adv	I like it **though**.
when (where)	I wonder **when** it will happen.	Adv	He left **when**?
whether	I wondered **whether** it would happen.	-	
while	She played soccer, **while** he slept.	N	A short **while**

5.2.1 Complementizer features

In Chapter 2, I provided an introduction to complementizers. Here we look at a few in more depth. Table 5.1 lists the most common complementizers in English. The first eleven are in head positions, and the last three are in specifier positions. Almost all of them have another function, in most cases an older function. The reason I list the other function is that the features of these more lexical words were modified historically to become the complementizer.

In Chapter 2, we looked at the features of some, e.g. *after*. We'll now discuss the features of a few of these, namely *that*, *for*, *whether*, and *while*.

In Chapter 2 and later, I argue that the complementizer *that* has uninterpretable mood features and uninterpretable tense features on the C. Using the split CP model, the mood features go into Force and the tense features in the Fin, as in (17a). The former look up to the higher verb, and the latter serve as a probe and require a T that has valued its features, as in (17b). This works well, since the tree is built up bottom to top.

(17)

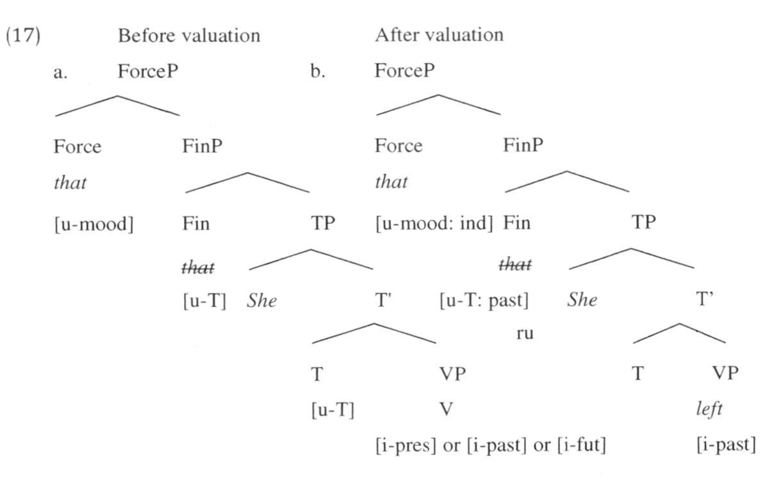

Many people talking about this issue simply use the CP-Layer, rather than the split CP. Occasionally, I will also do this where the expanded CP is less relevant. Pesetsky and Torrego (2001; 2004; 2007) develop the idea that the [u-T] features of C/Fin must be checked by *that*, or a nominative DP (that has valued its [u-T] with T), or an auxiliary. Their reasoning starts with the oft-noted difference between subject and object *wh*-elements. In (18), *who* moves to the Spec of the CP without the need for an auxiliary to be added, whereas, in (19), both *what* and an auxiliary appear in the CP.

(18) **Who** bought the book?

(19) **What did** he buy?

The reason Pesetsky and Torrego give for this difference between subject and object *wh*-movement is that C has [u-T] and [u-*wh*] features, and that moving *who* satisfies both features, but that moving *what* satisfies only the [u-*wh*]. As a result, the auxiliary has to check the [u-T] in (19) but not in (18).

They account for the ***that*-trace effect** in a similar way. As is well known, (20) and (21) are grammatical, but (22) is not, at least in some varieties of English.

(20) Who did John say [~~who~~ will buy the book]?

(21) What did John say [~~what~~ (that) he will buy]?

(22) *Who did John say [~~who~~ that will buy the book]?

Various explanations have been given over the years. Pesetsky and Torrego argue that the complementizer *that* is a T that moves to C, checking [u-T] and [u-*wh*] features of the embedded C. In (20), *who* checks both [u-T] and [u-*wh*]; in (21), *what* checks the [u-*wh*] and *that* the [u-T]. The ungrammaticality of (22) follows from the fact that *who* can check both [u-T] and [u-*wh*] features, rendering *that* superfluous. I'll leave the derivations given by Pesetsky and Torrego in (23) to (25) for you to look at and do not go into this issue further. In the years to come, the *that*-trace data will no doubt be given another analysis, because there are a lot of language-specific assumptions in Pesetsky and Torrego's proposal.

(23) Who$_i$ did John say [CP [*who +wh, uT*]$_i$ [C, *u*T, *u*Wh] [IP *who*$_i$ will$_j$ buy the book]]?

(24) *Who$_i$ did John say [CP [*who +wh, uT*]$_i$ [T that]$_j$+[C, *u*T, *u*Wh] [IP *who*$_i$ will$_j$ buy the book]]?

(25) What*i* did John say [CP what*i* [T that]*j*+[C, *u*T, *u*Wh] [IP Mary will*j* buy what*i*]]?

What I would like to stress in this section are the features of *that* and where they come from. Cross-linguistically, many complementizers derive from demonstratives, and demonstratives are acquired before complementizers. This cannot be a coincidence. The most salient features of a demonstrative are deictic features and phi-features. I have argued elsewhere (van Gelderen 2011) that the T feature of the complementizer *that* derives from the deictic features of the demonstrative, as in (26). In English, the phi-features of C are inherited by T, but in many languages the C checks agreement, as we'll see in Section 5.5, and C has phi-features as well as T features.

(26)	Demonstrative	>	complementizer
	[i-loc]		[u-T]
	[i-phi]		([u-phi])

That can of course also be used in subjunctive clauses, as in (27a). In these – now uncommon in English – *that* selects a TP without tense or agreement features. It may be the case that there is no split CP because (27b) is impossible. A possible tree is given in (28).

(27) a. I suggest (that) you read this book.
b. *I suggest that this book you read (it).

(28)

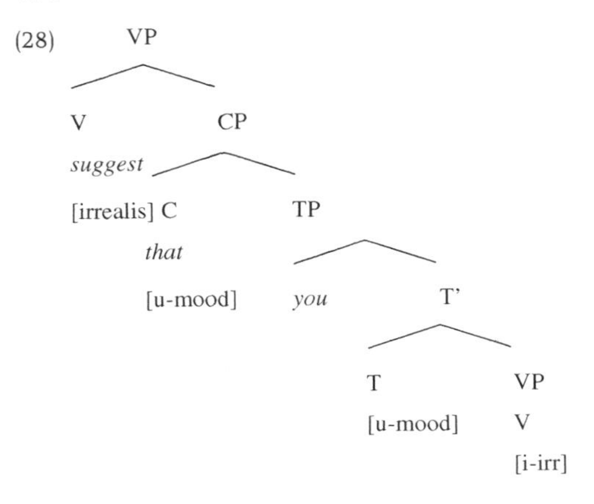

The word *for* is very versatile and has an interesting history, starting out as a spatial preposition, then temporal preposition, then as a purposive non-finite complementizer, a causal finite complementizer, and now a general non-finite complementizer, as in (29), with a tree as in (30).

(29) I would like **for** you to do your homework.

(30)

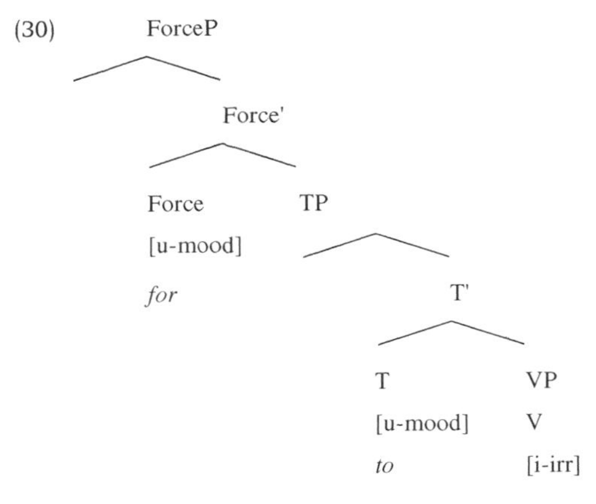

In Chapter 1, I show that children first acquire the preposition and then the complementizer use of *for*. This suggests that they first acquire semantic and interpretable features before figuring out that they can use the same lexical items but with fewer features.

The origin of *whether* is complex. In Old English, it is used as a complementizer, as an adverb with the meaning of 'however,' and as a *yes/no* marker. The first two functions are shown in (31) and the third in (32).

(31) *nast ðu* ***hwæðer*** *beoð þæs rican mannes ban.* ***Hwæðer*** *þæs þearfan*
not.know you whether be of.that rich man's bone or of.that poor
'Don't you know if they are of the rich man's bone or of the poor man's?'
(Aelfric, *Homilies I*, Thorpe 256, Clemoes, p. 324)

(32) ***Hwæðer*** *þara tweȝra dyde þæs fæder willan?*
which the.GEN two did the.GEN father will
'Which of the two did the father's will?' (*Anglo Saxon Gospel, Matthew* xxi. 31)

The origin of *whether*, according to the *OED*, is a comparative pronoun, which is still visible in Old English (32). It keeps the interrogative use, as in (33), until the eighteenth century and the complementizer use till the present.

(33) ***Whether*** *doth doubting consist in embracing the affirmative or negative side of a question?*
'Does doubting consist of embracing the affirmative or negative side of a question?' (Berkeley, *Hylas* I, 173, 10 from 1713)

So, the original features suggest a polar question 'which of the two,' which is then reanalyzed as an interrogative complementizer and *yes/no* marker.

The origin of *while* is a noun, used as an adverbial in Old English (34), and this use continues up to the present time. By late Old English, it is used as in (35), and it acquires its modern shape in early Middle English.

(34) ***Lytle hwile*** *sceolde he his lifes niotan*
little while should he his life enjoy
'For a little while he might enjoy this life.' (Junius, *Genesis* 486)

(35) *Eall hie us þyncað þy leohtran* ***ða hwile þe*** *þa oncras fæste bioð*
All they us seem the lighter the while that the anchors fast are
'They all seem the lighter to us, as long as the anchors are fast.'
(Alfred, *Boethius* x, Sedgefield 23, 14–15)

In present-day English, *while* is used as a temporal adverbial, as in (36), and as a CP adverbial, as in (37), synonymous with *although*. The two uses are sometimes referred to as central and peripheral adverbials, respectively.

(36) He mowed the lawn **while** it rained.

(37) **While** we understand a lot . . .

If we want to phrase the difference in terms of the features, they are durative in (36) and adversative in (37). In Cinque's tree, the central one would be in the VP, and the peripheral use isn't listed in the Universal Hierarchy of Chapter 4.

Having looked at some of the features, we now will look at the exact positions of some of the complementizers, i.e. how we know if they are in Force or in Fin.

5.2.2 Complementizer positions

Often, for reasons of convenience, we assume that the complementizers in 5.2.1 are in C. When we talked about the split CP, we identified the high Force and the lower Fin, and we should therefore look more carefully at the exact position of the Cs. I will show they can be in Force, or in Fin, or move from Force to Fin.

Rizzi maintains that, in Italian, the finite complementizer *che* is in Force, but that the infinitival *di* occupies Fin. The evidence for this comes from topicalization and left dislocation. The finite complementizer *che* precedes the Topic, as in (38), whereas the infinitival one follows *di*, as in (39), both from Rizzi (1997: 288).

(38) *Credo* **che** *il tuo libro, loro lo apprezzerebbero molto*
believe that the your book they it appreciate much
'I believe that they would appreciate your book a lot.'

(39) *Credo, il tuo libro,* **di** *apprezzarlo molto*
believe the your book for appreciate-it much
'I believe I like your book very much.' (Chiara Lage p.c.).

A tree for a sentence such as (38) would look like (40), where I have added features.

(40)
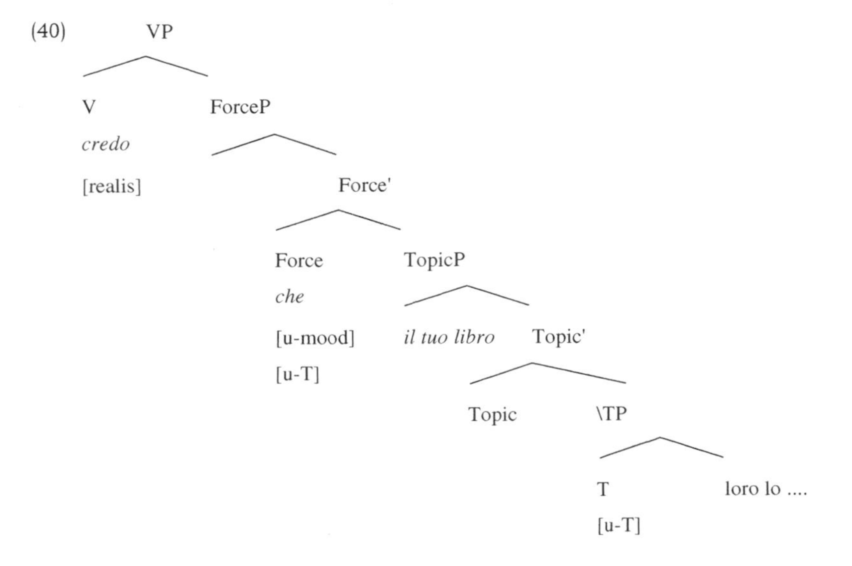

Poletto (2000: 129) says that speakers accept *che* on the other side of the topic as well, which may mean optional movement of *che* from Fin to Force.

The English finite complementizers *that* and *for* behave like *che*, as (41) (taken from McCloskey 1991) and (42) show, and allow topicalization (though not doubling, as indicated in brackets). That shows both Cs are in Force.

(41) She maintains **that** Irish stew she sort of likes (*it).

(42) I am buying spicy ingredients **for** Hungarian stew I sort of like (*it).

Historically, finite *for* has probably always been in a high position. It is first attested as a finite complementizer around 1200, and, since topics and adverbs follow *for*, the latter is in Force in (43) and (44). *That* is now in Force, but in Fin probably until about 1500, as (45) shows, with *when* preceding *that*.

(43) *For hardely I hym heete*
'For indeed I threaten him.' (*York Plays*, 11, 286).

(44) *For frenshippe we haue foune*
'Because friendship we have (indeed) found.' (*York Plays*, 10, 12).

(45) *She loved Arcite so | That [when that he was absent any throwe]*
Anon her thoghte her herte brast a-two
'She loved Arcite so much that when he was absent she thought her heart would break.' (Chaucer, *Anelida and Arcite* 377.92–94).

Further evidence for *for* in ForceP and *that* in FinP between 1200 and 1500 is the frequent occurrence of *for that*, as in (46).

(46) *and forþi we clepeð him fader for þat he us feide here*
and therefore we call him father because that he us fed here
'and we call him father because he fed us here' (*Trinity Homilies* HC-ME1).

Compatibility with an embedded topic is less grammatical for factive verbs, as in (47), and for non-finite *for*, as in (48).

(47) *I regret **that** Irish stew she likes. (from McCloskey)

(48) a. *I expect **for** your homework you to do.
b. *I expect your homework **for** you to do.

In Chapter 2, I suggested a structure of a bare CP for factives in English. That would explain the ungrammaticality of (47). The reason for (48a) to be ungrammatical is that *you* cannot be case-marked by *for*, and for (48b) to be ungrammatical the reason is that *for* is in the ForceP and cannot have a Topic higher than Force.

The position of the other complementizers is less easy to see. I will test the possibilities with *whether* and *while* but leave the others in Table 5.1 for you to check. Many clauses probably do not distinguish Force from Fin, i.e. may not split their CP.

Whether isn't considered a head since it can be augmented by "or not." Using a simple CP, that means it is in the specifier of a CP, and *wh*-movement across it is expectedly blocked, as (49) shows, unlike in the case of *that*, as in (50).

(49) *Who did you wonder **whether** he met ~~who~~?

(50) Who did you think that he met ~~who~~?

Using a split CP, however, *whether* also occupies the specifier position that the *wh*-element moves through and blocks *wh*-movement that way. Since *whether* is quite high, as (51) shows, i.e. above a Topic and *that*, it would have to move to Force as well. This is shown in (52).

(51) I just wondered **whether** that [as a next step] we might look to see why this seems to be the case. (CSE-FACMT97)

(52)

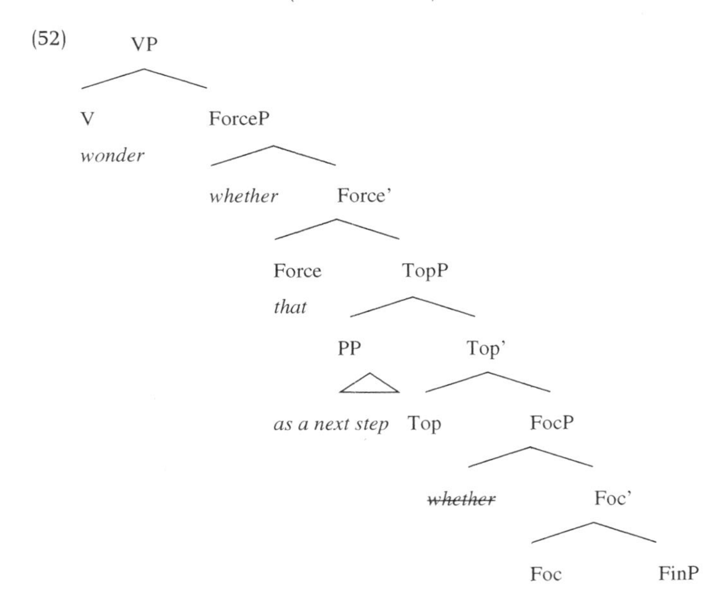

As we saw above, the complementizer *while* has two functions, a durative one and an adversative one. The former is not compatible with embedded topics and may therefore be an unsplit CP; the latter has topics and so might be in the head of the ForceP.

We'll now turn to cases where the C isn't present and the T is therefore "defective." These are clauses that are very transparent.

5.2.3 Transparent clauses and defective T

So far, most of our trees have had a CP and TP. However, in Chapter 2 we looked at clauses that lack a C or an independent tense or subject, and we called them transparent. Here, we'll examine two transparent constructions in English, namely ECM and Raising constructions, in more detail.

Chomsky (2000: 102; 2007: 20) argues that the T **inherits** the phi- and T features from C in main clauses and finite clauses. If T is selected by C, it will have case and phi-features and be a probe; if T is selected by a higher V, it will be defective, although it has EPP features. The phi-features and tense features are inherited by T, making it a probe; if C isn't there, the features cannot be inherited and the T is defective.

Let's look at an ECM construction in (53) with a tree as in (54), where I ignore the exact structure of the VP, the split CP, and the mood features in the embedded clause. In (54a), I show the features before valuation and, in (54b), after valuation, with the derivation going bottom to top.

(53) We believe them to be nice. = ECM

(54a) Before valuation

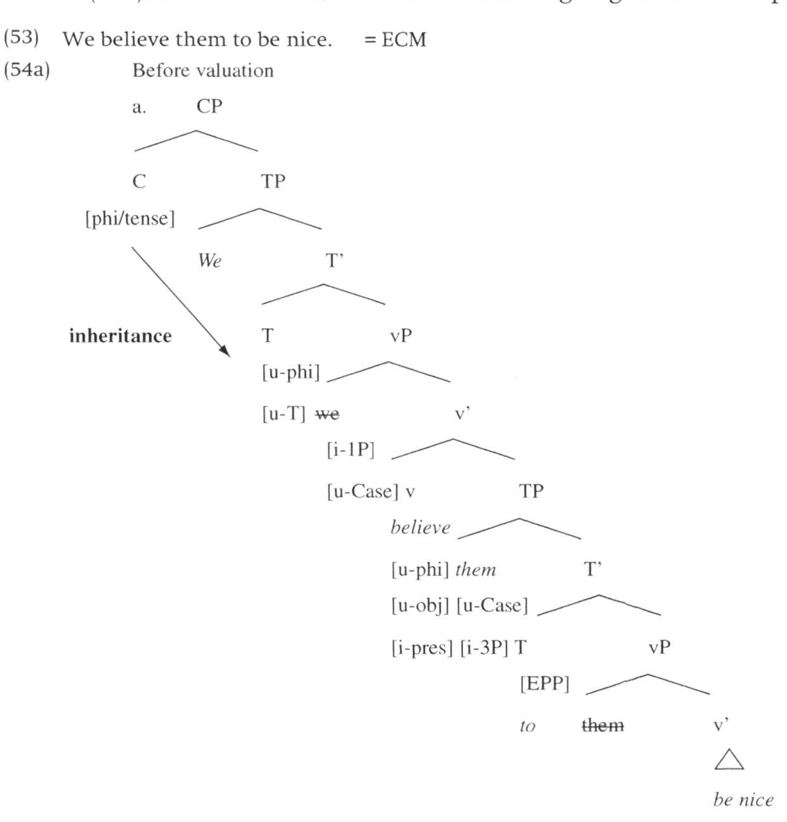

(54b) After valuation

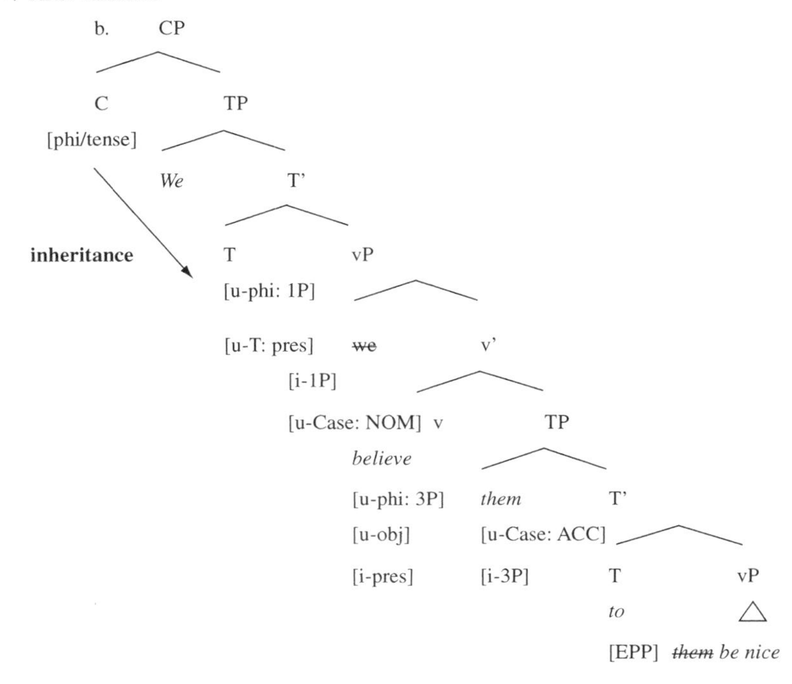

Ignoring the beginning of the derivation, *them* merges with the v at one point and moves to the Spec of the TP because T has EPP features, but this defective T cannot value the case on *them*. Once the higher v is merged, this v is a probe and values its own phi-features, and *them* values its case. The T of the higher clause is not defective, so its subject can be valued in the way familiar from Chapters 1 and 4.

Let's now look at a **Raising** construction, such as the Chomskian (55), with a tree before valuation in (56a) and after in (56b). Again, I simplify the tree for reasons of space and ignore the passive.

(55) Several prizes are likely to be awarded.

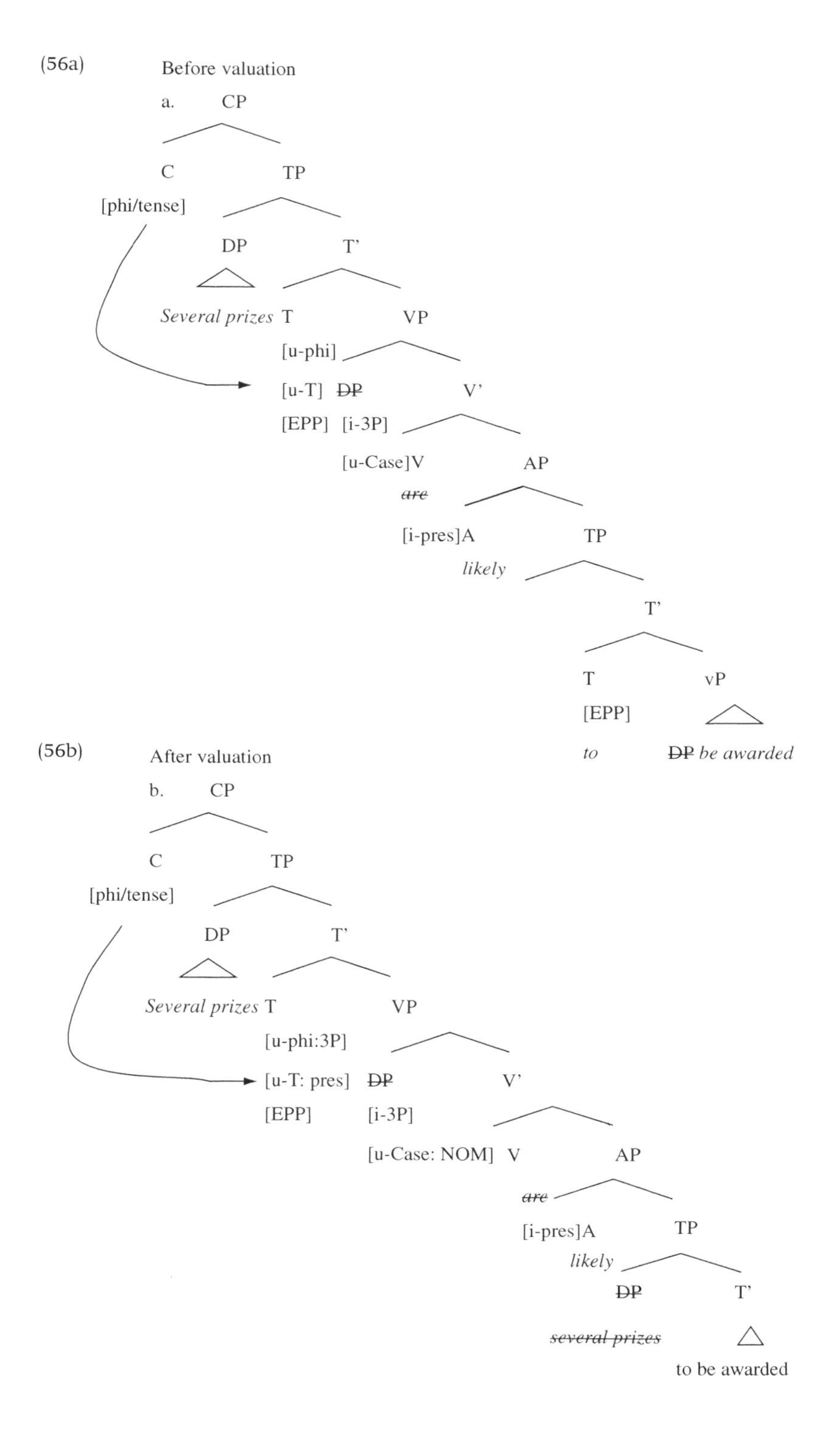

(56a)
Before valuation
a. CP
C
[phi/tense]
TP
DP
Several prizes
T'
T
[u-phi]
[u-T]
[EPP]
VP
DP
[i-3P]
[u-Case]
V'
V
are
AP
[i-pres]
A
likely
TP
T'
T
[EPP]
to
vP
DP be awarded
(56b)
After valuation
b. CP
C
[phi/tense]
TP
DP
Several prizes
T'
T
[u-phi:3P]
[u-T: pres]
[EPP]
VP
DP
[i-3P]
[u-Case: NOM]
V'
V
are
AP
[i-pres]
A
likely
TP
DP
several prizes
T'
to be awarded

In (56), after the DP *several prizes* merges with the vP, and the defective T *to* is merged but only triggers the movement of the DP to the Spec of the lower TP. There are no features checked, so the DP remains unchecked and active. The higher predicate *be likely* happens to be adjectival, i.e. without a full set of features. The T of the main clause therefore ends up being the probe for the DP *several prizes*, mutually valuing the case and phi-features, and finally the DP moves to the Spec of the highest TP for EPP checking.

In this section, we have discussed the most obvious component of the CP-Layer, namely the complementizer. We looked at the features of a few in more detail and also at the exact position. Embedded Cs can be absent and we looked what happened in ECM and Raising cases. The choice of C is connected to mood, although in main clauses the choice of mood is often not visible. We'll turn to mood now.

5.3 MOOD AND CP ADVERBS

The TP-Layer involves auxiliaries, adverbials, and grammatical roles; the CP-Layer includes mood, and focus and topic heads, as well as adverbials. In Section 5.3.1, we'll examine mood and in 5.3.2 CP adverbials.

5.3.1 Mood

In this section, we'll talk about the characteristics of the main moods in English, namely the indicative, interrogative, imperative, and exclamative moods.

The declarative or **indicative** mood is not usually marked overtly, except that the verb has to be finite in those languages that mark finiteness. The indicative is a **realis** mood, as opposed to the irrealis of the other moods. We have seen sentences with the indicative mood, and I have represented it by [i-ind] and [u-T] on C. Using a split CP, the [i-ind] feature is represented on the Force head and the [u-T] is in the Fin head.

The **interrogative** mood is overtly marked in most languages in the left-periphery or by intonation. English is a good example where questions involve the fronting of *wh*-words or auxiliaries or both to the CP. Some *wh*-questions are provided in (57) and (58), where the crossed-out copies tell you the original position of the moved *wh*-elements.

(57) Where will you move ~~where~~?

(58) Where did you say that she went ~~where~~?

The tree for (57) is given in (59). I have put the interrogative features [i-Q] in the ForceP because it is a main clause. Unlike Rizzi, I will argue that the *wh*-element moves only as far as Spec FocusP. The evidence for this movement is that *wh*-questions and Focus have a lot in common. In both cases the verb moves and in both a variable is left, as we'll see in Section 5.4.

(59)

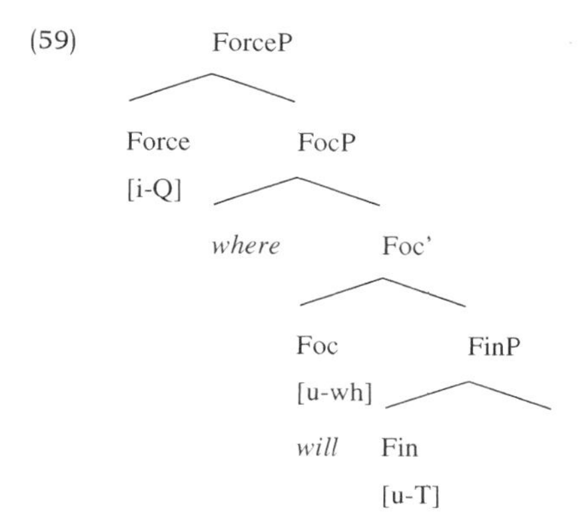

The derivation of (58) is more complex. The *wh*-word originates in the subordinate clause and needs to move using small steps, as we've briefly seen in Chapter 1 when we discussed phases.

The left-periphery marks questions in a number of head-final languages as well, such as Urdu/Hindi (60). The lack of verb movement shows the particle is in the relevant head position.

(60) ***Kya*** *ram* *ja-ta* *hę?* Urdu/Hindi
Q ram go-3SM AUX
'Is Ram going?'

Imperative mood is marked overtly in English and many other languages, and here too it is assumed that the CP-Layer is responsible for the features. There are still many unresolved issues. For instance, we are not sure where the optional subject is and if the imperative *do* moves to the CP.

Imperatives often "hide" their subjects, as in (61), have an optional *do*, as in (62), show restricted use of mood adverbials, as in (63), and are not embeddable, as (64) shows.

(61) a. You, be off!
b. Be off!

(62) (Do) be off!

(63) *Unfortunately be off!

(64) *I want that be off.

Because the imperative verb has so little inflection, Platzack and Rosengren (1998: 193) argue that the structure of an imperative is without a FinP, TP, or MoodP. As Potsdam (1998) shows, however, the subject of an imperative in (65a) seems to be in the same position as the subject of a finite clause in (65b). In these sentences, the quantifier *both* indicates the base position of the subject in Spec vP, although (65b) is pragmatically a little odd.

(65) a. You be **both** waiting for me promptly at three!
b. You are **both** waiting for me. (from Potsdam 1998)

Thus, the question is where is *you* in (61a) and (65a)? Platzack and Rosengren argue that *you* is the subject of the light verb *do*, which is covert in these sentences but overt in (66). When *do* is overt, as in (67), the pause between *you* and the rest of the sentence is longer, indicating it is a topic that is fairly far on the left and not in Spec vP.

(66) **Do** be off!

(67) You, **do** be off!

So, it looks like the *do* is in v and moves to a position in C, as in (68), which I have labeled as Force, but which may be lower, as (69) gives evidence for.

(68)
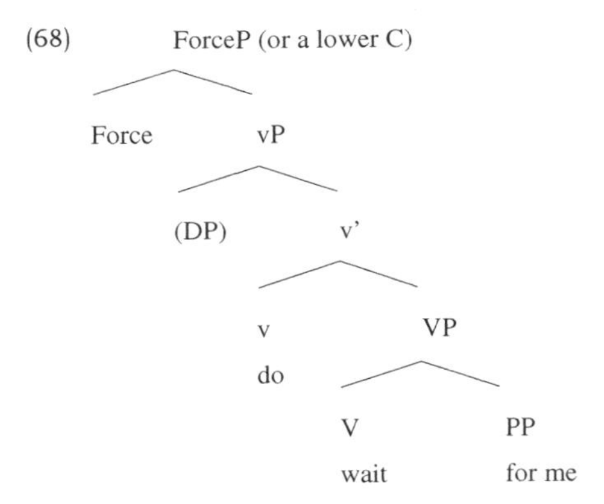

(69) The tie, you give it to Bill. (adapted from Potsdam)

Interestingly, the type of topic is very important in (69). If I add what we'll see is a Hanging Topic (HT), as in (70a), or a non-doubled topic, as in (70b), this results in ungrammaticality for most speakers.

(70) a. *As for the tie, you give it to Bill.
b. *The tie, you give to Bill! (unless it is in a list)

Since (69) is grammatical, the ungrammaticality of (70ab) must have to do with the absence of certain projections, e.g. the FinP may be involved in hosting the topic in (70b).

What happens with the auxiliaries in sentences such as (64) if there is no TP-Layer? There could be an ASPP between ForceP and vP or inside of the vP. Evidence for this position is given in (71), where the *do* is optional. Auxiliaries in imperative constructions work quite differently from those in finite clauses since they are not moving to T to check agreement, as (72) shows.

(71) (Please,) do be waiting for me at three!

(72) *Be not waiting!

As I said, imperatives pose many challenges. We don't know what the function of *do* is, where it moves to, and where the optional subject is situated.

Having looked at the three most common clause types, we'll briefly discuss English **exclamatives**. If we assume that English exclamatives are located higher in the CP-Layer than *wh*-elements are, we derive the fact that they do not trigger verb movement. Interrogatives trigger verb movement to the CP in most languages, as (59) above shows, but other clause types do not always trigger verb movement, as we know from English topics in (73). Exclamatives are similar to topics, as (74) shows.

(73) **Broccoli**, I hate (it)!

(74) **How lovely** that car is!

The reason for the non-inversion is because the verb isn't moving so high, as in (75) for (74).

(75)

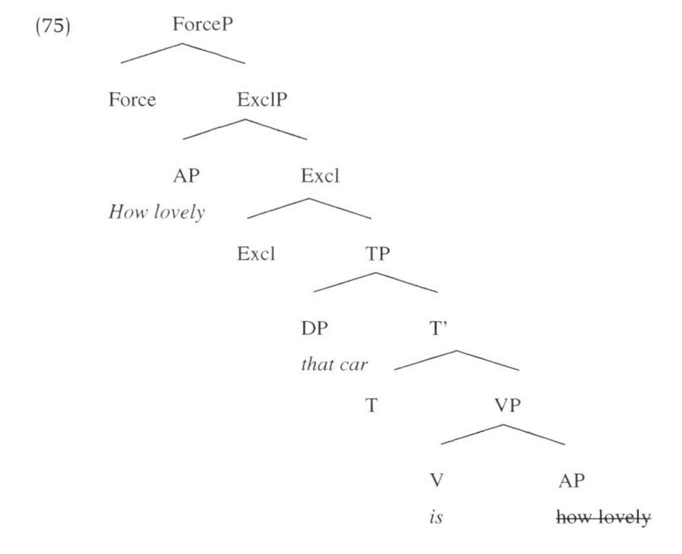

I use an Excl(amative)P(hrase), but it could be a special topic position as well. Unique about exclamatives is that they only prepose phrases with *how* and *what* in English, and in many languages, e.g. Arabic, exclamatives have a special ending.

So, mood in the main clause is represented through features on the Force. Indicatives need not move, but *wh*-questions, topics, and exclamatives do, although not all of them trigger verb movement.

I'll now turn to mood in the embedded clause. Although we've already seen some of this before, here we focus on mood using the split CP. Embedded clauses typically have a more condensed CP-Layer because their mood and tense usually depends on that of the main clause. This means they cannot mark all clause types, e.g. the imperative, as (63) above shows, repeated here as (76a), and the indicative, as in (76b).

(76) a. *I want that be off.
     b. *I want that he goes.

Indicatives are grammatical after certain verbs, but, as I show in Chapter 2, there are major restrictions, and many verbs prefer non-finite and irrealis clauses. How is the mood represented in the embedded split CP?

As mentioned in Chapter 2, we mainly focus our attention on embedded argument clauses in this book. Because adverbials are interesting in their abilities to expand the CP, we'll add a little more on them here. Haegeman (2006) argues there is a difference between central and peripheral adverbial clauses. The former structure the event, as in (77), whereas the latter structure the discourse, as in (78). *While* can have both functions, but some complementizers are specialized for either one of the two functions.

(77) These men worked for Clinton, [**while** he was governor].

(78) [**While** his support for women priests might label him a liberal], this would be a misleading way to represent him. (both adapted from Haegeman 2006: 29)

Central adverbials cannot include markers of mood, since they are more closely connected with the main clause, as (79) shows, whereas peripheral adverbials can, as the *might* in (78) shows.

(79) *These men worked for Clinton, [while he **may** have been governor].

Having discussed the representation of grammatical mood, I turn to adverbs, also responsible for mood but lexicalized.

5.3.2 Adverbials

In addition to sentence type, mood adverbs need to be accommodated in the CP: speech-act adverbs (*frankly, honestly*), evaluatives (*(un)fortunately*), evidential adverbs (*allegedly, evidently*), and modal affixes in certain languages. The full range of the CP adverbs is given in (80). I have added the epistemic TP adverb as well.

(80)

Mood $_{\text{speech act}}$	Mood $_{\text{evaluative}}$	Mood $_{\text{evidential}}$	Mod $_{\text{epistemic}}$
Frankly	fortunately	allegedly	probably

(from Cinque 1999: 107)

Cinque (1999) does not use Rizzi's categories, but, testing the compatibility of these adverbs with topics and focus, one finds (81) and (82). Even though (81) seems slightly odd, it is acceptable to native speakers, with the speech-act adverb *honestly* in ForceP and *those books* in the topic. (82) nevertheless presents a problem in Cinque's approach, since the speech-act adverb *frankly* is higher in the tree than the evaluative, evidential adverb *surprisingly*, but, unexpectedly, the two cannot occur together in (82).

(81) ?Honestly, those books, he should have read (them) before class.

(82) *Frankly, surprisingly, he read those books.

The examples Cinque gives with multiple adverbs are as in (83), but here one of the adverbs is inside the TP.

(83) Honestly, I am unfortunately unable to help you. (Cinque 1999: 33)

This lack of multiple adverbs and the reluctance by native speakers to have a topic and *wh*-element in the same sentence suggest that the English CP is restricted. In the 100 million-word BNC, *frankly* and *fortunately* never co-occur; nor do *fortunately* and *allegedly*, or *allegedly* and *frankly* (even though the adverbs occur frequently by themselves). The same is true in the four-times larger COCA corpus.

This restriction on multiple adverbials is also true for subordinate clauses, but, as (84) and (85) show, adverbials and topics do co-occur.

(84) I actually think **that fortunately** with all the different media that we have, people have the choice of both of those. (COCA 2000 CNN)

(85) McCain: Oh, I think **that frankly** any person who's the vice-presidential nominee, it's his job, his or her job to get along with - with the nominee. (COCA 2000 ABC)

In (84) and (85), the adverbial precedes a topic, which in the case of (85) is actually a left-dislocated topic and therefore quite high, as we'll see in the next section.

To finish this section, I'll give Haumann's (2007: 408) tree which combines the topic and focus positions and the adverbials. She has a slightly different Cartography from Rizzi because of the Prominence Phrase (or PromP) for the preposed adverbials.

(86)
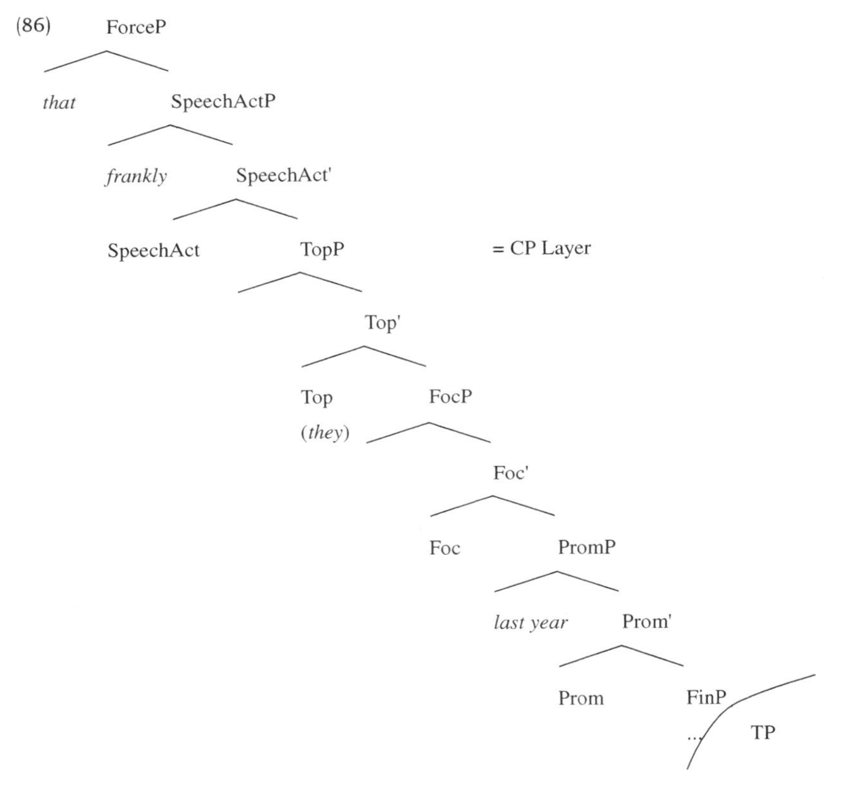

I provide this tree to accustom the reader to a variety of trees but will suggest a tree using special layers later on.

5.4 TOPIC AND FOCUS

In this section, we examine the specific pragmatic roles that DPs can have when they are topic and focus. They can bear these roles in the main clause as well as in the embedded clause, but, cross-linguistically, their occurrence is more restricted in the subordinate clause. Much of the current work gets its inspiration and basis from work in the more functionalist literature, in particular work by Tom Givón (e.g. 1983) and Ellen Prince (e.g. 1981).

First, in Section 5.4.1, I give a very basic definition of topic and focus and then, in Section 5.4.2, I go into some debates on how to label the various topics that have been identified in languages such as Italian, German, and Chinese. Finally, in Section 5.4.3, we discuss differences in topic and focus placement between the main and embedded clause in English.

5.4.1 Topic and focus

The main difference between topic and focus is providing old information and new information, respectively. Old and new information can be put in terms of theme and rheme (Abraham 1995) or backgrounded and foregrounded as well. Topics are definite and they may have a pronoun double or epithet in the main clause, as in (87).

(87) a. **That guy**, I hate **him**.
b. **That guy**, I hate **the idiot**.

A focus is often prosodically marked, indicated by small caps, and provides the answer to a *wh*-question, as in (88).

(88) **Q** **What** did you bring yesterday?
A I brought COOKIES.

The answer in (89) to the same question is pragmatically strange (indicated by a #) because the focus in English is not usually the first element.

(89) **A** #COOKIES I brought.

(Certain) topics in English can be preceded by *as for*, as in (90), and focus by *only*, as in (91). Focus also appears in a cleft, as in (92), or pseudo-cleft, as in (93).

(90) **As for me, I** am rooting for my beloved Red Sox to win the World Series. (www.was.org/Usas/USChapter_files/Newsletter/October04.pdf)

(91) I brought **only cookies**!

(92) It was **cookies** I brought.

(93) What I brought was **cookies**.

Topics are either base generated in the CP-Layer or moved there, but focus-elements are always moved.

Focus movement leaves a **variable**, as in (94a), so that it is interpreted as in (94b) (adapted from Chomsky 1977a: 203–204).

(94) a. Beans, I like.
b. The x such that I like x – is beans.

This variable is similar to that left in *wh-* movement, as in (95), and in quantifier movement, as in (96).

(95) a. What do I like?
b. Which x, x an entity, I like x.

(96) a. Every banker has his reasons.
b. For all x, x a banker, x has his reasons.

The final distinction between topic and focus is of course the word order. As we've already seen, the topic doesn't bring about movement of the verb to the CP-Layer, but the focus, when it is overtly positioned in the CP, does. That makes the focus and the *wh*-element similar.

We'll now look at more complex distinctions that have been made.

5.4.2 Labels for topic and focus

So much for the relatively simple contrast between topic and focus. We can make finer distinctions in topic and also in focus.

Over the last fifteen years, there have been many proposals for finer splits among topics. For instance, you might see the terms contrastive topic, hanging topic, left dislocation, framing or frame-setting topic, aboutness topic, shifting topic, familiar topic, given topic, and continuing topic. These terms appear because languages have different strategies. Rather than go through the many proposals, I will synthesize the work and come up with a set of criteria that we can use. However, when you read a proposal in the literature, the terms may not completely agree with the ones I am using and how I use them.

I will suggest, in the spirit of Benincà and Poletto (2004: 71), that the Cartography should express frame, Theme/given, and then focus elements. This is also based on insights from the functionalist literature. Even though a distinction is made between contrastive topic and contrastive focus, this is practically hard to distinguish, as indicated in (97). Note that the Theme here is different from that in Chapter 3!

(97) Frame/Scene – Theme/Given – Contrastive Topic/Focus

Cinque (1990) and others provide criteria to differentiate between the various topics. These are: (a) whether or not they move to the CP-Layer or are base generated there; (b) if a pronoun or epithet appears in the clause and if the case is different; (c) what phrase the topic is (DP or PP);

Table 5.2 *Two different Topics*

	Frame/Scene	Theme/Given
Position	Above ForceP	below ForceP
pronoun	obligatory	optional
same case	no	yes
DP or PP	only DP	DP or PP
recursion	no	no/yes
Island Sensitive	no	yes

and (d) whether or not the topic is recursive. These differences have led people to suggest different positions in the CP: Some topics are situated above the Force and some below.

Table 5.2 lists some of the differences between two different types of topic. The left-most sets the scene and is sometimes referred to as the Frame or the HT; the one in the "middle" of the CP provides the old information, i.e. what the conversation is about, and is therefore referred to as Given, Theme, Left-dislocated, or topicalized. Some languages may split these areas, but I am trying to generalize. I have also added island-sensitivity, which is relevant to predicting movement.

We'll now look at some examples and then decide which they are. The topic in (98) is a Frame because: (a) there is a pronoun with a nominative case (*I*) that refers back to the topic but is different from the accusative case of the topic; (b) the topic is a DP; and (c) there cannot be more than one of this particular topic, as (99) shows.

(98) **Me**, I've been a night person longer than I can remember. (BNC-GVL 335)

(99) *(As for) **me**, (as for) you, they didn't like us.

These characteristics suggest that the topic is base generated in a relatively high position.

In contrast to (98), (100) lacks a doubled pronoun, so can't be a Frame. It cannot be extracted from an island, as (101) shows, and is therefore moved to the CP-Layer. As a result, it is a given topic or a contrastive topic, depending on the pitch.

(100) **That man**, I hate.

(101) *That man, I heard the rumor that she met.

The Frame vs. Theme is often tested in situations such as (102). In (102), we have a topic that is given in the question, i.e. the Theme *Mary*, and therefore typically does not set the scene, as the pragmatic awkwardness of (102b) shows.

(102) What can you tell me about Mary?
 a. About Mary I know nothing! = Theme
 b. #As for Mary, she loves to eat! = Frame

Hence, having the PP *about Mary* is ok in (102a) because that is typical for a given/Theme topic, but the *as for*, typical for a Frame topic, is not grammatical.

German has the possibility of (103) and (104). In (103), the case of the topic and the doubled pronoun is the same, so the topic is more connected to the clause, whereas the topic in (104) has a different case and is more of a Frame.

(103) ***Den Knud, den*** *mag jeder.* = Theme German
 The.ACC Knud, that.ACC likes everyone
 'Knut, everyone likes (him).'

(104) ***Der Knud, den*** *mag jeder.* = Frame German
 The.NOM Knud, that.ACC likes everyone
 'As for Knut, everyone likes him.' (adapted from Frey)

Frey (2003: 12) gives the following data from German in which *Hans* is first introduced and continues the topic in (105a). The Frame construction in (105b) shifts the topic, which makes no sense in the context and is therefore strange (indicated by #).

(105) *Ich habe etwas in der Zeitung über Hans gelesen* German
 I have something in the newspaper about Hans read
 'I have read something in the paper about Hans.'
 a. *Den Hans, den will der Minister zum Botschafter*
 the.ACC Hans that.ACC wants the minister to ambassador
 ernennen = Theme
 appoint.
 'The minister wants to appoint Hans ambassador.'
 b. *#Der Hans, der Minister will ihn zum Botschafter*
 the.NOM Hans the minister wants him to ambassador
 ernennen = Frame
 appoint.
 'The minister wants to appoint Hans ambassador.'

In Italian, we have (106) and (107). In (106), a PP appears which shows that the phrase moved.

(106) ***A Leo (gli)*** *parlerò domani.* = Theme Italian
 to Leo to.him talk.FUT.1SG tomorrow
 'I will talk to Leo tomorrow.' (Frascarelli 2007: 698)

(107) ***Leo*** ***gli*** *parlerò* *domani* = possible Frame Italian
Leo to.him talk.FUT.1SG tomorrow
'Leo, I will talk to him tomorrow.'

Though the distinction between high and low topic may seem straightforward in the examples given so far, there is a lot of debate, especially about the function of each of the topics. The trouble is that most of these distinctions can only be seen in languages other than English. I'll therefore discuss that more in Section 5.5.

Turning to focus, it has only one position in (15), but here too there have been proposals for more than one type of focus, e.g. Kiss (1998) has identificational and information focus, where **identificational focus** is exhaustive, as in the clefted (108). This focus is also called **contrastive** and is making a selection from a limited set of answers.

(108) **Q** Who did Mary dance with at the party?
A It was BILL she danced with.

Informational focus need not be exhaustive but can be the answer to a regular *wh*-question, and is then often called ordinary focus. Benincà (2001) and Benincà and Poletto (2004) similarly divide the focus into what they refer to as **contrastive** and informational, with the former giving a contrast or correction and the latter the answer to a *wh*-question. (109) shows that the two kinds of focus are in different positions, but only one focus can be expressed per sentence.

(109) [[HT][[Scene Setting] [[LD] [[Contr Focus] [[Inf Focus]]]]]]
(adapted from Benincà and Poletto 2004: 71)

Again try to think of this in terms of high and low focus, and don't get too into all the different terms for topics.

Belletti (2001; 2004) argues that the high contrastive focus is in the CP but that the information focus is just above the vP, as in (110).

(110) **Q** *Chi* *ha* *parlato?* Italian
Who has spoken
'Who spoke?'
A **a.** *Ha* *parlato* *Gianni* = Information Focus
has spoken Gianni
b. #*GIANNI* *ha* *parlato* = Contrastive Focus
Gianni has spoken
'Gianni spoke.' (Belletti 2001: 3)

English uses clefts, as in (108), and intonation to indicate focus. Languages in which both topic and focus can appear sentence-initially display the sequence of (15), e.g. (111) from Bulgarian.

(111) *Filma* *Marija* *li* *gleda* Bulgarian
film Marija FOC watch
'As for the film, is it Marija who is watching it'?

In (111), the topic is *filma* and the focus is *Marija*. The focus is always followed by *li*. This means *li* is in the head and the focused DP is in the Spec of FocusP.

Chomsky (1971; 1976) and Jackendoff (1972) argue for focus movement, as I have shown before. Chomsky argues that focus-elements are like quantifiers and *wh*-elements, and introduce an operator-variable chain at LF. The evidence for the actual movement of the focus is **weak crossover**. In (112a), *he* cannot refer to *John* because *John* is a focus, but in (112b) it can, because *John* isn't a focus. The reason for the difference is that a pronoun may not be bound by an antecedent to its left, and only if *John* moves is the pronoun preceded and hence ill-formed.

(112) a. *The woman he loved betrayed JOHN. (with *he* and *John* coreferential)
b. The woman he loved BETRAyed John.

In (113) and (114), the movement of the *wh*-element and quantifier, respectively, result in having the pronoun *he* be preceded by its antecedent. There are a number of ways to make this precedence condition more principled, but I won't do that here.

(113) *who did his mother see ~~who~~. (if *who* and *his* are coreferential)

(114) *Everyone their mother loves ~~everyone~~. (if *everyone* and *his* are coreferential)

Concluding, the main difference between a topic and focus is that the latter moves and leaves a variable; topics may move or be base generated in the CP-Layer. The placement of both topic and focus elements to the left of the matrix subject and verb is possible in many languages. Multiple topics are also possible, although English generally restricts it to one.

5.4.3 Topic and focus in the main vs. the embedded clause

So far most of our examples of topic and focus have been from the main clause. Notice, however, the differences in word order between main and embedded clauses, as in (115) and (116). The auxiliary *should* is in the "best" position, according to my informants, and I have also put *to* in if it made it better.

(115) a. Leonard what should we give (him) on his retirement?
b. *What Leonard should we give (him) on his retirement?

(116) a. I wonder what to Leonard we should give.
b. *I wonder to Leonard what should we give.

The word order in (115a) is expected if the topic position that *Leonard* occupies is a position higher than the FocP, i.e. the position *what* occupies. Movement by *what* to ForceP leads to ungrammaticality, as (115b) shows. In the embedded clause, the *wh*-element is best in a higher (Force) position, as (116ab) show. See also Radford (2009: 328–329) for more sentences showing the asymmetry between main and subordinate clause as to where the *wh*-element is. In main clauses, it is in a relatively low position, indicating that it is asking about new/focal information; in subordinate clauses, it is in the ForceP.

As for complement clauses to factive verbs, Haegeman (2006: 37) claims that they lack a Force because they presuppose something but do not make an assertion. A Topic and Focus depend on having a Force, and therefore (117) is ungrammatical.

(117) *I regret that **this book** they don't sell.

Above, I suggested that factives have a CP only, and that boils down to the same.

In English, the infinitival complementizer *for* in (118) is similar to Italian *di* in (39) in that a topic cannot follow it. The reason is that *for* needs to be adjacent to the subject for case reasons. However, it is unlike *di* in that a topic cannot precede it either, as the ungrammaticality of (119) shows. This is unexpected if *for* is in Fin.

(118) *I expect for [her homework] her to do.

(119) *I expected [her homework] for her to do.

If we test the position with other non-finite complementizers, the result is the same, i.e. topics cannot precede them, as in (120) and (121), or follow them, as in (122), where the crossed-through words indicate the original position of the topic.

(120) *He swam the channel [to England] in order to get ~~to England~~.

(121) *I wonder [to Alaska] whether to go ~~to Alaska~~.

(122) *I wonder whether [to Timbuctoo] to go ~~to Timbuctoo~~.

Thus, non-finite complementizers in English do not fit readily in the expanded CP. It seems as if only the non-finite complementizer can be present, not a topic or focus. As we'll see in the next section, only finite clauses have multiple complementizers as well. This is indicative of their reduced clausal status.

In connection to the mood in an embedded clause, I mentioned in Sections 5.2.1 and 5.3.1 that central adverbials are the most restricted.

McCloskey (2006) notes an interesting point about complementizers that can have a topic and those that can't. If we look at (123) and (124), we see that temporal/central ones cannot, whereas clauses that modify the entire sentence can.

(123) ***After** [last year] she went to Paris, she became a different person.

(124) **Because** [many times] he doesn't notice a difference, he is seen as insensitive.

The ones that cannot have a fronted topic are the ones that are more integrated into the main clause and cannot express independent mood.

In conclusion to Section 5.4, both main and embedded clauses have a topic and focus in English, though not all native speakers like these. Other languages are more CP-oriented than English is. Not all CPs are split either, e.g. certain adverbial clauses and complements to factives may not be. Focus gives new information, and topic provides old or given information.

5.5 CROSS-LINGUISTIC OBSERVATIONS

Because English topic and focus constructions are rather limited, we have already seen a lot of examples of focus and topic constructions from other languages. In this section, I therefore look cross-linguistically at complementizers, verb movement in V2 languages and *wh*-questions, imperatives, and a little more on topics and focus elements. The major point to watch for is the extent to which the CP can be expanded.

5.5.1 Complementizers

Complementizers of some kind or other are found in all languages. Here I will look at multiple complementizers and at Cs that check features. The complementizer is in Force or Fin, and, cross-linguistically, they are variable in the CP: some languages have high complementizers and others low.

Roussou (2000) presents evidence that Modern Greek has many complementizers, each with a unique function. In addition to the three complementizers *oti*, *pu*, and *an*, there are three particles that occur in the low C, the future *θa*, the subjunctive *na*, and the hortative *as*, with the latter two optionally moving to higher positions. The combinations of these words and the use of topic and focus elements reveal three complementizer positions, according to Roussou.

Take a sentence such as (125). Since *oti* can either precede or follow the topic *ta mila* and *tha* is in the lowest C, there may be three Cs. In (126), *na* can only follow the topic and is in the "middle" position.

(125)	*nomizo*	(***oti***)	*ta mila*	(***oti***)	*ðen*	**tha**	*ta*	*fai*	*o*	*petros*	Greek
	think.1S	that	the apples	(that)	not	FUT	them	eat-3S	the	Peter	

'I think that Peter won't eat the apples.' (Roussou 2000: 76)

(126)	*elpizo*	*ta mila*	***na***	*min*	*ta*	*fai*	*o*	*petros*	Greek
	hope.1S	the apples	PART	not	them	eat	the	Peter	

'I hope that Peter won't eat the apples.'

So, in addition to Force and Fin, there is a complementizer position between the topic and the focus.

Other languages similarly have more options than English. For instance, Dutch has several overt complementizers as well, as (127) shows. However, it is not totally clear to me if (127) has a split CP and if *of dat* are two or one.

(127)	*Ik*	*weet*	*niet*	***wie***	***of***	***dat***	*ze*	*gaan*	*verkiezen*
	I	know	not	who	if	that	they	will	elect

'I don't know who they'll elect.'

I'll now turn to inflected Cs. As mentioned above, T inherits features from C, and in some languages these features are visible. Varieties of Dutch, for instance, have Cs with agreement features, as (128) shows, and so does Standard Arabic, as (130) and (131) show.

(128)	*Ik*	*wist niet*	*dat-**de***	*gij dat*	*ging*	*doen!*	(West) Brabant Dutch
	I	knew not	that-2P	you that	go	do	

'I didn't know you were going to do that!'

Standard Arabic has three complementizers *ʔanna*, *ʔinna*, and *ʔan*, and it is most likely that the former two are checking case and agreement. The least-marked complementizer *ʔan* has a subjunctive verb following it, whereas the former two do not allow a verb to follow them. A typical example of a complementizer is (129), where the DP that follows *ʔanna* has accusative case.

(129)	*yabduu*	***ʔanna***	*l-awlaad-a*	*saafar-uu*	Arabic
	seem	that	the-boys-ACC	depart-3P	

'It seems that the boys departed.' (Mohammad 1989: 121)

ʔanna is followed by a finite clausal complement, whereas *ʔinna* occurs as a root clause or as complement of the verb *qaala* 'say.' Both show agreement with the subject.

(130) *zaʕamtu* ʔanna-**hu** *kataba* *r-risaalat-a* Arabic
claimed that-3MS wrote the-letter-ACC
'I claimed that he wrote the letter.'

(131) ʔinna-**haa** *qaraʔ-at* *al-banaat-u* *r-risaalat-a* Arabic
that-3FS read-PST.3FS the-girls-NOM the-letter-ACC
'Indeed, the girls have read the letter.' (Mohammed Al-Rashed, p.c.)

In (131), *-haa* is an inflection that always marks for singular number, even though its gender features are determined by the subject NP, which is, in this instance, plural. This is reminiscent of the VS and SV asymmetry that we discussed before, namely if there is no Spec-Head checking, number is not checked. It is also possible for *ʔinna* to be inflected for masculine singular instead of feminine singular, i.e. *ʔinna-hu* rather than *ʔinna-haa*. This suggests person features in the C, as indicated in (132).

(132) CP
C
[u-phi]

5.5.2 V to C movement and *wh*-movement

We have mentioned V2 languages frequently but not yet given an analysis of the T to C movement that is involved. The preposed elements in these constructions are not topicalized, and the verb moves to a fairly low CP head, namely FinP, as in (133) for the Swedish sentence, meaning 'He bought the book.'

(133)

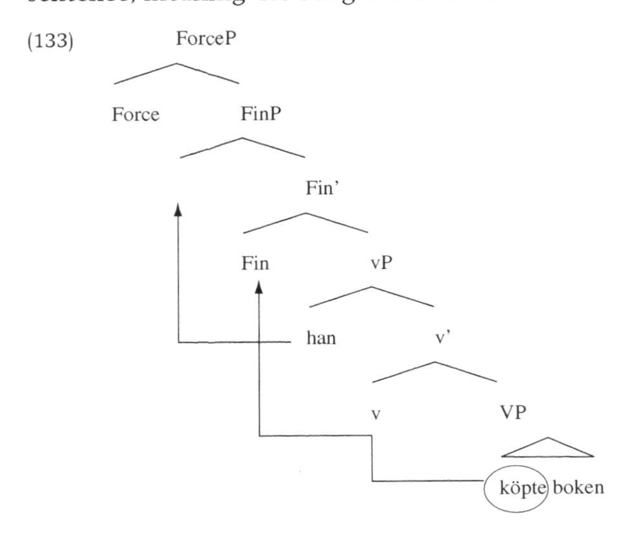

As I mentioned, it has been widely agreed upon that V2 involves movement to CP. After the split of the CP into Force and Fin, there is a tacit agreement that the verb is in the Fin, but there isn't much overt evidence for this. The fronted phrase is not in a Focus or Topic phrase since there are no pragmatic restrictions on this phrase, but it isn't clear why it couldn't move to ForceP.

Turning to *wh*-questions, these differ a lot whether or not the *wh*-element has to move or not. This used to be expressed as a parameter (cf. Chapter 1). I will not go into an explanation of the differences but just describe a few of them.

There are many languages that move one *wh*-element, as in English (134). English has the option to leave the *wh*-element **in situ**, as in the echo-question in (135).

(134) Where did you go?

(135) You went WHERE?

Echo-questions do not really ask for new information, however.

There are languages that can only leave the *wh*-element in situ and where the *wh*-element does ask for new information. Chinese is such an example, as (136) shows.

(136) *Zhangsan yiwei Lisi mai le* ***shinwe****?* Chinese
Zhangsan thinks Lisi bought PF what?
'What does Zhangsan think Lisi bought?'

As in English, this sentence cannot mean (137), although that is possible in both languages with the verb *wonder*, as (138) and (139) show. This means the verb *wonder* in both languages has a *wh*-feature. Even though the *wh*-element in Chinese doesn't have to move to C, it shows the same restrictions.

(137) Zhangsan thinks what Lisi bought.

(138) Zhangsan wonders what Lisi bought.

(139) *Zhangsan xiang-zhidao Lisi mai le* ***shenme*** Chinese
Zhangsan wonders Lisi bought PF what
'Zhangsan wonders what Lisi bought.' Huang (1982)

Thus, matrix clauses can licence [i-Q] freely, but, in embedded clauses, the C has to be licensed by a higher verb.

At the other extreme, there are languages that move all their *wh*-elements to the CP-Layer. An example is Macedonian, in (140).

(140) ***Koj shto na kogo*** *e dal?* Macedonian
who what to whom is given
'Who gave what to whom?' (Daniela Kostadinovska p.c.)

Between these two extremes, there are lots of variants. Hindi/Urdu and German have a complex system where the scope has to be marked, and Malay has partial movement. See the volume edited by Lutz, Müller, and von Stechow (2000) for more.

5.3 Imperatives and the expansion of layers

Above, we argued that imperatives lack some TP structure in English. Cross-linguistically, they are similarly reduced. Russian, however, marks aspect, i.e. it has perfective and imperfective imperatives, as in (141), but this is to be expected if ASP is possible in imperatives, and even English has (142).

(141) *pishi* Russian
write.IMPF.IMP.2S
'Write!'

(142) Keep writing!

I haven't found a tensed imperative.

In some languages, imperatives have special inflection, as in (143), and are also inflected for the subject.

(143) *iga*-***gi-t*** Greenlandic
cook-IMP-2
'Cook (something).' (Payne 1997: 303)

Without going into an analysis for that, it seems likely that this mood and the agreement are marked in the CP. This is yet another sign of how different the CP can be.

5.5.4 Topics

Above we have discussed several types of topic. Frascarelli and Hinterhölzel (2007: 88) argue that at least three types of topic have to be distinguished in Italian: aboutness (or shifting), contrastive, and familiar topics, and they occur in the following hierarchy.

(144) Aboutness-Shift Topic (ST) > Contrastive Topic (CT) > Familiar Topic (FT)
(Frascarelli and Hinterhölzel 2007: 89)

The aboutness topic is a newly introduced or newly changed-to topic; the contrastive topic "induces alternatives which have no impact on the focus value"; and the familiar topic is typically non-stressed and pronominal. Evidence for the ordering is provided for Italian in (145) and (146), where Frascarelli and Hinterhölzel use pitch levels to make a distinction between the various topics. I haven't shown the pitch levels, but let's assume they are correct in their labels.

(145) ***Io***, ***inglese*** *non* *l'avevo* *mai* *fatto* Italian = ST > FT
I English not it have never done
'I never studied English before.'

(146) ***Io***, ***una cosa che ho trovato positiva***, *è stata la comprensione*
I, one thing that have found positive, is been the comprehension
Italian = ST >CT
'As for me, one thing I considered positive was the comprehension part.'
(Frascarelli and Hinterhölzel 2007: 96)

In addition to these, Italian has a frame topic as well.

Frame-setting topics are very frequent in East Asian languages, as in (147) to (149), although they even occur in English (150). Most of these occur in very high topic positions, but, since the framing is very vague, they cannot be repeated by means of pronouns.

(147)

Pihengi-nin	*747-ka*	*khi-ta*	Korean
Airplane-TOP	747-SBJ	big-STAT	

'As for airplanes, the 747 is big.' (Li and Thompson 1976: 468)

(148)

Hua,	*wo*	*zui*	*bu*	*xihuan*	*meiguihua*	Chinese
flowers	I	most	not	like	roses	

'Among flowers, I dislike roses very much.' (Badan and del Gobbo 2011: 78)

(149)

Zhangsan,	*wo*	*gei*	***na***	***ge***	***shazi***	*ji*	*le*	*yi*	*feng*	*xin*	Chinese
Zhangsan,	I	to	that	CL	imbecile	send	PF	one	CL	letter	

'Zhangsan, I sent a letter to that imbecile!' (Badan and del Gobbo 2011: 74)

(150) **Speaking of hiking**, it is great living in Apache Junction.

With Frames too, we have arguments that there are several different types. Badan and del Gobbo (2011) distinguish the HTs in (147) from the Aboutness Topic in (148). According to Badan and del Gobbo, the main reason to distinguish Aboutness from HT is that there is usually only one HT and Aboutness topics can recur. I won't give further evidence for their claim but remind the reader of the three basic topics in (97), repeated here as (151a) with the alternative below it in (115b), as suggested in e.g. Frascarelli and Hinterhölzel and Badan and del Gobbo.

(151)

a.	Frame	Theme	Contrast
b.	HT > ForceP >	AboutnessShiftP >	ContrP > FocP > FamP > FinP

What our discussion has shown is that languages differ a lot as to where the topic is located and as to which types of topic occur. Frames or HTs are generally high in the CP-Layer and can have *as for* in English; the lower ones are sometimes referred to as Left Dislocated Topics (LDTs); and then we also have the topics that move to the CP, and they may be the lowest.

5.6 CONCLUSION

In this chapter, we have looked at the CP-Layer where clausal mood (indicative, subjunctive, etc.) and pragmatic roles (topic and focus) are marked. Here, I'll come back to the issue that's central to the book, namely how a bottom-to-top derivation is compatible with top-to-bottom approaches. In Chapter 4, I suggested that having scope determine where elements are was preferable to having an innate Cartography. Can we come up with something like that for topic and focus as well?

Frascarelli (2007) and Sigurðsson (2011) are concerned with what licenses pro-drop and attempt to find a third-factor principle licensing empty subjects and objects. The third factor they argue for is an Edge-Principle. Without going into their account of pro-drop, we could think that there is a principle that requires each DP to be connected to a role in the CP-Layer. This would be a requirement of pragmatic interpretation at the C-I interface. As a sentence is interpreted at the interface, the copies of earlier positions are still visible, so that semantic and grammatical roles can be identified, as well as the pragmatic ones. While I think that the Cartographic approach outlined in this chapter gives a great description of the CP-Layer, we need to think along the lines of Frascarelli and Sigurðsson to explain why the order is the way it is.

I will end with a tree for a *wh*-question with a topic. The interpretable features in the Force are interpreted at C-I, the preposed PP as topic, and the *wh*-element as focus. I have concentrated on the top part of the tree.

(153)

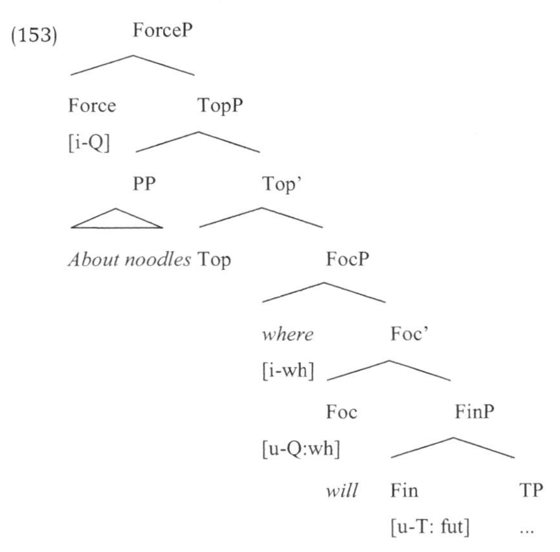

Keywords

CP, split CP, Force, Fin, left-periphery, declarative, interrogative, imperative, exclamative, verb-second (V2), Topic, HT, Frame/Scene, Theme/Given, Focus, double C, sentence adverbials, Raising, ECM

DISCUSSION POINTS

1. What happens to subject *wh*-questions? Does the *wh*-element move? What is the evidence?

    (1) Who left?

2. Draw a tree for (2) and justify your choices. Add features.

    (2) I asked if they could clean up.

3. In the following newspaper article, find where possible the complementizers, *wh*-movement, T-to-C movement, topic and focus elements, ECM and Raising verbs, and CP-adverbs.

    (3) Gene scans for everyone? Not so fast. New research suggests that for the average person, decoding your own DNA may not turn out to be a really useful crystal ball for future health. Today, scientists map entire genomes mostly for research, as they study which genetic mutations play a role in different diseases. Or they use it to try to diagnose mystery illnesses that plague families. It's different from getting a genetic test to see if you carry, say, a particular cancer-causing gene. But as genome mapping gets faster and cheaper, scientists and consumers have wondered about possible broader use: Would finding all the glitches hidden in your DNA predict which diseases you'll face decades later? Under best-case scenarios, most people would be told they had a somewhat increased risk of at least one disease, said Dr. Bert Vogelstein, a Hopkins cancer geneticist and the study's senior author. (Adopted from *East Valley Tribune*, April 2, 2012)

4. Some languages can have tensed imperatives (van der Wurff 2007: 21, 47–48). How would you analyze these?

    (4) *Had it dat maar gedaan!* Dutch
    Had I that but done
    'I wish I'd done that.'

5. In (Lebanese) Arabic, topicalized elements are always doubled, as in (5). What else would you ask native speakers to figure out which kind of topic this is?

    (5) ***Naadya*** *ßeef-**a*** *Kariim mbeeri* Lebanese Arabic
    Nadia saw.3SG.M-her Karim yesterday
    'Nadia, Karim saw her yesterday.' (from Aoun and Benmamoun 1998)

6. We discussed the difference between Raising and ECM verbs. The verbs in (6) are known as **control verbs** because their complements can have empty subjects controlled by the higher subject.

   (6) *try*, *like*, *start*, *want*, and *expect*.
   Provide some sentences that show this control. How would you analyze *tend*, *appear*, and *manage*?

7. We have discussed that *while* can introduce a peripheral or central adverbial. Use the COCA (http://corpus.byu.edu/coca/) to look at twenty instances (e.g. the first twenty) of *while* to see which kind is more frequent. You may want to play around with the part-of-speech feature of the interface. For instance, if I just wanted complementizer *that*, I'd use (7).

   (7) that.[cs*]

SUGGESTIONS FOR FURTHER READING

Bybee (1985) on mood, Zanuttini & Portner (2000) on clause types, and Enç (1987) on the anchoring of the tense.

Van der Wurff (2007) adds more to the theoretical background regarding imperatives; Isac (2012) suggests a finer-grained division of the imperative cross-linguistically.

Read Cinque (1990) on various islands and Gallego (2010) on the *that*-trace effect.

Biskup (2011) and Shu (2011) are insightful on CP adverbials and Frascarelli (2007) on how topics license pro-drop.

Earlier ideas on topics can be found in Prince (1981), Givón (1983), and Abraham & de Meij (1986).

6 Connecting the layers

The three layers form neat independent chunks in the sentence, with the vP-Layer being the most similar cross-linguistically. These three layers, however, also "communicate" with each other, and that's how the CP-TP-VP order arises. We'll now look at the ordering of the three layers and the links between them.

As for mood, we have seen mood in the CP in the form of indicative or subjunctive or imperative and in the TP in the form of evaluative/epistemic mood. An indicative mood is not compatible with an epistemic modal, but a subjunctive mood is. There are thus links between the various moods in the three layers, as well as between the mood in the C and the tense in the T, in that only an indicative mood is compatible with past or present tense. As for aspect, there is a high aspect (grammatical aspect in the TP-layer) and low aspect (lexical aspect in the VP-Layer), and they communicate as well, in that states do not typically occur as progressives. Focus involves the vP/VP and CP, and negation may involve all layers, and some languages have high negation and others relatively low negation.

In Section 6.1, we'll look at how the ordering of the three layers comes about. In Section 6.2, we discuss the link between the tense and mood in the CP and TP- and vP-Layers. In Section 6.3, we discuss the links between aspect and the verb, and Section 6.4 examines negation. Section 6.5 shows how topic and focus are distributed throughout the clause, and Section 6.6 is a conclusion.

6.1 KEEPING THE CP, TP, AND VP TOGETHER

In top-to-bottom derivations, a C selects a TP and a T selects the VP; in bottom-to-top derivations, the C and T probes look for goals by way of their features, so these are very similar processes. I'll briefly review some of the changes in how we've connected the layers in Generative Grammar.

Using phrase structure rules, as in Chomsky (1965, but even up to 1981), the CP selects the T and the VP, as we have seen in earlier chapters. An early 1980s-style rule would be the one in (1).

(1) CP → NP T VP

After extending X'-structure to all categories, which happens around 1986, the tree is as in (2) – by now very familiar.

(2)

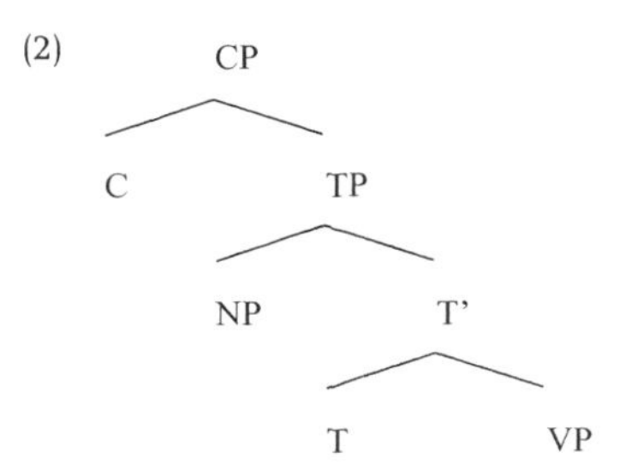

In this model, the C selects a TP and so on. As the tree gets more complicated in the late 1980s and 1990s, the selection becomes more specific. Cartographic structures, such as the ones we've seen in Chapters 4 and 5, make the selection even more complex.

Bare phrase structure derivations, i.e. those going from bottom-to-top, go as follows. The selection from the lexicon for an English finite clause includes a C to mark mood, a T for tense, a v/V, and some DP arguments. As I have quoted above, Chomsky (2001: 12) says "[a]ssume that substantive categories are selected by functional categories. V by a light verb, T by C." The verb would first merge with its arguments, possibly because of uninterpretable features, as suggested in the conclusion to Chapter 3. The VP would then merge with T and C because of the uninterpretable features of C and T, namely the [u-T] of the CP-Layer and the inherited [u-phi] of the TP-Layer. If these features didn't get valued, the clause would not be interpretable at the C-I level.

Having briefly sketched that the selection of the VP and TP by T and C, respectively, is not automatic but needs to be negotiated through features, I now turn to the connection between C and T and V where mood is concerned.

6.2 MOOD THROUGHOUT THE CLAUSE

Different mood domains have been recognized in the literature, namely speech act, propositional, and event-modality. These correspond to the three layers discussed in this book. The first domain concerns what we have put in the ForceP, for instance, imperative and interrogative mood; the second has to do with the speaker's attitude towards the proposition and has been put in the TP; and the third has to do with conditions imposed on the Agent of the main event and belongs to the VP. The three mood domains appear in work by Bybee and Fleischman (1995), Palmer (2001), and many others. We have also seen it in Chapters 4 and 5. Thus, mood is present in all layers, although more of it is centered in the CP and higher TP. In this section, we will first briefly discuss the connection between the mood in the CP and TP and then the relation between mood in the VP and TP by looking at the well-known distinction between deontic and epistemic modals.

Typologically, there is a connection between realis mood and (present and past) tense on the one hand and irrealis and negative, future, interrogative on the other. I have represented this by having a C with interpretable mood but uninterpretable tense features that need valuation by features from T or M. The link is obvious from the complementizers *that* and *for* in English, the one reserved for indicative-tensed CP and the other for irrealis non-tensed ones.

Chomsky argues for a C-T link for tense inheritance (as we've seen in Chapter 5, Section 5.2.3) but, since he only talks about declarative clauses, we'd have to add mood-inheritance for clauses with a modal. Some proposals do not consider C and T as separate but as one phase head. Combining the C and T was especially popular in the literature on Germanic in the 1980s (e.g. Platzack 1983), although this was done more because there was little evidence for an actual T position.

Turning to the VP and TP connection, English has a set of modals that is homophonous between deontic and epistemic uses, as we've seen in Chapter 4, with the deontic use more V-like and the epistemic more T-like. For instance, *may*, *must*, and *can* can be used with a root or deontic meaning, as in (3), as well as with an epistemic meaning, as in (4).

(3) You may/must/can/ go. = deontic

(4) It may/must/can/ be raining there now. = epistemic

Because the deontic meaning is more verbal, it is often called situational. Van der Auwera and Plungian (1998) suggest a four-way distinction which I have simplified as Table 6.1.

Table 6.1 *Types of modals*

	possibility	**necessity**
epistemic	can, may	must
situational	can, may	must

Not all languages display the same homophony as English. There may be homophony across horizontal lines instead, and some languages use different forms for all four.

The question that is relevant to this section is how the various modals "communicate" with each other. The epistemic ones are higher, connected to the TP-Layer, whereas the situational ones are lower, connected to the VP-Layer. In Modern (standard) English, however, we cannot have both, as (5) shows, although this is possible in varieties of English and earlier stages, as (6) shows.

(5) *He must can do it

(6) *ye* ***schall can*** *lyve lyke a jentylman*
you shall can live like a gentleman
'You'll be able to live like a gentleman.' (1475 *Paston Letters*, #292)

If both are not possible, the reason may be that the deontic modal has to move to a higher position. So although the deontic is verbal, it also bears irrealis mood.

(7)

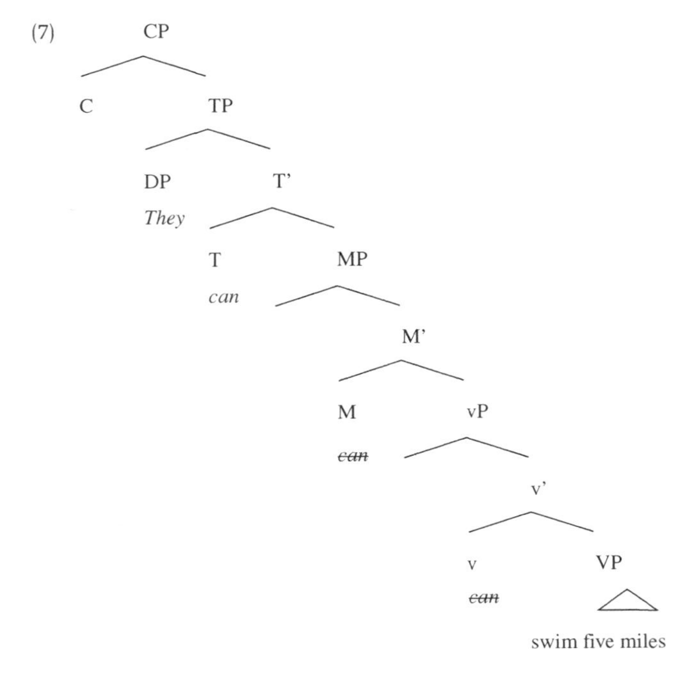

To be honest, I am not sure that (7) is the best solution. We'd have to look at languages with double modals and inflected modals to think about the incompatibility of Modern (standard) English more. I leave that for future research.

Tense and mood are mainly represented in the higher regions of the clause. If we think of deontic verbs as marking mood in a lexical way, it is also present in the VP. We'll now turn to aspect, which is located in the lower part of the TP and in the VP.

6.3 ASP, v, AND V

Aspect is marked in the lower layers of the clause. In the TP, auxiliaries (*have* and *be*) and adverbs (*often*, *again*, etc.) are used; in the VP-shell, adverbials (mostly PPs) are, and semi-lexical verbs (*start*, *begin*, and *finish*). In Chapter 4, the Functional Hierarchy of (16) puts habitual, repetitive, frequentative, celerative, terminative, continuative, perfect, retrospective, proximative, and durative aspect in the TP, whereas it puts generic, prospective, completive, celerative, repetitive, frequentative, and completive in the VP-Layer. Some of the TP aspect markers (e.g. frequentative and celerative) are repeated in the VP-Layer.

All of these auxiliaries and adverbs constitute outer aspect or external aspect or **grammatical aspect**. Cinque doesn't connect the various aspects. I have suggested that there are layers of aspect, as in (8), repeated from (23) in Chapter 4.

(8)

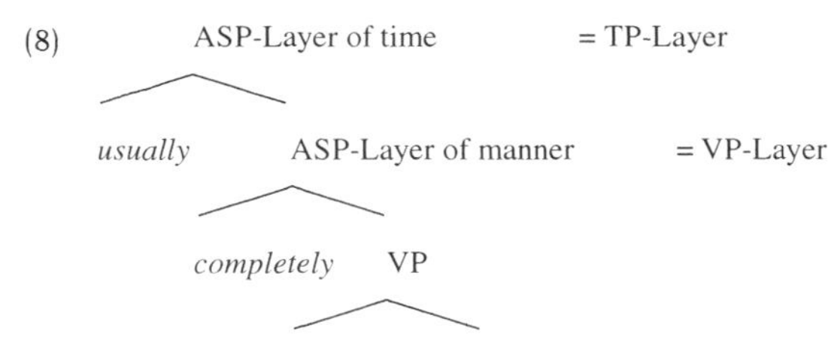

Some of the adverbs and auxiliaries can occur together, as we've seen in Chapter 4. The connection between time aspect and manner aspect is relatively free.

There is a clear connection between the external or grammatical aspect and the internal aspect or **Aktionsart** of the verb and the event structure in the vP-Layer. In Chapter 3, we discussed Vendler and Verkuyl in this connection, and I will just review that discussion briefly. If we think of the Aktionsart features of the verb as +/– durative and +/– telic, this will have an impact on the compatibility with the higher layers. Thus, if a verb is non-durative, it will not be compatible with a progressive, i.e. durative, external aspect, and if it is atelic, it can't combine with an *in an hour* adverbial. In Chapter 3, I represented this connection as in (9).

(9)

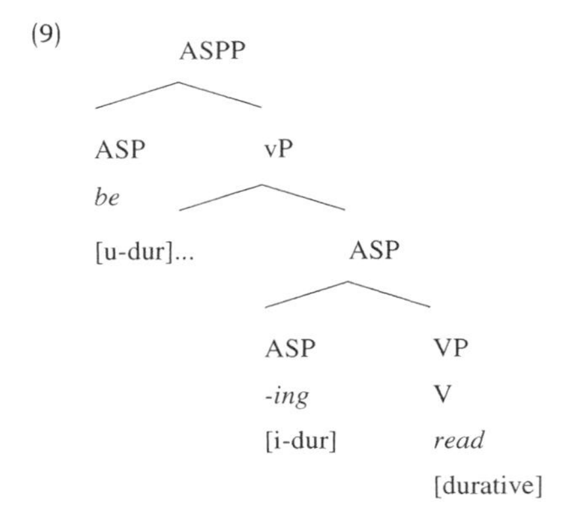

Linguistic aspect marks "different ways of viewing the internal temporal consistency of a situation" (Comrie 1976: 3), and we therefore expect it to be marked in and around the verbal area. This is in fact what we see reflected in the hierarchies of Chapter 4, represented also in (10) in a simplistic manner.

(10)

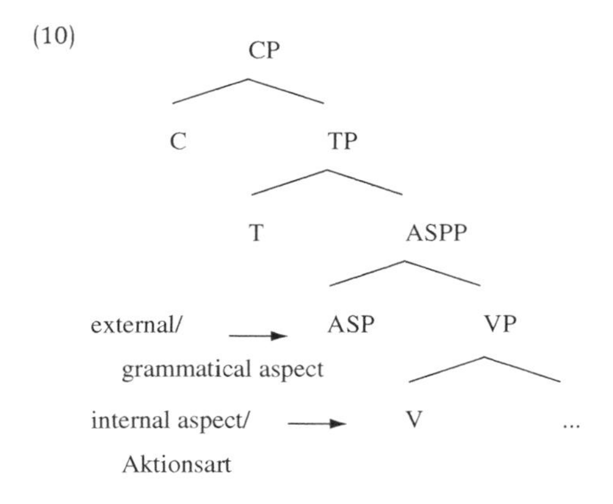

We'll now turn to negation.

6.4 NEGATION

In English, negation is represented throughout the clause. We'll first look at the distribution of English negatives and then at a structure for negatives using a NegP.

Negation may involve all the three layers. In English, it can be in the CP, in the TP, and in the VP. These possibilities are shown in (11) to (13), with a tree in (14) showing the various positions, although these do not all occur in the same sentence, which makes it obvious that the various negatives communicate with each other across the layers.

(11) **Never** had he seen such amazing ruins.

(12) I did**n't** see any ruins.

(13) I saw **no**body.

(14)

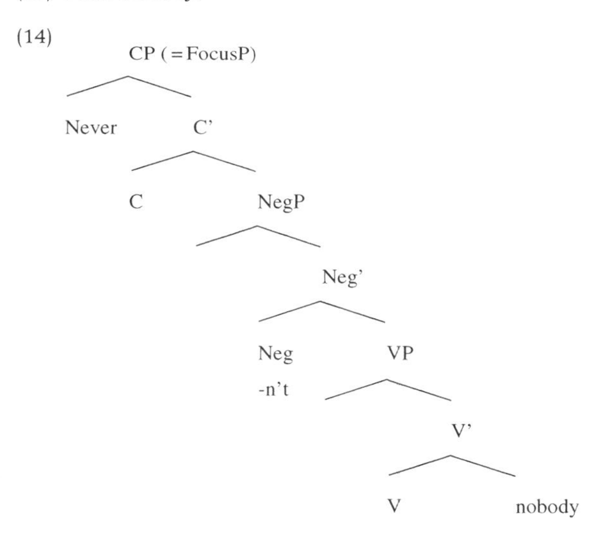

In (11), *never* is in the specifier of the Focus Phrase, as we've seen in the previous chapter; in (12), we'll see that the negative *-n't* is in the head of a NegP, situated somewhere in the TP; and in (13), *nobody* is a lexical item. Of these, only the negation using NegP is considered grammatical, whereas *never* in (11) is an adverb that's been preposed and *nobody* is a negative quantifier. So, one question to answer for each language is (a) which layer is sentential negation represented in and is it grammatical or lexical? Three other questions are (b) is the negative a head or a phrase, (c) what features are checked, and (d) how do the layers communicate?

As to (a), the negative force is arguably only present in the VP in (13). As is well known, NPIs (e.g. *ever*, *any*, *anybody*, *anything*) need to be c-commanded by a negative or question word. The reason that there is no NegP in (13) is that objects, such as *nobody* in (15), don't license NPIs (*ever* in (15)). I therefore assume there is no higher NegP present in (13) or (15) to which the quantifier could move and license *ever*.

(15) *I ever saw **nobody**.

In (12), *any ruins* is c-commanded by *-n't* but in (15) *ever* is not c-commanded by *nobody* and obviously not by anything in a NegP.

Negation can also be present in the TP area, and then we assume there is a NegP. The latter varies in position, as Ouhalla (1990) argues. Zanuttini (1997) claims that varieties of Italian have more than one structural NegP. If the negation appears in NegP, we consider it grammatical; if elsewhere, it is lexical.

As to question (b), since Pollock (1989) and Ouhalla (1990) most people have assumed that English *-n't/not* is an independent head that needs a lower head to move to it on its way to T. That means *-n't* is a clitic, as in (16) (although Zwicky and Pullum (1983) argue that the *-n't* is not a clitic but an inflectional affix).

(16)

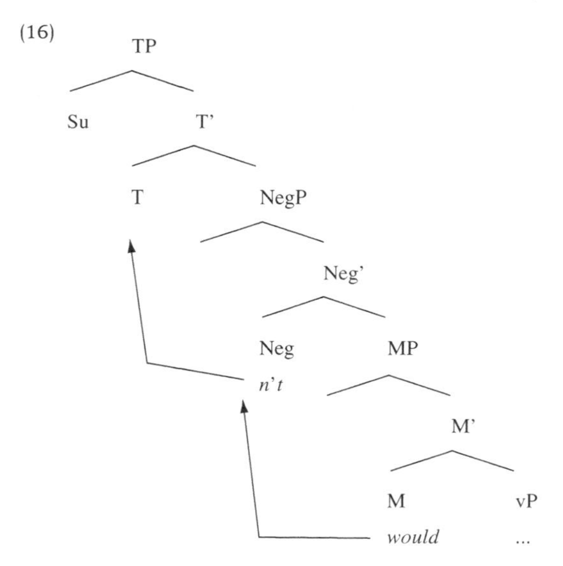

If the negative were in the specifier position, the auxiliary would be able to move across it, as *heeft* 'has' does in Dutch (17).

(17) *Heeft hij dat* ***niet*** *gedaan?* Dutch
Has he that not done
'Hasn't he done that?'

Haegeman (1995) therefore assumes *niet* in (17) is a specifier of the NegP.

This structure with a NegP works particularly well for languages with a two-part negation, such as standard French, where *ne/n'* are in the head and *pas* in the specifier of the NegP, as in (18), for standard French (19). In this tree, the verb attaches to the negative head, and then the two move to T.

(18)

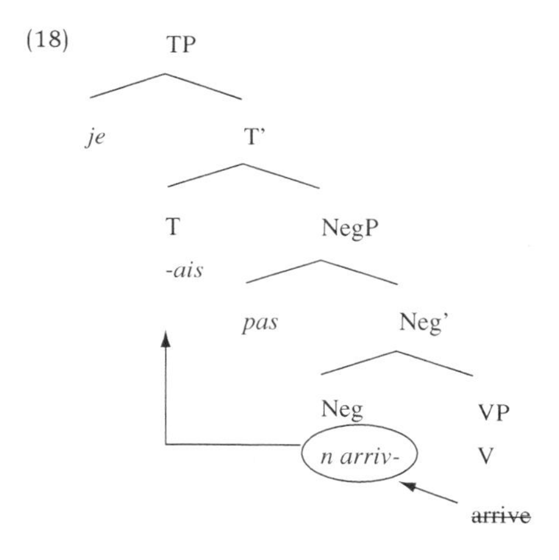

(19) *Je* ***n'****-arriv-ais* ***pas****.* Standard formal French
1S NEG-arrive-1S.PST NEG
'I didn't arrive.'

The position of the NegP in French is relatively low, as (20) shows for (21), although if the main verb has to right-adjoin to Neg in (18), perhaps the auxiliary could do so as well, and then the NegP could be higher.

(20)

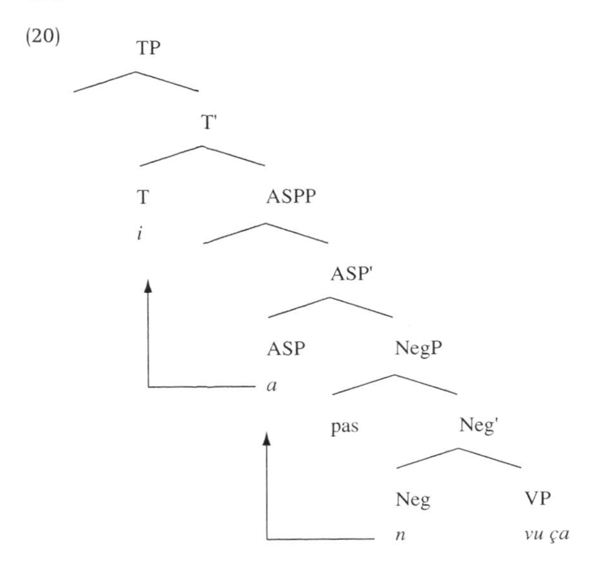

(21)	*Je*	***n'ai***	***pas***	*vu*	*ça*	Standard French
	I	NEG-have	NEG	seen	that	

'I haven't seen that.'

If negation is represented by a NegP, it can be in the specifier or the head, as French shows. How do the various negatives "communicate" with each other? This leads us to an answer to questions (c) and (d). In Standard English, a sentence with a quantifier and a negative result in double negation, i.e. the one negative cancels out the other negative, as in (22). In languages with negative concord, as in Non-standard English (23), the negative quantifier has a feature that is checked with a [u-Neg] in Neg. These are represented as (24a–b) respectively.

(22) I didn't see nobody! Standard English
'I saw someone.'

(23) I didn't see nobody! Non-standard English
'I didn't see anyone.'

(24)

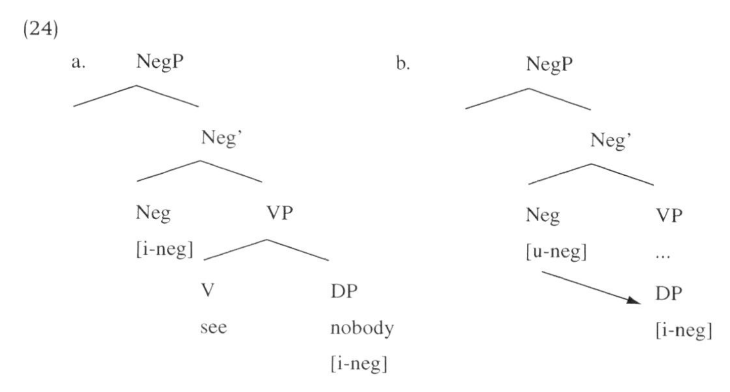

In (22), there are two real negatives, and they do cancel each other out. In (23), the negative quantifier's [i-Neg] features value the [u-Neg] of the head. Modern Standard English is a very artificial language in this respect (normative pressure keeping it from adopting (24b)) and has a (prescriptive) ban on having a Neg with [u-Neg].

In Section 6.4, I have shown that negatives can appear in all layers, but that they communicate through the NegP, as, for instance, in (24). It is the features of the NegP and the quantifier that are interpreted at C-I.

6.5 TOPIC AND FOCUS

In this section, we look at the representation of Topic and Focus throughout the clause.

We have seen that in Italian there can be many topics but that they tend to be in the left-periphery. Topical material in the form of pronouns or definite nouns is often shifted to the left in e.g. Germanic (25), but *dat boek* 'that book' presumably stays in the TP.

(25)	*dat hij* ***dat boek/*een boek***	*gisteren*	*weer*	*een keer*	*las*	Dutch
	that he that book/a book	yesterday	again	one time	read	
	'that he read that book/a book again yesterday.'					

Even though the CP looks like the prime area for topic positions, there are factors in the sentence that push certain arguments into topics. De Cat (2007: 64ff.) provides some evidence that Individual Level predicates force the "subject" into a topic position and "cause" clitic doubling, as in (26a), while Stage Level predicates do not, as in (26b).

(26) a. *Le* *malais* ***c'est*** *difficile* French
DEF Malay it-is difficult
'Malay is difficult.' (De Cat 2007: 77)
b. *Le* *directeur* *est* *là* French
'The director is there.' (De Cat 2007: 77)

Thus, there is a link between the verb type in the VP and possibly whether an ASPP is present and the extension to a topic.

Turning to focus, as we've seen, focus can be in the CP when it is contrastive or above the vP when it is informational (see Belletti 2001; 2004). There is a restriction of one focus per clause. I haven't said much about the low focus, but Belletti uses the low focus position to explain postverbal subjects, so prevalent in Romance pro-drop languages. Sentences with a postverbal subject, such as (27), receive an analysis as in (28), where the subject is in a low Focus position.

(27) *ha parlato* ***Gianni*** Italian
has spoken Gianni
'Gianni spoke.'

(28) [CP.. [TP... ha... parlato [TopP [***FocP*** Gianni [TopP [vP...]]]]]]
(adapted from Belletti 2008: 245)

This is only possible in languages without the EPP. English and French have other strategies for informational focus. French uses a cleft, and the structure Belletti proposes for French (29) is given in (30).

(29) Q *Qui a* *parlé?* French ((reduced) Cleft)
who has spoken
'Who spoke ?'
A *C'est* *Jean* *(qui a parlé)*
It-is John who has spoken
'John spoke.'

(30) [TP Ce... [TopP [***FocP***[TopP[vP être [sc Jean [CP qui a parlé]]]]]]
(Belletti 2008: 245)

The English focus strategy, according to Belletti, is given in (31). This focus comes about through the "activation of a DP internal (new information) focus position" (Belletti 2008: 247).

(31) Q Who spoke? English (SV/(in situ focalization))
A JOHN came/spoke
or: JOHN did (Belletti 2008: 242)

A problem with this account is that too much is possible. Both French and English speakers allow the cleft and the in situ focus as alternatives. Belletti (2008: 247) says, "in English-type languages as well the cleft French-type strategy can be resorted to in some cases, thus indicating that access to the low vP peripheral focus position is generally available across languages." Thus, (32) is possible in English, with a low focus.

(32) Q Who is it at the door?
A It's John (at the door).

Lambrecht (2010: 78–79), not working in a Cartographic approach, examines the Focus strategies of English and French. English strongly favors subjects that are pronouns, i.e. topics: it can put an accent on the subject *in situ*, as in (33). The answer in French is different, as also shown.

(33) Q You look upset. What happened?
A My CAR broke down.

J'ai	*ma*	*VOITURE*	*qui*	*est*	*en panne*	French
1S.have	my	car	which	is	broken	

'It is my car that broke down.' (Lambrecht 2010: 79)

The above focus constructions have involved subject focus. What happens if the object is new information? Here, English, French, and Italian do not show a difference; the objects are all as in English (34).

(34) Q What have you bought?
A I've bought a book.

This uniformity is predicted if the objects move to the low focus position (and all verbs move across that!). Object clefts have a different function and position. They are more contrastive and occupy the focus position in the copula's CP complement, according to Belletti (2008). The cleft in Italian is always used for contrastive focus, but in French and English it can also be used for information focus.

6.6 CONCLUSION

In this book, we have introduced features on C and T to indicate mood and tense. In this chapter, we saw how some of these layers communicate through feature checking. The C and T transmit mood and tense, the ASP and v/V aspect, negative features appear in a NegP which interacts with material in the VP, and Topic and Focus are also found throughout the clause.

Keywords

external mood, internal mood, external aspect, internal aspect/ Aktionsart, tense, negation, TP focus

DISCUSSION POINTS

1. Which data, in addition to (1), would you like from a native speaker of Sami to decide how to represent negation in Sami? Note that the related Finnish is (2).

(1) ***Idtjim*** *daejrieh* Southern Sami
NEG.PST.1S know
'I didn't know.' (from Bergsland 1994: 44)

(2) *Liisa* ***ei*** *osta-nut kirjaa* Finnish
Liisa NEG.3S buy-PST book
'Liisa did not buy a/the book.'

2. In Basque, we have a *ba* morpheme in (3). How would you analyze this?

(3) *Irune* **ba** *-da* *etorri* Basque
Irune so-has arrived
'Irune has arrived.' (Laka 1994: 77)

SUGGESTIONS FOR FURTHER READING

Palmer (2001) and Nordström (2010) provide good information on modality in general, and Van der Auwera and Plungian (1998) on cross-linguistic modality.

Pesetsky and Torrego (2004; 2007) are crucial reading on the connection between C and T.

Ouhalla (1990) is a classic where the NegP is concerned.

Jayaseelan (2001) discusses low focus and topic, and Lambrecht (2010) provides additional information on the cross-linguistic differences regarding topic and focus.

7 Conclusion: description, explanation, and "beyond"

This book provides a Minimalist description of the clause. It uses three clausal domains that are quite distinct in their characteristics. One way of characterizing each layer is by using the term pragmatic for the CP, grammatical for the TP, and semantic for the VP, but that is of course an overgeneralization. Each of these three layers has been examined in detail, and a Cartography has emerged. What I have tried to emphasize, however, is that this Cartography is descriptive, i.e. it is descriptively adequate and is not an explanation for why the order of phrases is the way it is and how it came to be this way, i.e. how it is explanatorily adequate and "beyond" explanatorily adequate. Cartography and Minimalism are different ways of approaching the problem: the one is descriptive, the other explanatory.

I have therefore also suggested ways to envisage an explanation in terms of third factors, as is now common in Minimalism. Here, I have been much vaguer, and that's why Minimalism is programmatic at this point. A complete account is not yet feasible. In addition to third factor effects, however, I have suggested a bigger role for Universal Grammar than is currently the case. Innate semantic concepts and features guide the child in its extraordinary acquisition of lexical items.

In this conclusion, I will point out the major functions of each of the three layers, the challenging issues in each layer, and a few areas that may in fact have the beginnings of a third factor explanation.

7.1 FUNCTIONS OF THE LAYERS

In this section, I summarize a few of the functions that phrases and heads in each of the layers play.

First of all, the DPs can be marked for semantic role (Agent, Theme, etc.), grammatical function (Subject, Object, etc.), and pragmatic role

(Topic and Focus). Structure (1) shows the three layers, where this marking on the DPs is shown by arrows.

(1)

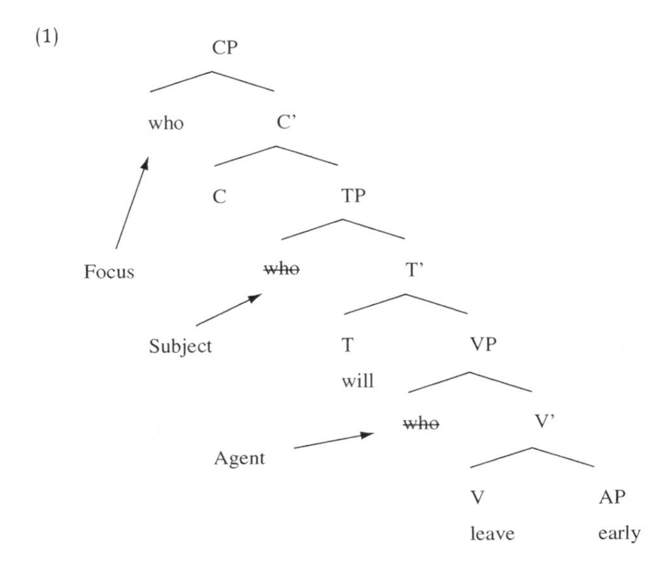

Secondly, we can represent tense in the CP and TP, and mood and negation in all three layers, although negation is grammaticalized in the TP-Layer, and aspect in the low TP and VP. This is shown in (2).

(2)

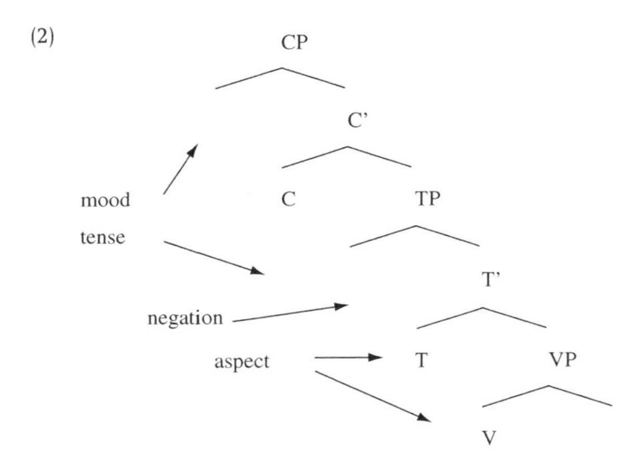

7.2 MAJOR ISSUES IN EACH LAYER

In this section, I will give a brief overview of the most important issues in each layer.

The VP-Layer centers around the verb in the projectionist, lexicalist approach, but around the light verbs in the constructionist approach. The major question is how the derivation "knows" which heads and phrases to merge first. In Chapter 3, we have examined a few mechanisms. In the projectionist approach, the Thematic Hierarchy and the UTAH are responsible for interpreting the DPs as Agents or Themes or as other semantic roles. If the derivation first merges the Agent, as in (3), it will incorrectly be interpreted as a Theme at the C-I Interface.

(3)
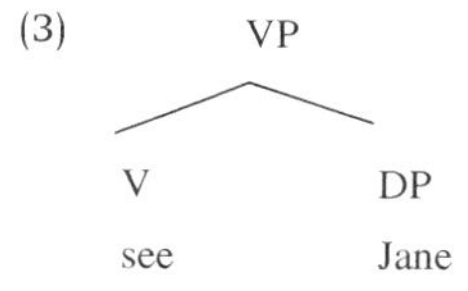

The Interface will also have to pay attention to the verb, however, to see that it has a Theme and Agent to assign, and not just a Theme. In the constructionist approach, the different functional categories will have to be ordered as well, and it is not immediately clear to me how.

The major issue in the TP-Layer is again the order of phrases, but also the number and type of features needed. As to the order, in Chapter 4 I cited a few attempts to derive the order from third factor principles such as scope. As to the features, I mentioned in Chapter 1 that children develop/refine cognitive concepts such as cause, time, and place, and that these will be abstracted as grammatical features. Universal Grammar will have to provide some input other than Merge, since these features are linguistic, but again this is an area in need of more work.

The major issue in the CP-Layer is how the derivation "knows" when to move topic and focus elements to that layer. Frascarelli (2007) and Sigurðsson (2011) argue for a third factor Edge-Principle, which can be phrased in such a way that each DP needs to be connected to a role in the CP-Layer. There are still a number of problems with this approach. Do all DPs need to be linked; can they be linked without movement to the CP-Layer?

7.3 THIRD FACTOR EFFECTS AND UNIVERSAL GRAMMAR

As mentioned, in the last ten years or so the focus of Generative Grammar has not only been on descriptive and explanatory adequacy (what is language and how is it acquired), but also beyond explanatory adequacy (why is it the way it is). Such an approach attempts to use insights from the physical structure of the brain and evolution. Language is a relatively new phenomenon in our species, and a complex Universal Grammar is unexpected, since it hasn't had time to evolve. The emphasis has therefore shifted to third factors, although I have suggested, e.g. in Chapter 1, that semantic features may exist in proto-language and could therefore be innate.

The Thematic Hierarchy, the UTAH, and Reinhart's theta-roles are great candidates for being due to a third factor. As briefly mentioned above and in Chapter 3, Baker sees the UTAH as an interface principle. If we consider how it may have arisen, the animacy built into it is striking, and it could therefore be a syntactic way of expressing animacy restrictions, something not restricted to language but to cognition in general.

7.4 CONCLUSION

This book has described the basic backbone of the clause. This can be done in a constructionist, Cartographic approach or in a projectionist, derivational one. Each has its challenges, in particular in predicting the selection and order or elements. The ultimate question is how did language get to be the way it is!

Keywords

descriptive and explanatory adequacy, beyond explanatory, third factor, evolution

Glossary

accusative	typically the marking on the grammatical object.
active voice	a construction where all the arguments that a verb typically has are present, e.g. *read* will have its Agent and Theme expressed.
actor	*see* Agent
adjunct	alternative for adverbial.
adverbial	a phrase that is optional, often used to give additional information on the manner, time, or place when an event takes place.
Agent	the semantic or thematic role of a mentally present Causer of an action.
AGREE	the operation where a probe with uninterpretable features searches for a Goal with interpretable features.
Aktionsart	the internal temporal structure of a verb, also known as internal or lexical aspect.
analytic	a language with little morphology, e.g. Chinese.
anti-causative	*see* unaccusative
argument	a phrase that is obligatorily present with a particular verb; for instance, *they always loved him*, *they* and *him* are arguments because they cannot be left out, but *always* is not.

aspect	considering the internal temporal organization of an event or situation, e.g. if the event is telic or durative.
assertive verb	a verb whose complement is an assertion.
auxiliary	a verb that needs another verb and that expresses the mood or aspect of a sentence.
binary branching	when each node in a tree has two branches.
bind/bound	an antecedent, such as *they*, binds an anaphor, such as *themselves*, in *They saw themselves*.
boundary	an imprecise way of saying that the VP, TP, and CP have edges that may stop movement etc.
case	morphologically, the difference between nominative *she* and accusative or dative *her*; syntactically, the licensing of arguments through uninterpretable features on a T or v probe.
causative verb	verb with a Causer theta-role.
causer	the semantic or thematic role of the causer of an action.
c-command	a way to define the relation of sisterhood in a tree.
circumstantial adverb	an adverb of manner, time, or space, usually expressed as PP.
clause	contains at least a lexical verb.
cleft	a construction in which one element is focused, e.g. *it was JOHN who left*.
clitic	a (phonologically reduced) word that needs another word to support it, e.g. *'im* in *I see 'im*.
complement	sister to X in X-bar theory; alternative for argument.

complementizer	introduces a clause, e.g. a subordinate one such as because, or a main clause by means of features on C.
complex sentence	a sentence with more than one lexical verb.
conjunction	a word that connects two clauses.
control verb	a verb with a clausal complement that has an unspecified subject that is identical to its own subject and is expressed as PRO, e.g. I tried PRO to leave.
coordination	a word that connects two independent clauses where neither fulfills a function in the other.
copula	a linking verb that combines a subject and an adjective or noun.
copy	when a word or phrase moves, or remerges, a copy is left behind, indicated by means of cross-through.
dative	the case that goes with a Goal in many languages.
declarative	*see* indicative.
default	the unmarked case, in English accusative.
defective	used for clauses when they do not have a C.
Definiteness Effect	the requirement that the postverbal argument in existential constructions be indefinite.
deontic	used for verbs as well as for modal auxiliaries when they express volition, ability, permission, and necessity.
dependent marking	a language which marks grammatical relations such as subject and object on the arguments, not on the verb.
derivation	syntactic operations that result in a sentence.

direct object	if a verb only has one object, it is the direct object.
durativity	a continued or unbroken action.
echo question	questions something just said by leaving the *wh*-word in place.
ECM	clauses in which the subject gets case from the outside, e.g. *him* in *I believe him to be nice.*
edge	used in connection with phases, the edge is the accessible part of a phase.
epistemic	used for verbs as well as for modal auxiliaries when they express the possibility, likelihood, or degree of certainty of the sentence being true.
EPP	the requirement that a clause has a specific structural position for grammatical subjects.
exclamative	mood that signals that the speaker is surprised or excited.
existential	a construction with *there*, as in *There were five unicorns.*
expletive subject	a subject that has a grammatical function but no thematic role.
External Argument	the argument that is the highest in the Hierarchy and is used as grammatical subject (in English).
extraction	taking a phrase out of another phrase.
factive	a verb with a clausal complement whose truth is presupposed by the speaker.
feature	a grammatical/morphological property, such as person, number, tense, and case.
finite	a very language-specific term. In English, a verb or clause with marking for agreement with the subject and tense.
FinP	Finite Phrase.

first Merge	Merge is when a head and a phrase are combined; first Merge is when the heads and phrases haven't merged before.
floating quantifier	*all* and *both* can float in English, i.e. do not need to stay together with the element they modify, as in *They may have all been happy*.
focus	can be a position to which a phrase moves that is new information.
force	a CP indicates the mood of a sentence, and this is often referred to as the force.
fragment	not a complete sentence, e.g. lacking a finite verb or a subject.
free word order	the phenomenon where languages seem not to have a preferred word order.
fronting	moving a phrase to an initial position.
function	usually grammatical function.
fut	future features.
Goal	theta-role; to check features with.
Government and Binding	a stage in Generative Grammar represented by Chomsky (1981) with an emphasis on case and agreement that leads into Minimalism.
head	the head of the verb phrase is the verb, and the head of the noun phrase is the noun, etc.
head marking	a language which marks grammatical relations such as subject and object on the verb, not on the arguments.
headedness	every phrase must have a head, and that's a principle; for a long time it was argued that headedness was a parameter that could be set as head-first or head-last.

I(NFL)	the name of a position dedicated to inflectional elements.
identificational Focus	contrastive Focus; making a selection from a limited set of answers.
imperative	the mood related to an order or command.
inchoative	used as unaccusative in the causative/unaccusative alternation; also refers to the beginning of an action.
Inclusiveness Condition	a principle that restricts new elements from being introduced into the derivation.
in situ	a word or phrase that stays in its first-merged position, e.g. *I saw who?*
interface	the grammar needs to connect with the sensorimotor and conceptual systems, and these connections are called interfaces.
interpretable	a feature that is relevant at the C-I interface.
interrogative	a mood expressing a question.
intransitive	a verb with one argument, e.g. *swim*.
irrealis	the opposite of real, hence moods that express uncertainty.
island	a constituent from which extraction is not possible.
labile verb	the same verb form is used for causative and unaccusative meanings, e.g. *boil* and *grow*.
left periphery	the highest area of the clause where pragmatic information is provided.
light verb	the higher verb in the vP-shell; a verb like *make*.
Linear Correspondence Axiom	a translation between hierarchy in the tree and linear spell-out.

locality	the idea that syntactic operations cannot occur between positions too far apart, as in extractions from islands.
main clause	a clause that has a finite verb and a subject, at least in English.
Merge	combining a head and a phrase.
Minimalism	a form of Generative Grammar prevalent since the early 1990s.
modal	an auxiliary that expresses possibility, necessity, etc.
modifier	an alternative term for adverbial, or for a non-essential element in the DP, usually an adjective phrase or relative clause.
mood	the mood of a clause can be indicative, interrogative, imperative, or exclamative.
move	selecting a word or phrase already merged in the derivation and merging it in another position.
multiple *wh*-question	having more than one *wh*-element in a clause.
negative concord	when two negatives result in an interpretation of one negative.
Negative Polarity Item	a word or phrase that needs to be in a certain environment, e.g. a negative one.
Negative Raising	a phenomenon where a negative can either modify the subordinate verb or the matrix verb.
nominative	the case used for the subject, e.g. *s/he* in English.
null subject	a subject that bears a theta-role but is not pronounced, represented as pro or PRO.
object	a grammatical role that is marked accusative in many languages.

object shift	used in the literature on Scandinavian languages for the movement of the definite object to the left.
parameter	ways in which languages differ from each other, e.g. in being head-initial or head-final.
passive voice	the result of the movement of a non-Agent or non-Causer to subject position.
Patient	*see* Theme
performance	reflective of what we hear and see of language; performance errors are often characterized as slips of the tongue.
phi-features	person and number and gender features.
phrasal verb	a combination of a verb and an adverb that usually has an unpredictable meaning.
pres	present features
Principle	a universal property of language.
Principles and Parameters	a stage in Generative Grammar represented by Chomsky (1973) where cross-linguistic variation comes to be important.
pro	the empty subject argument of a finite verb.
PRO	the empty subject argument of a non-finite verb.
probe	a head with uninterpretable features that searches for a Goal to value its features.
probe-goal checking	the valuation of the probe's uninterpretable features with the probe's interpretable ones.
pro-drop	a term used for null-subjects, especially for languages such as Italian and Spanish.

Projection Principle	the requirement that the properties of a verb's argument structure must be preserved in a derivation.
quantifier	words like *some*, *all*, *every*, and *any* that describe a quantity.
quantifier float	certain quantifiers can appear away from the noun they modify; this was initially seen as a "floating" to the right but is currently seen as a stranding; see Chapter 1.
raising verb	a verb with one clausal argument, e.g. *seem*.
realis	mood indicating that something is actually the case.
rheme	that which comments on the topic or theme of a sentence.
role	usually a semantic or thematic role
scope	certain words can have scope over other words in their c-commanding domain.
scrambling	when, for pragmatic reasons, subjects and objects are moved to grammatically unexpected positions; not relevant in a strict word order language such as English.
serial verb construction	a combination of two lexical verbs where neither is subordinate to the other.
specifier/spec	phrase that is contained in another phrase but not the complement; see Chapter 1.
spell-out	when the derivation is pronounced.
Subjacency	a principle that restricts movement across two boundaries, e.g. DP and CP.
subject	grammatical role that is marked nominative in many languages.

superiority	the principle that, for instance, selects the *wh*-element closest to the CP for movement to that CP.
T	tense head of the TP.
telicity	having a goal or end-point.
tense	relation between the event or action and the time of speech, e.g. present and past tense.
that-trace effect	the restriction (in some languages) that a complementizer cannot be followed by an empty subject position.
Theme	name of a theta-role; see Chapter 3.
theta-role	semantic role such as Agent or Theme.
Top	the head of a Topic phrase; see Chapter 5, Section 5.3.
Top(ic)	a DP that expresses old or given information.
transitive	a set of verbs that have two arguments, e.g. *hit*.
unaccusative	a set of intransitive verbs with just a Theme argument, e.g. *arrive*.
unergative	a set of intransitive verbs with just an Agent argument, e.g. *swim*.
valency	the number of arguments connected to a verb.
value	used as a verb, it means to check the uninterpretable features.
variable	an empty position that is bound by a particular element to its left, e.g. a *wh*-element.
voice	passive and active voice manipulate the expression of arguments in certain positions; e.g. a passive allows the Theme to function as grammatical subject.
VPISH	originally, it stated that subjects start out in the VP; but it is now taken to mean that all arguments originate there.

weak crossover	constructions such as *Who did his mother see*, with *who* and *his* coreferential, i.e. referring to the same person.
wh-movement	movement of a *wh*-element, usually to the specifier of the CP.
wh-question	a question whose answer is not just *yes* or *no* but informational.
X-bar theory	the generalization of the phrase structure rules so that each phrase looks similar, with a head, a specifier, and a complement.
yes/no question	a question whose answer is *yes* or *no*.

References

Abels, K. 2003. Successive Cyclicity, Anti-Locality, and Adposition Stranding. Doctoral dissertation, University of Connecticut.

Abney, S. 1987. The English Noun Phrase in its Sentential Aspect. Dissertation, MIT.

Abraham, W. 1995. Structural Properties of Information Packaging in German and in Universal Grammar. In E. Hajičová, M. Červenka, O. Leška and P. Sgall (eds.), *Prague Linguistic Circle Papers*, vol. I, 125-156. Amsterdam: John Benjamins.

1997a. Kausativierung und Dekausativierung: Zu Fragen der verbparadigmatischen Markierung in der Germania. In T. Birkmann and O. Werner (eds.), *Vergleichende germanische Philologie und Skandinavistik: Festschrift für Otmar Werner*, 13-28. Tübingen: Niemeyer.

1997b. The Interdependence of Case, Aspect, and Referentiality in the History of German: The Case of the Genitive. In A. van Kemenade and N. Vincent (eds.), *Parameters of morphosyntactic change*, 29-61. Cambridge University Press.

Abraham W. and S. de Meij. 1986. *Topic, Focus, and Configurationality*. Amsterdam: John Benjamins.

Adger, D. 2007. *Core Syntax*. Oxford: Blackwell.

Adger, D. & G. Ramchand. 2001. Phases and Interpretability. In K. Megerdoomian and L.A. Bar-el (eds.), *WCCFL 20 Proceedings*, 101-104. Somerville, MA: Cascadilla Press.

Akmajian, A., S. Steele, and T. Wasow. 1979. The Category AUX in Universal Grammar. *Linguistic Inquiry* 10: 1-64.

Aoun, J. & E. Benmamoun. 1998. Minimality, Reconstruction and PF-Movement. *Linguistic Inquiry* 29.4: 569-597.

Aoun, J. & A. Li. 1989. Scope and Constituency. *Linguistic Inquiry* 20: 141-172.

Authier, M. 1992. Iterated CPs and Embedded Topicalization. *Linguistic Inquiry* 23.2: 329-336.

Auwera, J. van der & V. Plungian. 1998. Modality's Semantic Map. *Linguistic Typology* 2: 79-124.

Babyonyshev, M., J. Ganger, D. Pesetsky, and K. Wexler. 2001. The Maturation of Grammatical Principles: Evidence from Russian Unaccusatives. *Linguistic Inquiry* 32.1: 1-44.

Badan, L. & F. del Gobbo. 2011. On the Syntax of Topic and Focus in Chinese. In P. Benincà and N. Munaro (eds.), *Mapping the Left Periphery*, 63–90. Oxford University Press.
Baker, Mark. 1988. *Incorporation*. Chicago University Press.
1997. Thematic Roles and Syntactic Structure. In L. Haegeman (ed.), *Elements of Grammar*, 73–137. Dordrecht: Kluwer.
2001. *The Atoms of Language*. New York: Basic Books.
2008a. *The Syntax of Agreement and Concord*. Cambridge University Press.
2008b. The Macroparameter in a Microparametric World. In Theresa Biberauer (ed.), *The Limits of Syntactic Variation*, 351–374. Amsterdam: John Benjamins.
Baltin, M. 2004. Remarks on the Relation between Language Typology and Universal Grammar. *Studies in Language* 28.3: 549–553.
Basse, G. 2008. Factive Complements as Defective Phases. *WCCFL 27 Proceedings*, 54–62. Somerville, MA: Cascadilla Press.
Bech, G. 1955. *Studien über das deutsche Verbum infinitum*. Copenhagen: Munksgaard.
Belletti, A. 2001. Inversion as Focalization. In A. Hulk and J.-Y. Pollock (eds.), *Subject Inversion in Romance and the Theory of Universal Grammar*, 60–90. Oxford University Press.
2004. Aspects of the Low IP Area. In L. Rizzi (ed.), *The Structure of CP and IP: The Cartography of Syntactic Structures*, 16–51. New York: Oxford University Press.
2008. Answering Strategies: New Information Subjects and the Nature of Clefts. In *Structures and Strategies*, 242–265. London: Routledge.
Belletti, A. and L. Rizzi. 1988. Psych-Verbs and Theta-Theory. *Natural Language and Linguistic Theory* 6: 291–352.
Benincà, P. 2001. The Position of Topic and Focus in the Left Periphery. In G. Cinque and L. Renzi (eds.), *Current Studies in Italian Syntax*, 39–64. Amsterdam: Elsevier.
Benincà, P. and N. Munaro. 2010. Introduction. In P. Benincà & N. Munaro (eds.), *Mapping the Left Periphery*, 3–15. Oxford University Press.
Benincà, P. & C. Poletto. 2004. Topic, Focus and V2: Defining the CP Sublayers. In L. Rizzi (ed.), *The Structure of CP and IP*, 52–75. Oxford University Press.
Bergsland, K. 1994. *Sydsamisk grammatik*. Karasjok: Davvi Girji o.s.
Besten, H. den. 1983. On the Interaction of Root Transformations and Lexical Deletive Rules. In W. Abraham (ed.), *On the Formal Syntax of the Westgermania*, 47–131. Amsterdam: John Benjamins.
Biberauer, T. & M. Richards. 2006. True Optionality: When the Grammar doesn't Mind. In C. Boeckx (ed.), *Minimalist Essays*, 35–67. Amsterdam: John Benjamins.
Bickerton, D. 1990. *Language and Species*. University of Chicago Press.
Biskup, P. 2011. *Adverbials and the Phase Model*. Amsterdam: John Benjamins.

Boeckx, C. 2008. *Bare Syntax*. Oxford University Press.

Borer, H. 1984. *Parametric Syntax: Case Studies in Semitic and Romance Languages*. Dordrecht: Foris Publications.

1994. The Projection of Arguments. In E. Benedicto and J. Runner (eds.), *University of Massachusetts Occasional Papers in Linguistics* 17, 19–47. Amherst: GLSA.

2005a. *In Name Only. Structuring Sense*, vol. I. Oxford University Press.

2005b. *The Normal Course of Events. Structuring Sense*, vol. II. Oxford University Press.

Bošković, Ž. 2002. A-Movement and the EPP. *Syntax* 5: 167–218.

Bowerman, M. 1974. Learning the Structure of Causative Verbs: A Study in the Relationship of Cognitive, Semantic, and Syntactic Development. *Papers and Reports on Child Language Development*, 8: 142–178.

Bowers, J. 2010. *Arguments as Relations*. Cambridge, MA: MIT Press.

Bresnan, J. 1972. Theory of Complementation in English Syntax. Doctoral dissertation, MIT.

Bril, I. (ed.). 2010. *Clause Linking and Clause Hierarchy*. Amsterdam: John Benjamins.

Butler, J. 2003. A Minimalist Treatment of Modality. *Lingua* 113: 967–996.

2004. On Having Arguments and Agreeing: Semantic EPP. *York Papers in Linguistics* 2.1: 1–27.

Bybee, J. 1985. *Morphology*. Amsterdam: John Benjamins.

Bybee, J. and S. Fleischman (eds.). 1995. *Modality in Grammar and Discourse*. Amsterdam: John Benjamins.

Carnie, A. 2007. *Syntax*. Oxford: Blackwell.

Carstens, V. 2012. Delayed valuation: A Reanalysis of "upwards" Complementizer Agreement and the Mechanics of case. Unpublished manuscript.

Chocano, Gema 2007. *Narrow Syntax and Phonological Form: Scrambling in the Germanic Languages*. Amsterdam: John Benjamins.

Chomsky, N. 1955. The Logical Structure of Linguistic Theory. Manuscript. Published in 1975. New York: Plenum Press.

1957. *Syntactic Structures*. The Hague: Mouton.

1965. *Aspects of the Theory of Syntax*. Cambridge, MA: MIT Press.

1970. Remarks on Nominalization. In R. Jacobs and P. Rosenbaum (eds.), *Readings in English Transformational Grammar*, 184–221. Waltham: Ginn.

1971. Deep Structure, Surface Structure and Semantic Interpretation. In D. Steinberg and L. Jakobovits (eds.), *Semantics: An Interdisciplinary Reader in Linguistics, Philosophy and Psychology*, 183–216. Cambridge University Press.

1973. Conditions on Transformations. In S. Anderson and P. Kiparsky (eds.), *A Festschrift for Morris Halle*, 232–285. New York: Holt, Rinehart, and Winston.

1975. *Reflections on Language*. London: Fontana.

1997a. *Essays on Form and Interpretation.* New York: Elsevier North-Holland.

1977b. On *Wh*-Movement. In P. Culicover, T. Wasow, and A. Akmajian (eds.), *Formal Syntax*, 71–132. New York: Academic Press.

1981. *Lectures on Government and Binding.* Dordrecht: Foris.

1982. *Some Concepts and Consequences of the Theory of Government and Binding.* Cambridge, MA: MIT Press.

1986a. *Knowledge of Language.* New York: Praeger.

1986b. *Barriers.* Cambridge, MA: MIT Press.

1989. Some Notes on Economy of Derivation and Representation [reprinted as chapter 2 of Chomsky 1995, and references to that].

1992. A Minimalist Program for Linguistic Theory. *MIT Occasional Working Papers in Linguistics.*

1993. *Language and Thought.* Wakefield: Moyer Bell.

1995. *The Minimalist Program.* Cambridge, MA: MIT Press.

2000. Minimalist Inquiries: The Framework. In R. Martin, D. Michaels, and J. Uriagereka (eds.), *Step by Step: Essays in Syntax in Honor of Howard Lasnik*, 89–155. Cambridge, MA: MIT Press. [originally published 1998]

2001. Derivation by Phase. In M. Kenstowicz (ed.), *Ken Hale: A Life in Language*, 1–52. Cambridge, MA: MIT Press.

2002. *On Nature and Language.* Cambridge University Press.

2004. Beyond Explanatory Adequacy. In A. Belletti (ed.), *Structures and Beyond*, 104–131. Oxford University Press.

2005. Three Factors in Language Design. *Linguistic Inquiry* 36.1: 1–22.

2007. Approaching UG from Below. In U. Sauerland and H.-M. Gärtner (eds.), *Interfaces + Recursion = Language?*, 1–29. Berlin: Mouton de Gruyter.

2008a. The Biolinguistic Program: Where does it Stand Today? ms.

2008b. On Phases. In R. Freidin, C. P. Otero, and M. L. Zubizarreta (eds.), *Foundational Issues in Linguistic Theory. Essays in Honor of Jean-Roger Vergnaud*, 134–166. Cambridge, MA: MIT Press.

2011. Problems of Projection. ms.

Chung, S. and J. McCloskey. 1983. On the Interpretation of Certain Island Facts in GPSG. *Linguistic Inquiry* 14: 704–713.

Cinque, G. 1990. *Types of A'-Dependencies.* Cambridge, MA: MIT Press.

1999. *Adverbs and Functional Heads.* Oxford University Press.

Cinque, G. and L. Rizzi. 2008. *The Cartography of Syntactic Structures*, ed. V. Moscati, CISCL Working Papers on Language and Cognition 2. 43–59. www.ciscl.unisi.it/doc/doc_pub/cinque-rizzi2008-The_cartography_of_Syntactic_Structures.pdf

Collins, C. 2005. A Smuggling Approach to the Passive in English. *Syntax* 8: 81–120.

Comrie, B. 1976. *Aspect.* Cambridge University Press.

1981. *Language Universals and Linguistic Typology: Syntax and Morphology.* Chicago University Press.

2006. Transitivity Pairs, Markedness, and Diachronic Stability. *Linguistics* 44.2: 303–318.
Crowley & C. Bowern. 2010. *An Introduction to Historical Linguistics*. Oxford University Press.
Cysouw, M. 2003. *The Paradigmatic Structure of Person Marking*. Oxford University Press.
2008. Generalizing Scales. In M. Richards & A. Malchukov (eds.), *Scales*, Linguistische Arbeitsberichte 86: 379–396.
Daly, J. 1973. *A Generative Syntax of Peñoles Mixtec*. Norman: University of Oklahoma Press.
Davidson, D. 1980. *Essays on Actions and Events*. Oxford University Press.
Davies, M. & D. Gardner. 2007. Pointing out Frequent Phrasal Verbs: A Corpus-Based Analysis. *TESOL Quarterly* 41: 339–359.
de Cat, C. 2007. *French Dislocation*. Oxford University Press.
Diesing, M. 1992. *Indefinites*. Cambridge, MA: MIT Press.
1997. Yiddish VP Structure and the Typology of Object Movement. *Natural Language and Linguistic Theory* 15.2: 369–427.
Dillon, M. & D. ó Cróinín. 1961. *Irish*. London: The English Universities Press.
Dixon, R. & A. Aikhenvald. 2006. *Serial Verb Constructions: A Cross-Linguistic Typology*. Oxford University Press.
Donohue, M. 1999. *A Grammar of Tukang Besi*. Berlin: Mouton de Gruyter.
Drach, E. 1937. *Grundgedanken der deutschen Satzlehre*. Frankfurt: Diesterweg.
Dryer, M. 1992. The Greenbergian Word Order Correlations. *Language* 68: 81–138.
2011a. Expression of Pronominal Subjects. In M. Dryer and M. Haspelmath (eds.), *The World Atlas of Language Structures Online*. Munich: Max Planck Digital Library, feature 101A. Accessed December 27, 2011.
2011b. Polar Questions. In M. Dryer and M. Haspelmath (eds.), *The World Atlas of Language Structures Online*. Munich: Max Planck Digital Library, feature 116A. Accessed December 27, 2011.
Emonds, J. 1976. *A Transformational Approach to English Syntax*. New York: Academic Press.
Enç, M. 1987. Anchoring Conditions for Tense. *Linguistic Inquiry* 18: 633–657.
Ernst, T. (2002). *The Syntax of Adjuncts*. Cambridge University Press.
Fillmore, C. 1968. The Case for Case. In E. Bach and R. T. Harms (eds.), *Universals in Linguistic Theory*, 1–88. New York: Holt, Rinehart, and Winston.
Folli, R. & H. Harley. 2007. Causation, Obligation and Argument Structure: On the Nature of Little *v*. *Linguistic Inquiry* 38.2: 97–238.
Fong, S. 2005. Computation with Probes and Goals. In A. M. DiSciullo (ed.), *UG and External Systems*, 311–333. Amsterdam: John Benjamins.

Forchheimer, P. 1953. *The Category of Person in Language*. Berlin: Mouton de Gruyter.

Frascarelli, M. 2007. Subjects, Topics and the Interpretation of Referential Pro. *Natural Language and Linguistic Theory* 25.4: 691–734.

Frascarelli, M. & R. Hinterhölzl. 2007. Types of Topics in German and Italian. In K. Schwabe & S. Winkler (eds.), *On Information Structure, Meaning and Form*, 87–116. Amsterdam: John Benjamins.

Frey, W. 2003. *On Some Dislocation Constructions in German and English*. http://amor.cms.hu-berlin.de/~h0594bbb/pdf-files/2003-Frey-Dislocation.pdf

Fukui N. & M. Speas. 1986. Specifiers and Projection. *MITWPL* 8: 128–172.

Gallego, A. 2010. *Phase Theory*. Amsterdam: John Benjamins.

Geach, P. 1957. *Mental Acts*. London: Routledge, Kegan, and Paul.

Gelderen, E. van. 1993. *The Rise of Functional Categories*. Amsterdam: John Benjamins.

1997a. *Verbal Agreement*. Tübingen: Niemeyer.

1997b. Structures of Tense and Aspect. *Linguistic Analysis* 27.3–4: 138–165.

2000. *A History of English Reflexive Pronouns*. Amsterdam: John Benjamins.

2004. *Grammaticalization as Economy*. Amsterdam: John Benjamins.

2010. *A Grammar of English*. Amsterdam: John Benjamins.

2011. *The Linguistic Cycle*. Oxford University Press.

Giannakidou, A. 1998. *Polarity Sensitivity as (Non)Veridical Dependency*. Amsterdam: John Benjamins.

Givón, T. 1971. Historical Syntax and Synchronic Morphology. *Chicago Linguistic Society Proceedings* 7: 394–415.

1978. Negation in Language. In P. Cole (ed.), *Syntax & Semantics* 9: 69–112. New York: Academic Press.

1980. The Binding Hierarchy and the Typology of Complements. *Studies in Language* 4: 333–378.

1983. Topic Continuity in Discourse: An Introduction. In T. Givón (ed.), *Topic continuity in Discourse*, 1–41. Amsterdam: John Benjamins.

1990. *Syntax: A Functional-Typological Introduction*. Amsterdam and Philadelphia: John Benjamins.

2006. Multiple Routes to Clause Union. ms.

2009. *The Genesis of Syntactic Complexity*. Amsterdam: John Benjamins.

Greenberg, J. 1963. *Universals of Language*. Cambridge, MA: MIT Press.

Gruber, J. 1965. Studies in Lexical Relations. Doctoral dissertation, MIT.

Guasti, M. 2002. *Language Acquisition*. Cambridge, MA: MIT Press.

Guimarães, M. 2000. In Defense of Vacuous Projections in Bare Phrase Structure. *University of Maryland Working Papers in Linguistics* 9: 90–115.

Hacquard, V. 2009. On the Interaction of Aspect and Modal Auxiliaries. *Linguistics and Philosophy* 32: 279–315.

2010. On the Event-Relativity of Modal Auxiliaries. *Natural Language Semantics* 18.1: 79–114.

Haegeman, L. 1995. *The Syntax of Negation*. Cambridge University Press.

2006. Argument Fronting in English, Romance CLLD, and the Left Periphery. In R. Zanuttini, H. Campos, E. Herburger, and P. H. Portner (eds.), *Crosslinguistic Research in Syntax and Semantics*, 27–52. Washington: Georgetown University Press.

Haiden, M. 2005. *Theta Theory*. Berlin: Mouton de Gruyter.

Haider, H. 2000. Adverb Placement - Convergence of Structure and Licensing. *Theoretical Linguistics* 26: 95–134.

Haiman, J. 2010. *Cambodian Khmer*. Amsterdam: John Benjamins.

Hale, K. 1992. Basic Word Order in Two "Free Word Order" Languages. In D. Payne (ed.), *Pragmatics of Word Order Flexibility*, 63–82. Amsterdam: John Benjamins.

Hale, K. and S. J. Keyser. 1993. On Argument Structure and the Lexical Expression of Syntactic Relations. In K. Hale and J. Keyser (eds.), *The View from Building 20*. Cambridge, MA: MIT Press.

2002. *Prolegomenon to a Theory of Argument Structure*. Cambridge, MA: MIT Press.

Harley, H. 1995. Subjects, Events, and Licensing. Doctoral dissertation, MIT.

2002. Possession and the Double Object Construction. *Linguistic Variation Yearbook* 2: 31–70.

Harley, H. & E. Ritter. 2002. Person and Number in Pronouns: A Feature-Geometric Analysis. *Language* 78.3: 482–526.

Haspelmath, M. 1993. More on the Typology of the Inchoative/Causative Verb Alternations. In B. Comrie & M. Polinsky (eds.), *Causatives and Transitivity*, 87–120. Amsterdam: John Benjamins.

2010. Ditransitive Constructions: The Verb "Give". In M. S. Dryer and M. Haspelmath (eds.), *The World Atlas of Language Structures Online*. Munich: Max Planck Digital Library, feature 105A. Accessed December 28, 2011.

Haumann, D. 2007. *Adverb Licensing and Clause Structure in English*. Amsterdam: John Benjamins.

Hazout, I. 2004. The Syntax of Existential Constructions. *Linguistic Inquiry* 35: 393–430.

Hegarty, M. 2005. *A Feature-Based Syntax of Functional Categories: The Structure, Acquisition, and Specific Impairment*. Berlin: Mouton de Gruyter.

Heine, B. & T. Kuteva. 2002. *World Lexicon of Grammaticalization*. Cambridge University Press.

Henry, A. 1995. *Belfast English and Standard English*. Oxford University Press.

Hoekstra, E. 1993. Dialectal Variation inside CP as Parametric Variation. *Linguistische Berichte* 5: 161–179.

Holmberg, A. 1986. Word Order and the Syntactic Features in the Scandinavian Languages and English. Doctoral dissertation, University of Stockholm.

Hooper, J. and S. Thompson. 1973. On the Applicability of Root Transformations. *Linguistic Inquiry* 4.4: 465–497.

Hopper, P. and S. Thompson. 1980. Transitivity in Grammar and Discourse. *Language* 56. 2: 251–299.
Hornstein, N. 1999. Movement and Control. *Linguistic Inquiry* 30.1: 69–96.
Huang, C.-T. James. 1982. *Logical Relations in Chinese and the Theory of Grammar*. Doctoral dissertation, MIT.
Iggesen, O.A. 2011. Number of Cases. In M. Dryer and M. Haspelmath, (eds.), *The World Atlas of Language Structures Online*. Munich: Max Planck Digital Library, feature 49A. Accessed December 27, 2011.
Ingram, D. 1978. Typology and Universals of Personal Pronouns. In J. Greenberg (ed.), *Universals of Human Language*, vol. III, 213–247. Stanford University Press.
Isac, D. 2012. Decomposing Force. In A.M. DiSciullo (ed.), *Towards a Biolinguistic Understanding of Grammar*, 87–116. Amsterdam: John Benjamins.
Jackendoff, R. 1972. *Semantic Interpretation in Generative Grammar*. Cambridge, MA: MIT Press.
1977. *X-bar-Syntax: A Study of Phrase Structure*. Cambridge, MA: MIT Press.
1990. *Semantic Structures*. Cambridge, MA: MIT Press.
2002. *Foundations of Language*. Oxford University Press.
Jayaseelan, K.A. 2001. IP-internal Topic and Focus Positions. *Studia Linguistica* 55: 39–75.
Jeong, Y. 2007. *Applicatives*. Amsterdam: John Benjamins.
Jespersen, O. [1922] 1959. *Language*. London: George Allen & Unwin.
Jones, M. 1992. Infinitives with Specified Subjects in Sardinian. In C. Laeufer & T.A. Morgan (eds.), *Theoretical Analyses in Romance Linguistics*, 295–310. Amsterdam: John Benjamins.
Kari, J. 1990. *Ahtna Athabaskan Dictionary*. Anchorage: Alaska Native Language Center.
Kayne, R. 1989. Facets of Romance Past Participle Agreement. In P. Benincà (ed.), *Dialect Variation and the Theory of Grammar*, 85–103. Dordrecht: Foris.
1993. Toward a Modular Theory of Auxiliary Selection. *Studia Linguistica* 47: 3–31.
1994. *The Antisymmetry of Syntax*. Cambridge, MA: MIT Press.
2005. Some Notes on Comparative Syntax, with Special Reference to English and French. In G. Cinque and R. Kayne (eds.), *The Oxford Handbook of Comparative Syntax*, 3–69. Oxford University Press.
2010. Why are there No Directionality Parameters? ms.
2011. Some Thoughts on Syntax in 2011. Talk, Potsdam.
Keenan, E. 1976. Toward a Universal Definition of "subject". In C. Li (ed.), *Subject and Topic*, 303–334. New York: Academic Press.
Kimball, J. & J. Aissen. 1971. I Think, You Think, He Think. *Linguistic Inquiry* 2: 241–246.
Kiparsky, P. 1998. Partitive Case and Aspect. In M. Butt and W. Geuder (eds.), *The Projection of Arguments*, 265–307. Stanford: CSLI Publications.

Kiparsky, P. & C. Kiparsky. 1970. Fact. In M. Bierwisch and K. E. Heidolph (eds.), *Progress in Linguistics*, 143–173. The Hague: Mouton de Gruyter.

Kiss, K. 1996. Two Subject Positions in English. *The Linguistic Review* 13: 119–142.

1998. Identificational Focus versus Information Focus. *Language* 74: 245–273.

2007. Topic and Focus. *Interdisciplinary Studies on Information Structure* 6: 69–81. www.sfb632.uni-potsdam.de/publications/isis06_4kiss.pdf

Koopman, H. & D. Sportiche. 1991. The Position of Subjects. *Lingua* 85.2/3: 211–258.

Koptjevska-Tamm, M. 1990. Finiteness. In K. Brown & J. Miller (eds.), *Concise Encyclopedia of Grammatical Categories*, 146–149. Amsterdam: Elsevier.

Koster, J. 1978. *Locality Principles in Syntax*. Dordrecht: Foris.

1986. *Domains and Dynasties*. Dordrecht: Foris.

1993. Towards a New Theory of Anaphoric Binding. ms, Groningen University.

2000. Extraposition as parallel construal. http://odur.let.rug.nl/koster/papers/parallel.pdf

2004. Syntaxis: Dynamisch of Cartografisch? *TABU* 33: 173–194.

2007. Structure Preservingness, Internal Merge, and the Strict Locality of Triads. In S. Karimi, V. Samiian, and W. K. Wilkins (eds.), *Phrasal and Clausal Architecture: Syntactic Derivation and Interpretation*, 188–205. Amsterdam and Philadelphia: John Benjamins.

Kratzer, A. 1996. Severing the External Argument from its Verb. In J. Rooryck and L. Zaring (eds.), *Phrase Structure and the Lexicon*, 109–137. Dordrecht: Kluwer.

Kuczaj, S. 1976. -Ing, -s, -ed: A study of the Acquisition of Certain Verb Inflections. Dissertation, University of Minnesota.

Kulikov, L. n.d. www.eva.mpg.de/lingua/tools-at-lingboard/pdf/Kulikov_Diachronic_Valency_Changing_rev_Version.pdf

Kural, M. 1993. V-to(I-to)C in Turkish. *UCLA Occasional Papers in Linguistics* 11.

Kush, D., A. Omaki, and N. Hornstein (in press). *Microvariation in Islands*. http://mind.cog.jhu.edu/~omaki/Kush_etal11_island_preprint.pdf

Laenzlinger, C. 2004. A Feature-Based Theory of Adverb Syntax. In J. R. Austin, S. Engelberg, and G. Rauh (eds.), *Adverbials: The Interplay between Meaning, Context, and Syntactic Structure*, 205–252. Amsterdam: John Benjamins.

Laka, I. 1994. *On the Syntax of Negation*. Outstanding Dissertations in Linguistics Series. New York and London: Garland Publishing.

Lambrecht, K. 2010. Constraints on Subject-Focus Mapping in French and English. In C. Breul and E. Göbbel (eds.), *Comparative and Contrastive Studies of Information Structure*, 77–100. Amsterdam: John Benjamins.

Landau, B. 1994. Where's What and What's Where: The Language of Objects in Space. *Lingua* 92: 259–296.

Landau, I. 2012. *The Locative Syntax of Experiences*. Cambridge, MA: MIT Press.
Larson, R. 1988. On the Double Object Construction. *Linguistic Inquiry* 19: 335–391.
Lasnik, H. 1999. *Minimalist Analysis*. Malden, MA: Blackwell.
2001. A Note on the EPP. *Linguistic Inquiry* 32.2: 356–362.
Lasnik, H. and M. Saito. 1992. *Move: Conditions on its Application and Output*. Cambridge, MA: MIT Press.
Leiss, E. 2000. *Artikel und Aspekt*. Berlin: Walter de Gruyter.
Letuchiy, A. 2010. Lability and spontaneity. In P. Brandt and M. G. García (eds.), *Transitivity*, 237–255. Amsterdam and Philadelphia: John Benjamins.
Levin, B. and Malka Rappaport Hovav. 1995. *Unaccusativity*. Cambridge, MA: MIT Press.
Li, C. and S. Thompson. 1974. An Explanation of Word Order Change: SVO > SOV. *Foundations of Language* 12: 201–214.
1976. Subject and Topic: A New Typology of Language. In C. N. Li (ed.), *Subject and Topic*, 458–489. New York: Academic Press.
1981. *Mandarin Chinese*. Berkeley: California University Press.
Lohndal, T. 2012. Without Specifiers: Phrase Structure and Events. Doctoral dissertation, UMD.
Lutz, Uli, G. Müller, and A. von Stechow. 2000. *Wh-scope Marking*. Amsterdam: John Benjamins.
Lyons, J. 1977. *Semantics I and II*. Cambridge University Press.
Macaulay, M. 1996. *A Grammar of Chalcatongo Mixtec*. Berkeley: California University Press.
Malchukov, A., M. Haspelmath, & B. Comrie. 2010. *Studies in Ditransitive Constructions: A Comparative Handbook*. Berlin: Mouton de Gruyter.
Marelj, M. 2002. Rules that Govern the Co-occurrences of Theta-Clusters in the Theta System. *Theoretical Linguistics* 28.3: 357–373.
2004. Middles and Argument Structure across Languages. Doctoral dissertation, Utrecht.
Markman, E. 1994. Constraints on Word Meaning in Early Acquisition. *Lingua* 92: 199–227.
May, R. 1985. *Logical Form*. Cambridge, MA: MIT Press.
McCloskey, J. 1991. Verb Fronting, Verb Second and the Left Edge of IP in Irish. Talk, Stuttgart workshop on Comparative Germanic Syntax.
2006. Questions and Questioning in a Local English. In R. Zanuttini, H. Campos, E. Herburger, and P. H. Portner (eds.), *Crosslinguistic Research in Syntax and Semantics*, 87–126. Washington: Georgetown University Press.
McGinnis, M. 2001. Variation in the Phase Structure of Applicatives. *Linguistic Variation Yearbook* 1: 105–146.
2004. Lethal Ambiguity. *Linguistic Inquiry* 35.1: 47–95.
Medeiros, D. 2011. Economy of Command. Doctoral dissertation, University of Arizona.

Mithun, M. 2000. The Reordering of Morphemes. In S. Gildea (ed.), *Reconstructing Grammar*, 231–255. Amsterdam: John Benjamins.
2008. Borrowed Rhetorical Constructions as Starting Points for Grammaticalization. In A. Bergs and G. Diewald (eds), *Constructions and Language Change*, 195–230. Berlin: Mouton de Gruyter.
Mohammad, M. 1989. The Sentential Structure of Arabic. Doctoral dissertation, University of Southern California.
Moro, A. 1997. The Raising of Predicates. Cambridge University Press.
Muysken, P. 2008. *Functional Categories*. Cambridge University Press.
Newmeyer, F. 2005. *Possible and Probable Languages: A Generative Perspective on Linguistic Typology*. Oxford University Press.
Nichols, J., D. Peterson & J. Barnes. 2004. Transitivizing and Detransitivising Languages. *Linguistic Typology* 8.2: 149–211.
Noonan, M. 1985. Complementation. In T. Shopen (ed.), *Language Typology and Syntactic Description*, vol. II, 42–140. Cambridge University Press.
Nordström, J. 2010. *Modality and Subordinators*. Amsterdam: John Benjamins.
Nunes, J. 2004. *Linearization of Chains and Sideward Movement*. Cambridge, MA: MIT Press.
Oehrle, R. 1976. The Grammatical Status of the English Dative Alternation. Doctoral dissertation, MIT.
Olsway, C. 2004. The Hungarian Verbal Complex: An Alternative Approach. In K. É. Kiss & H. van Riemsdijk (eds.), *Verb Clusters: A Study of Hungarian, German and Dutch*, 290–333. Amsterdam: John Benjamins.
Ouhalla, J. 1990. Sentential Negation, Relativized Minimality and the Aspectual Status of Auxiliaries. *The Linguistic Review* 7: 183–231.
Palmer, F. R. 2001. *Mood and Modality*. Cambridge University Press.
Parsons, T. 1990. *Events in the Semantics of English: A Study in Subatomic Semantics*. Cambridge, MA: MIT Press.
Payne, T. 1997. *Describing Morphosyntax: A Guide for Field Linguists*. Cambridge University Press.
Pérez-Leroux, A. T. 1995. Resumptives in the Acquisition of Relative Clauses. *Language Acquisition* 4: 105–138.
Perlmutter, D. 1978. Impersonal Passives and the Unaccusative Hypothesis. *Proceedings from the 4th Regional Meeting of the Berkeley Linguistics Society*, 157–189.
Pesetsky, D. 1995. *Zero Syntax*. Cambridge, MA: MIT Press.
Pesetsky, D. & E. Torrego. 2001. T-to-C Movement: Causes and Consequences. In M. Kenstowicz (ed.), *Ken Hale: A Life in Language*, 355–426. Cambridge, MA: MIT Press.
2004. Tense, Case, and the Nature of Syntactic Categories. In J. Guéron & J. Lecarme (eds.), *The Syntax of Time*, 495–538. Cambridge, MA: MIT Press.
2007. The Syntax of Valuation and the Interpretability of Features. In S. Karimi, V. Samiian, and W. K. Wilkins (eds.), *Phrasal and Clausal Architecture*, 262–294. Amsterdam: John Benjamins.

Pietroski, P. 2005. *Events and Semantic Architecture*. Oxford University Press.

Platzack, C. 1983. Germanic Word Order and the COMP/INFL Parameter. *Working Papers in Scandinavian Syntax* 2.

Platzack, C. & I. Rosengren. 1998. On the Subject of Imperatives: A Minimalist Account of the Imperative Clause. *The Journal of Comparative Linguistics* 1: 177–224.

Poletto, C. *The Higher Functional Field*. Oxford University Press.

Pollock, J.-Y. 1989. Verb movement, Universal Grammar, and the Structure of IP. *Linguistic Inquiry* 20: 365–424.

Postal, P. 2010. *Edge-Based Clausal Syntax*. Cambridge, MA: MIT Press.

Potsdam, E. 1998. *Syntactic Issues in the English Imperative*. Outstanding Dissertations in Linguistics. New York: Garland Publishing, Inc.

Prince, E. 1981. Toward a Taxonomy of Given-New Information. In P. Cole, (ed.) *Radical Pragmatics*, 223–56. New York: Academic Press.

Pylkkänen, L. 2008. *Introducing Arguments*. Cambridge, MA: MIT Press.

Radford, A. 2000. Children in Search of Perfection: Towards a Minimalist Model of Acquisition. *Essex Research Reports in Linguistics* 34. (http://privatewww.essex.ac.uk/~radford/PapersPublications/perfection.htm

2009. *Analysing English Sentences*. Cambridge University Press.

Ramchand, G. 2008. *Verb Meaning and the Lexicon*. Cambridge University Press.

Rappaport Hovav, M. and B. Levin. 1998. Building Verb Meanings. In M. Butt and W. Geuder (eds.), *The Projection of Arguments: Lexical and Compositional Factors*, 97–134. Stanford: CSLI Publications.

Reinhart, T. 2002. The Theta System: An Overview. *Theoretical Linguistics* 28:3: 229–290.

2006. *Interface Strategies*. Cambridge, MA: MIT Press.

Rice, K. 2000. Monadic Verbs and Argument Structure in Ahtna, Slave and Navajo. In T. Fernald & P. Platero (eds.), *The Athabaskan Languages*, 167–199. Oxford University Press.

Richards, M. 2007. Object Shift, Phases, and Transitive Expletive Constructions in Germanic. In P. Pica, J. Rooryck, and J. van Craenenbroeck (eds.), *Linguistic Variation Yearbook* 6, 139–159. Amsterdam: John Benjamins. www.uni-leipzig.de/~richards/MRichards_LinguisticVariation_Leipzig.pdf

2008. Two Kinds of Variation in a Minimalist System. Varieties of Competition. In F. Heck, G. Müller & Jochen Trommer (eds.), *Linguistische Arbeits Berichte* 87, 133–162. www.uni-leipzig.de/~asw/lab/lab87/LAB87_richards.pdf

Richards, M. & T. Biberauer. 2005. Explaining "Expl". In M. den Dikken & C.M. Tortora (eds.), *The Function of Function Words and Functional Categories*, 115–153. Amsterdam: John Benjamins.

Ritter, E. 1995. On the Syntactic Category of Pronouns and Agreement. *Natural Language and Linguistic Theory* 13: 405–443.

Rizzi, L. 1982. *Issues in Italian Linguistics*. Dordrecht: Foris.

1990. *Relativized Minimality*. Cambridge, MA: MIT Press.
1997. The Fine Structure of the Left Periphery. In L. Haegeman (ed.), *Elements of Grammar*, 281–337. Dordrecht: Kluwer.
2001. On the Position "Int(errogative)" in the Left Periphery of the Clause. In G. Cinque, L. Renzi, and G. Salvi (eds.), *Current Studies in Italian Syntax*, 287–296. Amsterdam: Elsevier.
2004. Locality and Left Periphery. In A. Belletti (ed.), *Structures and Beyond*, 223–251. Oxford University Press.
Roberts, I. 2010. *Agreement and Head Movement*. Cambridge, MA: MIT Press.
Roberts, I. & A. Holmberg (eds.). 2010. *Null Subjects: The Structure of Parametric Variation*. Cambridge University Press.
Rochette, A. 1988. Semantic and Syntactic Aspects of Romance Sentential Complementation. Doctoral dissertation, MIT.
Rosen, C. 1984. The Interface between Semantic Roles and Initial Grammatical Relations. In D. Perlmutter and C. Rosen (eds.), *Studies in Relational Grammar* 2, 38–77. Chicago University Press.
Rosenbaum, P. 1976. *The Grammar of English Predicate Complement Constructions*. Cambridge, MA: MIT Press.
Rosengren, I. 2002. EPP: A Syntactic Device in the Service of Semantics. *Studia Linguistica* 56.2: 145–190.
Ross, J. 1967. Constraints on Variables in Syntax. Doctoral dissertation, MIT.
Roussou, A. 2000. On the Left-Periphery: Modal Particles and Complementisers. *Journal of Greek Linguistics* 1: 65–94.
Ryan, J. 2012. *The Genesis of Argument Structure*. Saarbrucken: Lambert Publishing.
Sadock, J. and A. Zwicky. 1985. Sentence Types. In T. Shopen (ed.), *Language Typology and Syntactic Description*, vol. I, *Clause Structure*, 155–196. Cambridge University Press.
Schachter, P. 1976. The Subject in Philippine Languages: Topic, Actor, Actor-Topic, or None of the Above. In C. Li, *Subject and Topic*, 491–518. San Diego: Academic Press.
Schein, B. 1993. *Plurals and Events*. Cambridge, MA: Academic MIT Press.
Schweikert, W. 2005. *The Order of Prepositional Phrases in the Structure of the Clause*. Amsterdam: John Benjamins.
Shibatani, M. & P. Pardeshi. 2001. The Causative Continuum. www.lit.kobe-u.ac.jp/linguistics/KPL/3_2001/KPL_2001_shibatani-pardeshi.pdf
Shlonsky, U. 2010. The Cartographic Enterprise in Syntax. *Language and Linguistics Compass* 4/6: 417–429.
Shu, C.-H. 2011. Sentence Adverbs in the Kingdom of Agree. Doctoral dissertation, Stony Brook.
Siewierska, A. 2011. Verbal Person Marking. In M. Haspelmath, M. Dryer, D. Gil & B. Comrie (eds.), *The World Atlas of Language Structures Online*. Munich: Max Planck Digital Library, chapter 102. Accessed December 28, 2011.

Siewierska, A. & D. Bakker. 2009. Case and Alternative Strategies. In A. Malchukov and A. Spencer (eds.), *The Oxford Handbook of Case*, 290–303. Oxford University Press.

Sigurðsson, H. 2011. Conditions on Argument Drop. *Linguistic Inquiry* 42.2: 267–304.

Slobodchikoff, C. 2010. Alarm Calls in Birds and Mammals. In M. Breed and J. Moore (eds.), *Encyclopedia of Animal Behavior*, vol. I, 40–43. Oxford: Academic Press.

Solà, J. 1996. Morphology and Word Order in Germanic Languages. In W. Abraham, S. D. Epstein, Höskuldur Thráinsson, and C. J.-W. Zwart (eds.), *Minimal Ideas*, 217–251. Amsterdam: John Benjamins.

Sorace, A. 2000. Gradients in Auxiliary Selection with Intransitive Verbs. *Language* 76.4: 859–890.

Sportiche, D. 1988. A Theory of Floating Quantifiers and its Corollaries for Constituent Structure. *Linguistic Inquiry* 19.2: 425–451.

Stewart, O. 2001. *The Serial Verb Construction Parameter*. New York: Garland.

Stowell, T. 1981. Origins of Phrase Structure. Doctoral dissertation, MIT.

Stroik, T. 2009. *Locality in Minimalist Syntax*. Cambridge, MA: MIT Press.

Swartz, S. 1988. Pragmatic Structure and Word Order in Warlpiri. *Papers in Australian linguistics* 17: 151–166. *PL*, A-71.

Tenny, C. L. 1994. *Aspectual Roles and the Syntax-Semantics Interface*. Dordrecht: Kluwer.

2000. Core Events and Adverbial Modification. In C. Tenny and J. Pustejovsky (eds.), *Events as Grammatical Objects*, 285–334. Stanford: CSLI Publications.

Tomasello, M. 1992. *First Verbs*. Cambridge University Press.

Topping, D. 1973. *Chamorro Reference Grammar*. Honolulu: University of Hawaii Press.

Travis, L. 1984. Parameters and Effects of Word Order Variation. Doctoral dissertation, MIT.

Trudgill, P. 1974. *The Social Differentiation of English in Norwich*. Cambridge University Press.

Uriagereka, J. 2011. *Spell-Out and the Minimalist Program*. Oxford University Press.

Vendler, Z. 1967. Verbs and Times. *Philosophical Review* 66: 143–160.

Vergnaud, J.-R. 2008. Letter to Noam Chomsky and Howard Lasnik. In R. Freidin, C. P. Otero, and M. L. Zubizarreta (eds.), *Foundational Issues in Linguistic Theory*, 3–16. Cambridge, MA: MIT Press.

Verkuyl, H. 1972. *On the Compositional Nature of Aspects*. Dordrecht: Reidel.

Visser, F. 1963–1973. *An Historical Syntax of the English Grammar*, Vols I–IIIb. Leiden: Brill.

Watkins, L. 1990. Noun Phrase versus Zero in Kiowa Discourse. *International Journal of American Linguistics* 56.3: 410–426.

Watters, J. 2000. Syntax. In B. Heine & D. Nurse (eds.), *African Languages*, 194–230. Cambridge University Press.

Williams, E. 1981. Argument Structure and Morphology. *The Linguistic Review* 1: 81–114.
1994. *Thematic Structure*. Cambridge, MA: MIT Press.
Willie, M. 1991. *Navajo Pronouns and Obviation*. Dissertation, University of Arizona.
Willis, D. 2007. Specifier-to-Head Reanalyses in the Complementizer Domain: Evidence from Welsh. *Transactions of the Philological Society* 105.3: 432–480.
Wurff, W. van der. 2007. *Imperative Clauses in Generative Grammar*. Amsterdam: John Benjamins.
Yap, F. H., K. Grunow-Hårsta and J. Wrona (eds.). 2011. *Nominalization in Asian Languages: Diachronic and Typological Perspectives*. Amsterdam: John Benjamins.
Zagona, K. 2007. Some Effects of Aspect on Tense Construal. *Lingua* 117: 464–502.
Zanuttini, R. 1997. *Negation and Clausal Structure: A Comparative Study of Romance Languages*. Oxford University Press.
Zanuttini, R. and P. Portner. 2003. Exclamative Clauses: At the Syntax–Semantics Interface. *Language* 79.1: 39–81.
Zepeda, O. [1983] 1994. *A Papago Grammar*. Tucson: University of Arizona Press.
Zwicky, A. & G. Pullum. 1983. Cliticization vs. Inflection. *Language* 59.3: 502–513.

Index